Praise for *A Woman in Amber*

"This book, about the sufferings of civilians during the Second World War, is unlike most war books, because it deals with the long-term effects of war, and this makes it relevant now with more and more people in the world hurt by war. People who become disquieted about how much we are manipulated by experiences we might not even remember will find this perceptive book helpful. In using her memories in an effort of self-healing the author will show them the way. This is a powerful anti-war book. It is also a hopeful one. . . . I whole-heartedly recommend it."
   —Doris Lessing

"A brave and subtle confrontation with childhood memories of extreme horror. Agate Nesaule shows us, in disturbing but illuminating detail, how violence and cruelty register on the psyche from without, to haunt it later painfully from within. This beautifully written book makes us reckon anew with the deep costs of war, and reassures us that hope can be wrested from great suffering."
   —Eva Hoffman, author of *Lost in Translation*

Professor Nesaule's story is so honestly and beautifully told that it rises above whatever lessons may be drawn from it: it is her story, her family's, and that of other Latvians, and to read it is to enlarge one's own experience."
   —Garrison Keillor

"This rich, complex memoir is about war and its 'endless aftermath,' about memory, denial, the breaking of taboos and the difficulty women and people from small nations encounter in taking themselves seriously. . . . For those of us currently outside the war zone . . . she wrenches us out of our shamed TV-viewer passivity. . . . A remarkable book."
   —*Newsday*

"Mothers rule our destiny and this is true whether we live relatively peaceful lives or are plunged into war. Mother as archetype is the theme of this moving story."   —Edna O'Brien

"Like all the best modern memoirs, *A Woman in Amber* belongs to the quest literature of our times. . . . It draws the reader forward with the suspense of a novel, a tale told in the unmistakable voice of one searching urgently for integrity as if it were a cure. And in this memoir the cure is found."   —Patricia Hampl, *The New York Times Book Review*

ABOUT THE AUTHOR

Agate Nesaule graduated from Indiana University and received her doctorate from the University of Wisconsin. She is currently a professor of English and Women's Studies at the University of Wisconsin-Whitewater and lives in Madison. *A Woman in Amber* was selected for Outstanding Achievement Recognition by the Wisconsin Library Association Literary Awards Committee and won a 1996 American Book Award.

A WOMAN IN AMBER

◆◆◆

Healing the Trauma of War and Exile

AGATE NESAULE

PENGUIN BOOKS

PENGUIN BOOKS
Published by the Penguin Group
Penguin Books USA Inc., 375 Hudson Street, New York, New York 10014, U.S.A.
Penguin Books Ltd, 27 Wrights Lane, London W8 5TZ, England
Penguin Books Australia Ltd, Ringwood, Victoria, Australia
Penguin Books Canada Ltd, 10 Alcorn Avenue, Toronto, Ontario, Canada M4V 3B2
Penguin Books (N.Z.) Ltd, 182–190 Wairau Road, Auckland 10, New Zealand

Penguin Books Ltd, Registered Offices: Harmondsworth, Middlesex, England

First published in the United States of America by Soho Press, Inc. 1995
Published in Penguin Books 1997

1 3 5 7 9 10 8 6 4 2

Chapter 7, entitled "Mothers and Daughters," was published in a slightly
different form in *Northwest Review*.

The excerpt from "A Rose in the Heart of New York" from *A Fanatic Heart*,
copyright © 1984 by Edna O'Brien, is reprinted by permission of Farrar, Straus & Giroux,
Inc. The excerpt from "How to Tell a True War Story" from *The Things They Carried*,
copyright © 1990 by Tim O'Brien, is reprinted by permission of Houghton
Mifflin Co./Seymour Lawrence. All rights reserved.

THE LIBRARY OF CONGRESS HAS CATALOGUED THE HARDCOVER AS FOLLOWS:
Nesaule, Agate.
A woman in amber: healing the trauma of war and exile/Agate Nesaule.
p.   cm.
ISBN 1-56947-046-4 (hc.)
ISBN 0 14 02.6190 7 (pbk.)
1. Nesaule, Agate.   2. Latvian Americans—Biography.   3. Latvian Americans—Cultural
Assimilation.   4. Indianapolis (Ind.)—Biography.   5. Madison (Wis.)—Biography.
6. Refugees—United States—Biography.   7. World War, 1939–1945—Refugees.   I. Title.
E184.L4N47   1995
940.53´159´092—dc20
[B]   95–18907

Printed in the United States of America
Set in Stempel Garamond
Designed by Lisa Govan

With love and gratitude to the two
who helped me tell this story:
Ingeborg Casey,
who taught me that
the past is meaningful,
and John Durand,
who brought love, happiness
and peace to the present

"Her mother was the cup, the cupboard, the sideboard with all the things in it, the tabernacle with God in it, the lake with the legends in it, the bog with the wishing wells in it, the sea with the oysters and the corpses in it . . ."

—EDNA O'BRIEN,
"A Rose in the Heart of New York,"
A Fanatic Heart

"War has the feel—the spiritual texture—of a great ghostly fog, thick and permanent. There is no clarity. Everything swirls. . . . The vapors suck you in. You can't tell where you are, or why you're there, and the only certainty is overwhelming ambiguity. In war you lose your sense of the definite, hence your sense of truth itself, and therefore it's safe to say that in a true war story nothing is ever absolutely true."

—TIM O'BRIEN,
"How to Tell a True War Story,"
The Things They Carried

Author's Note

I have uncertainties about this story. I was only seven when some of the events took place, and there is so much that I have forgotten or I never knew or understood. But I have not been able to compare my recollections with others. No one in my family wants to talk about the war: they may have silent images, but they tell no stories. And no matter how hard I try, I cannot force myself to do research. I can only bear to read novels, as if they were safer, not factual accounts of the period.

I know that memory itself is unreliable: it works by selecting, disguising, distorting. Others would recall these events differently. I cannot guarantee historical accuracy; I can only tell what I remember. I have had to speculate and guess, even to invent in order to give the story coherence and shape. I have also changed some names and identifying details to protect the privacy of others.

The matter of inventing requires a special note. All memories, but especially traumatic ones, are originally wordless. Putting them into words inevitably transforms them (Judith Lewis Herman, *Trauma and Recovery*, Basic Books, 1992). One verbal form is not necessarily "truer" than another, yet many people naively prefer narration and summary over dramatization and dialogue. I have chosen to show the people from my past in action and I have allowed them to speak because that is how I see and hear them. Ultimately all memoirs are attempts at "inventing the truth" (William Zinsser, *Inventing the Truth: The Art and Craft of Memoir*, Houghton Mifflin, 1987). Yet they also test the writer's integrity and require constant striving for fairness and authenticity.

Why tell this story now, so many years after World War II? In all wars the shelling eventually stops, most wounds heal, memories fade. But wartime terror is only the beginning of stories. The small boy with arms raised in the face of guns, the girl forced to witness rape, the emaciated children begging for food, if they survive, all have to learn how to live with their terrible knowledge. For more than forty years, my own life was constricted by shame, anger and guilt. I was saved by the stories of others, by therapy, dreams and love. My story shows healing is possible.

Wars are never-ending, and so are their stories. I pray for an end to war, and I fervently hope for greater understanding for all its victims. I want tenderness for them long after atrocities end.

Part I

♦♦♦

◆ 1 ◆

Talking in Bed

We are talking in bed, friends again instead of lovers. Apricot-colored fern fronds wave against the pearl gray background of my flannel sheets. Both of us are surprised to hear thunder, thunder in February, in Wisconsin, over frozen ground and dirty snow. My hand rests lightly on his gray hair, our legs are still entwined. Soon we will turn away from each other, but our backs will touch, close enough to stay warm. We will dream different dreams. He will walk in the Sangre de Cristo mountains of New Mexico or drive over a wooded Wisconsin road towards Birch Island Lake. I will carry a baby away from a burning Latvian village, evade Nazi guards, catch the last train. When we dream about being seven, we speak different languages.

"Tell me a story," John says, "tell me a story before we go to sleep."

I can't think of one. I have told him many stories, but during the day I often feel we are strangers. I don't believe him when he says he loves me, I don't expect him until he returns.

"You first," I say.

"I told one last night." And it's true, he has. A Miss McPike, the choir director, has glared at two altar boys in Spooner, the small Wisconsin town where John grew up.

"I can't think of one, they're all gone. Or rather, I've told them all."

"Did you have a car in Latvia, before the war?" he prompts.

That's all I need, I am off. "No, no cars, just horses. And, of course, bicycles."

The Parsonage seemed immense. A long road wound through the park toward the trellised porch. Mock orange and lilacs bloomed close to the house, I remember the fragrance. In the fall the leaves from the tall gloomy oaks and red maples were strung on wire. Later, six or so at a time they would be placed under the unbaked loaves of sweet and sour rye bread. Sometimes there was a pattern of leaves on the bottom crust.

My mother had a new bicycle. It was shiny metal, with a large black leather seat and huge black handlebars. But it wasn't like a man's. It had blue and green and red crocheted skirt-guards and a round silver bell.

It was before the war got very close, I am sure of that. She would not have had time to learn to ride a bicycle once refugees and partisans started coming to the house. Gypsies came too. So did a lot of relatives. The adults sat up late and argued whether to sail to Sweden, stay in Latvia, go to Germany. No one cared if my sister and I stayed outside all night, no one made us go to bed. We fell asleep under the stars, sometimes we slept in the hay. But this was the year before the war came. I must have been five, my sister six.

My mother walked the bicycle by herself on the gravel path by the orchard. The apple trees had already finished blooming, but the tiny green fruit could hardly be called apples yet. She would run a little, try to mount, change her mind and slow down again. My sister, Beate, and I were holding hands, watching. My mother had told us to stay behind the orchard fence, well out of her way.

Sniegs walks out of the house, he is smoking a cigarette. His eyes are a washed-out blue. He is dressed in an immaculate suit, but he is wearing bedroom slippers. When he gets closer we can see that one of his shirt cuffs is unbuttoned and the sleeve is frayed. Once he was a promising concert pianist, but now he plays the organ in our father's churches. My father says that Sniegs has ruined his life; he has failed to live up to his earlier promise and taken to drink.

On Sunday mornings Sniegs lets my sister and me pump the organ. Perspiring and trembling after a dissipated night, he is nevertheless vigorous as he plays the hopeful Lutheran hymns. We love being up in the loft with him. It is better than sitting still in one of the pews, waiting for the sermon to be over.

Inhaling slowly, Sniegs watches my mother through narrowed eyes. She is wearing a linen blouse, trimmed with lace, and a full blue skirt that swings as she moves. Although it is summer, she is wearing magenta stockings and black shoes with delicate straps. The shoes are dusty, her face is flushed. She looks up at him, holds his gaze for a second or two, then drops her eyes.

Sniegs strides across the open expanse of lawn bordered by daylilies and irises. He swings across the fence rather than using the gate and stands very close to her. He says something so quietly that we cannot hear, and she laughs. He whispers again, and she laughs once more. Then he steadies the seat with one hand and blows out a final puff of smoke over her shoulders, vulnerable beneath lace and linen. We know she is wearing an ivory-colored camisole; the outline of a smooth satin strap is faintly visible beneath the chaste cool cloth. He grinds the cigarette into the gravel with his heel and puts his other hand on the handlebar. She seems to shiver slightly as she puts her feet on the first pedal, then the second. He soothes and steadies while she, protected by his arms, pedals clumsily at first, then confidently.

She does not look at us. I can feel my face flushing. Beate and I hold hands, our arms stiffly extended. We are trembling with rage. My sister brushes hair out of her eyes to see better.

My mother, shielded by Sniegs, has circled the orchard path a dozen times. She glances at him now and then, but she does not look at us. She has forgotten we exist. A strand of her dark hair has escaped from the chignon she wears. She lets it graze her cheekbone, to lift in the breeze, to partially obscure her vision. She does not hasten to restrain it.

Sniegs lifts first one hand, then the other from the bicycle. He allows her to ride alone for a moment, then his arms encircle her again. Finally she rides by herself. Sniegs lopes dreamily behind her. He does not notice us either. Her eyes are shining, she is exhilarated. She does not fall, although I want her to. I want the bicycle to veer sideways, trip Sniegs, throw her on her knees on the ground right in front of my sister and me. We would rush to comfort her, she would cry and put her arms around us. My sister and I continue holding each other's hands so hard our fingers hurt, but we do not let go.

"Stupid, stupid, stupid," my sister whispers.

"Stupid," I echo, willing my mother to look at me. She does not. She continues circling the orchard. Her eyes briefly meet Sniegs's, but mostly they are on the horizon, far away from the house.

In the twilight she sits on the sofa, covered with an afghan, surrounded by pillows, cups of tea, a tablecloth of peacocks and lilies she has been embroidering forever.

"Come and sit by me, precious," she says to me. "Come, my little love." How dare she say that? How dare she assume I would come? I take a step backwards, press myself into the wall. But it is impossible to resist her. Although I stiffen myself, I am pulled towards her. I throw my arms around her neck and hold on as tightly as I can. She lets me do that, then gently begins to free herself.

"Not so hard," she says.

She turns away, towards the window. I know she likes the blossoms of the apple trees in the twilight, but they are long gone. She sits motionless, watching the darkening distant trees. Her dark brown eyes are sad, though not nearly as sad and empty as they will become later.

"Go now," she whispers, "Go away, I want to be by myself. Go play."

Her black bicycle is leaning against the orchard fence. Next to it is the other bicycle she has persuaded my father to buy. Together they ride out into the country. Sometimes they bring back wild strawberries. Once they brought two trout.

While they are gone, Sniegs paces and smokes. He has begun composing again, so he spends a lot of time in the drawing room. He plays a phrase or two on the piano, marches around the sofa, goes out to have a cigarette, returns, tries again. Occasionally the chords flow together; a melody seems to be hovering just on the edge. He walks up and down the long drive through the park. He is wearing shoes, and his shirt cuffs are buttoned.

He takes an interest in my sister and me. He brings us halvah bars from Riga. He hands them over wordlessly, his other arm circling a briefcase with a broken clasp. We can hear the bottles clink. He brings a book of verse with a few gloomy pictures. A man is being pursued by his sins, represented as gray balls of yarn. It is Peer Gynt, who has lived a dissolute life. Saying it is too old for my sister, my mother puts it on the top shelf in the library.

On the next trip, he brings me an ugly black-and-white cast-plaster dog with drooping jowls. Saying it is breakable, my mother puts it on the top of the tall chiming clock in the dining room. One hot July afternoon, while everyone is resting, I push a chair over to the clock, reach up and grasp the dog. It is heavier and more slippery than I remember. The short neck and the pudgy body are hard to hold onto. I stand on tiptoe to lift it. It flies out of my hands and shatters on the parquet floor; the pieces fly off in a thousand directions.

She does not scold me. "Poor little thing," she says, "what will you do now without your little dog? How will you pass the time?"

She has not noticed that I have never played with the dog. She keeps her finger marking her place in her book.

My mother has one of her musical evenings. The maid lays out a white satin cloth, the delicate cups and plates with wreaths of pale violets and gold rims. The samovar gleams. She will serve tea, Russian style, in tall glasses, with slender long silver spoons. The platters are filled with raspberry meringues, apricot turnovers, dark red cherries. The torte looks disappointing to Beate and me; instead of being piled high with chocolate icing and whipped cream, it is flat and thin, with tiny almond half-shells and sugar roses on the mocha glaze.

The first to arrive is her former colleague, the village music teacher. He bows silently and hands her a single white lily. Then Elvīra, whose brother Ārijs is in the insane asylum; my mother is her only friend. Two high school teachers from town, in flowered dresses, with crisp white collars, lace handkerchiefs tucked into their gold watchbands. They dab at their faces, laugh and whisper with my mother. She used to take long Sunday walks with them, going from one Lutheran church to another to look at the new preachers, to see their faces and to sit through their sermons. My father was the handsomest and the smartest, so my mother married him. The doctor limps in, leaning on his cane. His driver carries in his cello and music stand and sets them up, while the doctor kisses my mother's hand and unwraps a bottle of cognac. Sniegs comes in last, looking rushed yet weary. He nods silently to my mother, strolls over, opens her piano, begins to play.

We are allowed to sit on the top steps. We listen to the women's sweet voices, accompanied first by the cello, then a flute, joined finally by the regular throbbing of the piano. The women sing separately, then together.

Tonight there is something special. Sniegs has written a song dedicated to my mother. He stands up, bows, speaks long and importantly, bows formally again and hands the music to my mother. She smiles into his eyes.

"It's a song about the comfort Christ can bring to those who long for him," he says.

"Like twilight to a dreamer
Like a goblet of cool water to the weary . . ."

The melody is plaintive, not energetic like the hymns in church. Sniegs plays the piano softly, letting his tenor voice rise and yearn. He sings all three verses alone, then my mother joins in. Together they sing the first verse. She leans over his shoulder to follow the music; her hand brushes his arm when she turns a page. After much applause and laughter, the two of them sing the entire song together again.

"How beautifully it expresses religious feeling," Elvīra says. The two school teachers whisper and giggle. Distracted from the music, my mother turns around, notices my sister and me, and firmly motions us up the stairs to bed.

"What happened to all those people?" John asks. "Where do you suppose they are right now? Do you think any of them are alive?"

I do not know. Sniegs was arrested by the Russians, deported to Siberia. My mother has been dead for more than ten years. My father is alive, remarried, living in a distant city, but then, of course, he wasn't there that night.

"What happened to the song? Did she ever sing it again?"

"Oh, yes, yes, she did. She used to hum it."

"Often? When?"

"Oh, sometimes. Her eyes would have that faraway look."

"Ah."

We are silent together.

"Tell me about one time when she hummed it," he says.

I am too surprised to speak. No one ever wants to hear about the painful parts of my past. People have hundreds of ways, both subtle and harsh, to reinforce my own reluctance to tell.

"I really want to know. Please tell me."

No wonder I love him. Sometimes I almost believe he loves me.

"Well, let's see . . ."

"Yes?"

We were in a basement in Germany. It seemed quiet for a moment. The Russian soldiers had gotten tired of threatening us, our possessions were all over the muddy floor—clothes, photographs, shattered crystal. We weren't allowed to pick anything up. All the women without children had been dragged away. My father was gone. It was chilly and getting dark.

"Please," I whispered, "I want to go away. Please."

"We can't," she said. "They are still shooting, and anyway, we don't have horses or cars."

"Please."

"Shush, poor little thing, shush."

"Then tell me everything will be all right," I beg. "Please smile at me. Say it will be all right."

She smiles down at me.

"Yes, yes, it will, precious."

She lets me put my head in her lap, she strokes my hair. I cling to her; my sister, Beate, clings to her other side. I close my eyes. I almost do not hear the women pleading behind the partition. The guns seem to recede, but there is a steady rumble in the distance.

"It will be fine," she says, "you'll see. But now you must not make the soldiers angry, you must not cry, you must not speak. You have to be very, *very* quiet."

I can feel the warmth of her hands on my hair, the warmth of her eyes on my face.

She starts humming, wordlessly at first, then she whispers the words.

"Like twilight to a dreamer,
Like a goblet of cool water to the weary . . .
Tu sapņotājam zilgans novakars . . ."

9

I know her eyes are sad, that she is looking toward the dark horizon. I want her to look at *me*, just me, so I hold on harder.

"Yes," he murmurs, "I can see that scene. You must have been very frightened."

We caress each other's eyelids and hair.

"I cherish you," he says.

I struggle to believe him. Outside the rain has changed to sleet. Snow will fall later. It will be treacherous driving or walking, the layer of ice under the deceptively soft snow. I have seen such changes in weather before. To keep the warmth in, I pull the apricot and pearl gray sheets tighter around us both.

Shielded by shadows, away from the world, in a safe and intimate setting, it is possible to talk. But later I regret the telling. To distract myself from my shame, I move into a ritual I have practiced for more than forty years. I am ashamed of it too, but I cannot stop.

I reach for my underwear in the cold and whisper, "Thank you." I repeat the words after every item of clothing I put on because now I will not freeze when I am shoved out into the cold drizzle by the soldiers. Sometimes they are Nazi guards with swastikas on their armbands, more often they are Russian soldiers with impassively cruel faces and slurred words. "Thank you," I murmur as I pull on my shoes and stockings because now I will not have to walk barefoot over frozen mud. I luxuriate in my thick soft sweater, I am relieved as I hurriedly button my skirt. I have made it, I will be warm in the camps, I am all right.

But on my way down the stairs, guilt sweeps over me. Dressed, warm, I move towards crusty bread, fragrant coffee, sweet oranges. My house feels solid and safe and orderly; hyacinths and narcissus bloom indoors here even in the dead of winter. I have everything that others packed onto trains, starving in camps, tortured, gassed, bludgeoned and shot do not. I move resolutely, willing for guilt to pass. I compose my face into a smile. I am known as a cheerful person.

In the summer I dress more quickly to cover my nakedness, shield myself from mud, mosquitoes and whips, before the truck carries me off. Faces from photographs of children from Vietnam, Afghanistan, South Africa, Guatemala, Ethiopia haunt me then. I must hurry.

I know these fantasies trivialize the suffering of millions who were awakened at night, shoved out on cold sidewalks, marched away as their homes and villages burned behind them. Separated from their families, they were packed onto trains headed for concentration camps in Germany, forced labor camps in Siberia, dilapidated shacks far from food and water in Asia, Africa, Central America.

My own experience of war and displacement was different, it was not so bad. How dare I visualize myself like them? How do the real survivors bear it? I ask the empty air.

How?

♦ 2 ♦

Broken Links

When John and I have spent an entire day together, which is seldom, we read in bed before turning out the lights to talk. As our eyes grow accustomed to the dark, we tell each other bits of plot, funny lines, odd facts. Some images remain remarkably vivid. Perhaps the retina retains more than we think, perhaps some kinds of light carry an afterlight.

He is reading a novel by a South African writer in which a little girl leans her head against her mother's knees, her mother's head is in the lap of her mother, her mother's head rests against the knees of her mother. The unbroken chain extends all the way back to the Great Mother.

I envy the chain. My mother did not speak to me for two years after I married, and I could never please her again. But already, years before that, my mother stayed in bed alone, reading late into the night, waiting only for me to finish speaking so she could return to her book.

I remember her in the dark damp cubicle, once the laundry room behind the kitchen, of the tiny house where we lived after coming to the United States in 1950. The narrow windows faced north, it smelled of mold. Sometimes the door was ajar and I would see her sitting absolutely still, staring into space, not reading at all. I was twelve when we came to Indianapolis, expecting an easier life than in the Displaced Persons' camps in Germany.

The two of us were seldom in the house together. On weekdays I would return from school as my mother was silently getting ready to go to work as a dishwasher at LaRue's Supper Club. We would exchange a few words, mostly directions about things to be done, dinner to be made for my father, clothes to be ironed. On Saturday nights I too worked at the supper club. I scraped cigarette butts and bloodied mashed potatoes off plates, dumped half-eaten steaks and broken lobsters into bins. As I lifted the heavy trays of steaming plates from the conveyor belt, I kept my eye on the door for the policeman I expected to arrest me. To work at all, one had to be fourteen; to work till one in the morning, eighteen. Later I would run breathless from the bus stop, expecting to be murdered, beaten, raped. It was almost two when I got home, but my mother's light was often on. She was reading or pretending to read. On other nights when my mother was working, I bent over my homework, trying to write a précis of "The Raven" or to make sense of the stilted language of "The Man Without a Country." I was very much alone. My sister did not get home from her housecleaning job until after dark. Both of us were grateful that the other children at school did not beat us.

One February afternoon during that first year in the United States my mother smiled at me. "I have something special for you," she said. "America really is a wonderful country. Imagine, buying something like this in the middle of winter. Melon. Melon in February."

She set a wedge of watermelon on the table.

"Beautiful," she said. The deep red flesh, the black seeds, the vivid green rind glistened. It *was* beautiful.

I bent to smell it.

"Don't bother, Agate. It doesn't have a fragrance, it isn't like a Siberian melon. Taste it instead."

My mother cut me a slice, then carefully scooped out the seeds. She rummaged in the cupboard, lifting out and rejecting one dish after another. Finally she sliced the red fruit into a plain glass bowl.

"Like crystal."

I was prepared for the familiar lines of pain in her forehead, but they weren't there.

"Isn't that pretty? Go on, taste it."

My mother bit into a piece herself. A trickle of juice ran down her arm. She looked at me and smiled again.

"Like it?"

"Yes, it's delicious."

"Like the melons in Siberia, almost."

Almost.

My mother is back in Russia. I can just see her if I close my eyes.

Her name is Valda, she is twelve years old, the same age as I. The shades are drawn throughout the house, everyone is resting. Valda's French governess is stretched out on a narrow bed with delicately curved legs, her parents are asleep in their four-poster, their heads on the same pillow. Velta, her beloved younger sister, is sleeping in her half-bed in the nursery; her two brothers, Gustavs and Jaša, are dozing in their rooms filled with toys and books and maps.

She alone is wide awake. She is anticipating a visit from Varvara, her best friend, who will arrive later this summer. Together with Varvara, Valda has endured ballet lessons, deportment lessons, Latin lessons, French lessons, English-style riding lessons, although both of them know how to ride bareback and often do. This summer they plan to ride long distances in the cool mornings. Her brothers will sometimes come along too. They will ride as hard as they can, then stop to drink cold water out of the crystal-clear rivers, to find raspberries and fragrant wild melons. Valda and Varvara have planned the visit while walking back and forth across the school courtyard with books balanced on their heads. Their postures by now are excellent. They bend their heads gracefully as they kneel each morning to pray for the welfare of the Czar and his family.

Valda's parents occasionally remark how nice it is that she has Varvara as a friend, such a well-brought-up girl from one of the best Russian families in the district of Omsk. Valda is not Russian but Latvian. Her parents say that they are living in a foreign country and they long to return to Latvia, but Russia is all that Valda knows and loves. She was born here and has never wanted to live anywhere else. To her it is home.

Valda's parents came to Russia from Latvia before she was born. Her father is a political refugee. Following a socialist uprising in Latvia, he came to Siberia to make a new life for himself. He has advanced ideas, including equal education and votes for women. Although his socialism has forced him to leave Latvia, his intelligence and industry have made him wealthy in Russia, an irony he cannot completely reconcile himself to, but which Lina, Valda's mother, finds cause for joy and gratitude. They speak Latvian at home, not Russian or French. Lina misses her mother and grandmother, who are in Latvia. She writes long letters every Sunday afternoon and hopes to return for a visit, as soon as the children are older, as soon as the estate, with its sugar beet farms, sawmills, dairies and vast forests, can take care of itself without her hard work and management.

In the heat Valda is restless. She is not allowed to play the piano during the hot afternoons while everyone sleeps. She has no one to talk to, she has finished copying her daily poem into her commonplace book, and her father has taken the newspaper upstairs to read out loud to her mother before they both doze off. Valda picks up *Anna Karenina*. She has already read it, but she likes rereading Vronsky's tender words to Anna.

Valda and Varvara adore officers, their impeccable manners, their formal bearing, their white uniforms. Their lives seem exciting, reckless, noble. Valda daydreams a little about the coming-out ball she is sure her father will give her. She will be sought after by university students and officers both, but she will prefer the officers. She will waltz all night with one white-clad officer after another, but she will be in love with just one, a combination of Vronsky and her father's younger brother, Žanis. Her white dress will swirl, gardenias will perfume the air, the music will be passionate, though a little sad.

Her reverie is interrupted by the sound of hooves on the long white road winding towards the house. The cloud of dust grows bigger and bigger. The lone rider is galloping furiously, sparing neither himself nor his horse. She parts the lace curtains and leans her forehead against the glass. Such haste is unusual on this road, which is sometimes empty for days, disturbed only by a rare decorous four-wheeled carriage of a far-distant neighbor on a family visit or a cart driven by a peasant to the mill. Perhaps there is a fire or illness at the nearest neighbor's house, which is more than an hour away, and someone has ridden to ask her father for help. He is generous and highly respected in the district.

The rider bursts into the courtyard; he reins the horse so hard it rears backwards and almost throws him on the ground. Dust swirls over the scandalized pigeons. The peacocks are startled out of the shade into the sunlight. They look outraged as they flee.

She recognizes his uniform first. It is Žanis, her only uncle, her father's younger brother, an officer in the Czar's palace guard. He has seen the Czar daily, retrieved a lost ball for the beloved Anastasia, played with Nicholas, the son suffering from hemophilia. Valda knows that Žanis must be a great favorite at court. He is handsome, tall and lively, he can make whoever he is with feel important. He always has time for her, seemingly all the time in the world. He asks her serious questions about her taste in clothes, her plans for the future, the habits of her horse Žubīte ("Little Finch").

Valda rushes down the steps into the courtyard. She expects him to bow to her a little formally before he kisses her on the cheek, then she will throw her arms around him.

"Fire," he is shouting at Fjodor, the peasant who is holding his horse. "Go build a big fire for me. Hurry."

Žanis looks through her as if she were part of the house and the trees. A thin fresh red scar extends from his left eye to the corner of his mouth. His eyes are swollen, he hasn't shaved. His beautiful white wool uniform is dirty, the buttons are torn off, she can see the smooth olive brown skin of his chest. The nakedness under his uniform shocks her more than anything.

"Uncle Žani." She touches his sleeve.

He recognizes her. He bows formally, then she is in his arms, they embrace. In the midst of her momentary relief, she knows everything is very different. She smells sweat and dust, instead of the familiar lemony fragrance of the English toilet water he likes.

He looks towards the drapes drawn across most of the windows of the house to keep out the sun. It is very still.

"You must be the only one awake." He caresses her cheek.

"Yes, they're all sleeping."

"The Czar has fallen," he says.

His words are shocking but meaningless. He sees that, so he adds, "The Czar has been imprisoned. All his family too. No one can save them now, it's too late." He touches his scar absentmindedly.

Fjodor runs back from the smokehouse. He falls on his knees before Žanis and tries to kiss his hand.

"I've started the fire for you, Your Excellency," he says.

Žanis laughs and pulls him to his feet. He tries to shake hands with Fjodor, but the peasant steps back, confused.

"In the great Russian Soviet Republic there won't be masters and servants, no excellencies, no hand-kissing. That's all finished."

Žanis takes Valda's hand and runs with her to the smokehouse. The horse ambles after them.

"Someone has to witness this," he says. "It's history."

But all Valda can see is the wound on his cheek, the dirt on his uniform, his chest naked under the white wool.

"It's nothing, precious. I'm alive, not like the others. The Czar may be dead by now as well."

He motions to Fjodor. "I need some of your clothes, a smock and some pants."

Fjodor backs farther away.

Žanis looks quickly over his shoulder, then back to Fjodor again.

"Yes, yes, I must have them. Here, you can have this." Žanis presses his gold watch into Fjodor's hands.

Fjodor stares at him, then slowly starts to pull off his loose blouse.

"Do that behind the oven," Žanis orders.

He opens his saddlebags, shoves aside a black revolver and takes out a handful of documents. "I want you to remember this," he says to Valda.

He burns his birth certificate, his university diploma, his officer's commission, citations for personal services to the Czar, ribbons, decorations, monogrammed handkerchiefs, a set of ivory brushes.

He goes behind the partition where Fjodor stands in his underwear, holding the watch to his ear. Žanis steps into the gray rough pants and loose shirt, ties the hemp belt tightly, then pulls the visored coachman's cap over his eyes. He bundles up his white uniform, throws it into the fire, slams the oven door. It doesn't latch properly; he slams it again, harder. He tries to pull on Fjodor's boots, but they are much too small, so he reaches for his own.

"I'll have comfortable shoes, that's something. Good walking boots." He looks very different.

"Where are you going? Where?"

"Into the forests. The beautiful vast forests of Mother Russia."

She has many questions, but he is in a hurry.

"When will you be back?"

"Ah, precious, I don't know. Maybe never."

He sees her tears, so he holds her chin with one hand and gently wipes her cheeks with the other.

"I'll try to come back, but tell them not to wait for me. Tell them to save themselves, that's the most important thing."

"Žani."

"I'll be fine. It's nice in the woods. Dark but full of mushrooms and berries, you could live in there forever and never have to come out."

"At least go tell my father," she pleads.

"No, I don't have time, they're after me." His hand reaches automatically towards the revolver in the saddlebag. But then he laughs. "Think the family would recognize me anyway?"

She is crying hard by now.

"Ah, don't cry," he says. "I don't intend to die. Adventure, love, pretty peasant maids, I'll have all that. You'll have little cousins playing in the forest. Don't cry."

He kisses her and swings onto his horse. Valda watches him until he disappears into the dark woods behind the house.

That was how I imagined my mother lost her beloved Russia, but I never knew for certain. I did know that her friend Varvara was arrested, then shot. After Valda's family had spent all the gold coins hidden in her thick braids, they collected salt to trade for food. Fearing constantly for their lives, they walked all the way across Russia to Latvia. Her father died the year they returned, so she never did get the university education he had promised her. "I'll see that you are educated just like your brothers, I love you just as much," he had always told her. "Besides, women should be educated, just like men."

She attended only a teachers' institute, then taught in a village school. She sent money to her mother, who in turn sent it to her sons so they could get university educations. She made exhausting train trips to Riga to carry back oxygen tanks for her younger sister, Velta, who died of TB the year that their older brother got his theology degree. She never saw her Uncle Žanis again. Then Latvia was occupied by the Russians in 1940, by the Germans in 1941 and the Russians again in 1944. The list of losses is unbearable; I am glad she does not talk about it.

We have finished the watermelon.

My mother says, "I am a little tired now. I'll lie down for just half an hour before I have to go to work."

She bends down and pulls off her shoes. Her feet are slightly swollen, though less so than in the summer. On the bottom of her left instep is a large scar, which looks like a mole, about the size of a quarter. The summer before the Revolution, she cut her foot on a sharp stone in one of the icy rivers that she swam in with her brothers. Some soil got trapped in the wound, then the skin healed over. My father and Uncle Jaša, her younger brother who was a surgeon, used to urge her in Latvia to have the sand removed, but she never did. "It's the soil of Mother Russia," she would say. No one refers to the scar now.

My mother climbs into the narrow bed, settles the pillows behind her and picks up a book. She will not read it, she is only holding it, waiting to be alone again. I wish she could comfort me, help me with my schoolwork, offer advice about making friends with the other children, buy me something to wear that would make me feel less odd. I miss the Displaced Persons camps in Germany, where at least I was among people like myself, rather than among strangers from whom I will always be different, as I now am in America.

The sound of sleet on the windows is vaguely comforting. As I am drifting off to sleep, I think of my son Boris, or Borisītis, as I called him when he was small. One Valentine's Day, when he was about seven, we were walking down State Street in Madison.

"We're having a good time, aren't we having a good time, Mommy?" he begged. "Say we're having a good time."

"Yes, yes, of course we are," I said automatically, as my mother had.

"Smile, please." He pulled cautiously on my coat, his eyes fixed on my face.

But I was too enmeshed in my own pain to give him the genuinely happy smile he needed. Instead, I forced my features into a wan imitation. Seeing through the pretense, my little boy let go of my coat and walked on silently with downcast eyes. I have never been able to forget that scene. More than anything else, I wish I could go back and relive it, then relive all the years when he was growing up. If only I had been a happier mother, if only I had not inflicted my own sadness on him. It's a long time before I can fall asleep.

◆ 3 ◆

The Starving Boy

I sleep by myself and dream. I am hurrying across a field because I am late for work when I notice John ahead of me. He is bending tenderly towards one of my women friends. They are planning a trip together, arranging where to meet, discussing what to bring. When they notice me coming towards them, they stop talking. I feel jealous and excluded, but I am ashamed to say so. I would like to cling to him, to talk with her. They are both logical and just a little brusque with me. I should know this is not a romantic encounter but work. I feel childish, unloved, banished, beyond the pale.

Suddenly I remember with terror that I have left a seven-year-old starving boy in a room by himself. I have promised that I will be right back, told him to wait, locked the door, but I have forgotten all about him. The boy's limbs are like sticks, his belly is swollen, he is holding an empty bowl in hands so thin they seem transparent, his face is resigned. He seems to be crying, but it is hard to tell because of the flies swarming around his eyes and mouth. Perhaps the moisture seeping from them is infection, not tears. The room is airless, the windows too high for him to open or to see out. He has been waiting for me for a very long time.

Overwhelmed by guilt, I start running towards the vast building. I must reach him before he suffocates.

John catches up with me and understands immediately.

"I'll go," he says, "I'll take him for a ride, I'll take him to visit my family." He is kind and helpful.

But I know this boy is my responsibility.

"No," I say, "I have to rescue him." Terrified he will be dead, I run, breathless and stumbling. The boy is very far away.

The dream stays with me for days, colors what I do, makes everything seem gray and hopeless. I am ashamed of it, ashamed of my jealousy especially. If I put it into words that John could leave me for someone else, he would. If I don't trust my women friends, who is there to trust? The boy stays locked in the room.

To comfort myself, I take a long warm candle-lit bath. In the steamy mirror in the half-light, my body seems smooth and strong, almost lovely. The fragrance of lily of the valley from the milk bath one of my women friends has given me fills the air. I dry myself gently, I almost feel better.

But when I blow out the candle and turn on the light, it is harsh, like a spotlight over barbed wire in a frozen field. I look at myself again. Why do I dream of starving children, when my body is so well fed? It refuses to melt into slenderness. No matter how hard I try to control it, it demands food in spite of me. My arms and legs are slender and long, but there is a small roll of fat below my waist. My stomach, in the candlelight a moonlike shape in the water, is now much too solid, the navel no longer a mysterious eye above the foam.

I draw in my breath sharply and hold it. I pummel myself with my fists, hard, a dozen times. It does not help. I pull on my nightgown, relieved when the tiny flannel roses hide the body I believe is monstrous, whose hungers fill me with shame. I force myself to make a cup of tea, to carry it upstairs, to read in bed, to be gentle with myself. It is very hard to do. I would like to gulp down everything sweet and filling in the house, then everything salty, to tear into bread, to use both hands to bring food to my mouth faster and faster. Then I could go to sleep, half-sick, sated, ashamed. I would like to stay in bed forever, curled under the covers, with the lights out, the drapes drawn. I wish I could stay in the twilight and never have to move, never have to talk to anyone. I long for a pill that would anesthetize me, a blow to the head to bring darkness.

From long experience I know I will feel a little better in the morning. I must not give in. But I am frightened. Although I have struggled with depression all my life, the episodes are becoming more frequent and more savage, rather than disappearing, as I had expected they would if only I found the courage to get a divorce.

I am talking to Ingeborg Casey, the therapist I have been seeing for help with my divorce, which I believe is my real problem. In her serene room, I have slowly come to feel safe. The late afternoon light is fading over the pale furniture and walls, over the dark red amaryllis on the windowsill, over Ingeborg's softly flowing clothes. We are enclosed here, we are safe, the noise of the traffic is far away.

I have talked to her about my guilt for leaving my husband, about the disgrace of bankruptcy brought about by his business ventures, about losing my garden and house. I have admitted my depression, ashamed though I am. Hundreds of thousands of women have lived through similar experiences without running to therapists. They do not have jobs like mine; because I am a tenured professor, I can pay for therapy. My privileged position allows me to indulge in self-pity and despair.

Whenever Ingeborg asks about my childhood, I give her the formula I always use: "I was born in Latvia, went to Germany during the war and came to the United States when I was twelve." It is all I can bear to tell, all that others have wanted to hear.

"Has anything unusual happened?" Ingeborg asks. "You seem sadder. Or am I imagining it?"

"Oh, it's nothing really. It's just that I can't lose weight. I try and try, but I don't. I hate my body." I pause. "I *despise* it."

How easy it is, after all, to say that to Ingeborg. She would still value me if I doubled in size, grew old and wrinkled, lost all my teeth.

"There is something else," she says.

"Yes. I had an awful dream."

Ingeborg's calm acceptance of whatever I say and the gathering twilight around us make it easy to talk. I tell the dream I have been hiding like a secret wound. John enters the room, the starving boy pauses by the door, an afterthought, a way to end the story.

"How painful," Ingeborg murmurs, "that starving boy especially. I wonder why you are dreaming about him."

Has Ingeborg missed the point of the dream, I wonder. Will John leave next week, next month, next year? I want her to promise that he won't, even though she does not know him.

"You've never told me," Ingeborg continues, "exactly what happened when you were a child. Where were you when you were seven?"

The room is safe, enclosed, protected from the harsh glare of artificial light. Moonlight will reign here after we leave.

"Where were you when you were seven?" Ingeborg repeats.

"In Germany. In the Russian sector." And because I know that she will never tell, I add, "Starving."

The Russian soldiers are mining the lake with hand grenades. They are impatient and angry. Some of them are Mongolians, their eyes are narrow, dark, cruel. When the dying and maimed fish float to the surface, they scoop up only the largest ones. A huge fire is roaring already. They will cook the fish, eat the sweet warm flesh with chunks of dark rye bread. They will drink, shout, sing and dance. The aroma of fish and bread will drift over the hungry children standing behind the barbed wire fence, watching, waiting.

Perhaps some of the smaller fish the soldiers have rejected will be floating on the water close to the shore, still fresh in the morning after the soldiers leave. It is early autumn, the lake is deep and cold, the soldiers cannot stay here forever. Perhaps after the soldiers have eaten all they want to, they will give some leftover bread and fish to the children. Only a few will get some, it is impossible to say who. Perhaps the soldiers will get angry at the staring, waiting children and drive them away with guns. They will come back to be driven off a second time. Perhaps. All they can do is wait.

Perhaps the soldiers will dump the fish heads, scales and even whole fish they do not want on the ground. The children will scramble for them; only a few will be lucky. Most will walk home later, ashamed that their buckets are empty. They will be ashamed if they have fought for the fish and won, even more ashamed if they have nothing. They know they are not worth feeding.

Standing in the line are two girls, seven and eight years old, sisters probably. Their hair is drawn back severely from their faces and braided. Their dark blue dresses with tiny white polka dots are very short, as if they have outgrown them, but they hang loose and frayed around their collarbones and arms. Their skin is pale, their arms and legs are like sticks. One of them has a large empty bowl under her arm, the other holds an empty bucket. The older sister has dark hair and eyes that under other circumstances might be lively and mischievous; the younger sister is blond, her eyes are more gentle and compliant.

Their eyes are on the pans of fish and the basket of loaves, but their faces are impassive. They hold hands gingerly to avoid putting pressure on the boils in their armpits. They keep their legs slightly apart so as not to bruise the boils under their too short dresses and thin cotton underpants. The firelight plays over them. They are no longer hungry, that passed weeks ago. They will wait here all night if they have to.

The soldiers are drinking vodka, passing the clear glass bottles from hand to hand, taking large gulps, shuddering and sighing with satisfaction. Their narrow eyes and high cheekbones, their swarthy skins seem even more foreign in the firelight. One starts playing a harmonica, the others form a circle. They take turns dancing, leaping, kicking. They dance the *kazačok*. With arms folded across their chests, they squat and kick their legs out vigorously, they compete to see who can keep his balance the longest. Others clap and shout. A few are already stumbling about, their voices harsh, their words slurred. They turn away from their comrades, towards the children, only to vomit or urinate. The two sisters wait.

The uniforms of the soldiers are a very dark green that looks gray, almost black in the firelight. Some are wearing gray undershirts, though it is hard to say whether that is their original color or whether they are dirty. Behind the soldiers are dark trucks and jeeps drawn up in a half-circle. In the distance are the bombed buildings of the village. The village church is gone, the orphanage is still standing, though one wing of it has been gutted by fire. Some raw stumps of pine trees recently felled are behind the barbed-wire fence between the children and the soldiers. The lake is very dark.

The only vivid color in the whole landscape is the last truck. Three women holding guitars and a balalaika sit in front of it. Inside the wagon is a sultan's paradise of red and gold cushions and blankets, flickering lanterns, billowing satin curtains. When the soldiers have drunk more, they will take turns going into the wagon with the women.

The women of the village wear frayed gray and black garments. They cover their heads with dark wool scarves, smear dirt into their cheeks to look older, drop their eyes when they meet soldiers, flatten themselves against walls, hide. Most of them have been raped anyway. The women in the wagon are colorful and bold. They wear bright orange, red and yellow gowns with billowing sleeves, their gold bracelets and necklaces jingle, their pendulous earrings swing back and forth. Their dark hair is shiny, their bodies soft and full, their eyes sparkling. They laugh when the soldiers look at them.

The three women strum and sing softly. They are a little bored waiting. The youngest one plays with her bracelet, holds it up to the light, admires her smooth plump arm, takes off the bracelet and dangles it in invitation towards the two solemn sisters standing behind the fence with the other children. The younger sister starts to move towards her, but the older one pulls her back.

"Don't," she says, "she's only teasing you."

They continue waiting.

"Ah, yes," says Ingeborg, "but try to say more. Who are those children? Why do you say *they*? Is that your sister and you? Try to own your own story, try to say *I* and *we*. And what do you feel?"

"I'm wasting your time," I retort. "I should be in Ethiopia, helping the starving and sick. Instead I'm sitting here, in great comfort, going on about my precious feelings, wondering why I stayed married for so long when I was so miserable."

"You'll probably understand that when you write your story. You must write it, not just for yourself, but for others too. That is what *you* can do for others. Stories can change the human heart."

When the Russian soldiers first arrived they smashed all the glass jars of preserves of plums, apples, gooseberries, tomatoes, tiny peas, strawberry jam, raspberry jam, cherry compote, potted meat, pigs' knuckles, tiny sausages. These were stored in the vast cellar of the main building of the Lobethal Institution for the Mentally Defective and carefully rationed out during the war. The soldiers ate the sauerkraut in the large barrels, urinated and defecated in the corners of the basement once filled with food for hundreds. Rotting food, excrement, broken glass had to be painstakingly cleaned up later.

What was there for us to eat? At first there were carrots, rows and rows of them, left in the ground from the year before. We ate them raw, boiled, grated. Carrots were good for the eyes. When the wild roses finished blooming, we collected the orange-red hips, carefully picked the skin off the compressed seeds. It made our hands and fingers itch, but the tiny pieces of red flesh were delicious. We did not wait for the fruit in the orchard to ripen. Plums and apples were stripped off, still green and hard, stolen, devoured, digested with pain. We hunted for mushrooms, boiled them in water, ate the glutinous mass slowly, wishing for salt. We ate green soup, made from the leaves of linden trees.

At first we were very hungry and more energetic. If we heard rumors that the Russian soldiers were slaughtering a pig a farmer had been hiding, women and children with empty buckets and bowls would walk for miles. Sometimes some of us would be given bones or kidneys or intestines or scraps of skin. Or a jeep would screech into the courtyard, and the soldiers would order the first woman or two to come milk some cows they had found. Other women and children would follow, for safety, for a chance we would be allowed to drink some of the milk or even carry it home. Sometimes we were, sometimes the drunk soldiers laughed as they kicked over our buckets. We watched as the rich milk seeped into dark ground.

"Why did you stop talking?" Ingeborg asks.

"I . . . I am so ashamed. It made me feel completely worthless to know I wasn't even worth feeding. I'm ashamed of all the rest of it too."

"What courage it must have taken to survive. You must have been a brave little girl. Tell me some things that you did."

My mother has an idea. She teaches me to recite two short children's verses in Russian.

"Petushok, petushok . . ."

She pushes me towards the soldiers, my sister's hand is pulled from mine. At first the soldiers ignore me, standing in isolation from the other children and women. My legs and arms tremble violently, but I do not cry. I repeat the words over and over.

A soldier notices me, bends down, cups his ear. He is a little older than the rest. He laughs delightedly when he understands and he motions to a few others. When I hesitate, he pulls me by the arm, even further away from my sister and mother. I try to resist, I can feel warm urine run down my legs uncontrollably, my face flames with shame and terror. I repeat the words again and again.

A few soldiers stop shouting and listen briefly, amazed, as if they were seeing a goose singing in a human voice or a wound-up top that continued spinning forever. They pat me on the head and throw a few chunks of raw meat into my bowl. The older soldier presses a chocolate bar into my hand, then pushes me towards the crowd of waiting women.

I see my mother with arms stretched out for me. I set the bowl down several yards in front of her, turn my back and run towards one of the few trees still standing. I hide behind it, press myself into the trunk as hard as I can, wishing to grow into it, hoping my mother will be sorry when I do. Nothing happens.

I have to go back to give the chocolate bar to my mother so that our family can share it. I face the condemning eyes of the other women and girls. My sister, separated from the group, has stepped forward. She stands alone, ready to hold my hand.

But my bowl stays empty most of the time, and it is even more shameful to beg and not to receive.

One day Beate finds a large goose egg on the ground. Has a wild goose grown desperate and confused by the disappearance of all grain and berries? Has one escaped from a farmer hiding it underground somewhere? The miraculous egg lies in the dust in the road, right in front of her and three German children, two bigger boys and a girl.

The children fight and push silently. One of them almost steps on the egg and shatters it. Beate scratches, kicks and wiggles as the two boys try to restrain her. When they start fighting with each other, she smartly trips the girl reaching for the egg. She runs as she has never run before, remembering nevertheless to hold the egg tenderly in her hand rather than clutching it.

She takes it to our room. It is down a long corridor, far away from the huge institutional kitchen. After everyone else has gone to bed, my mother tiptoes to the kitchen to boil the egg in the dark. She has a lid for the pan and a borrowed hot water bottle with her. She will say she is only heating water for one of us who is not feeling well.

She brings the boiled egg back to the room, peels it, slices it in five parts, gives my sister and me and my father the parts with the most yolk in it. She and Ōmīte, our grandmother, eat the ends. We drink the water for any calcium leached from the shell. We talk about other eggs, other wonderful dishes we have eaten in times past. The following day my mother buries the tiny pieces of shell in the cemetery.

A few weeks later we share three potatoes in the dark. My father has been working, digging a ditch for corpses in the meadow on the edge of the woods. The Russian soldiers are getting ready to boil potatoes, but they need kindling and smaller branches in addition to the logs they already have. They order him to find some. He spends the last few hours of the day dragging branches out of the woods, going back and forth slowly, hoping they will not order him to work even further away from home than he already is.

When they finally have enough wood, they light the fire and tell him to wash the mud-caked potatoes. He begs for some, but they refuse him. He steals three potatoes, concealing them in the pants and jacket that flap about his thin body. As he is leaving, one of the soldiers asks, "Have you taken anything?"

"No," he lies.

He, a man of deep integrity and a minister of God, has begged, stolen and lied. It shatters him.

He cries when he gives my mother the three potatoes. It is the second time that I have seen him cry.

When my mother returns from the kitchen with the boiled potatoes and the water bottle borrowed again for explanation, we eat the potatoes wordlessly.

But that seems long ago. Now the women and children watch quietly while the soldiers eat and drink, then slowly walk the long distances back to the Institution. Our buckets and bowls are almost always empty, but we are too ashamed to say anything to each other.

The blisters on our feet sting; our shoulders, arms and legs ache, but we hardly notice. Only our boils throb violently, insistently. When they burst, there is momentary relief. We do not mind the stench of our own pus and blood, but we do not like smelling someone else's, so we walk at arm's length from each other.

Behind the main building of the Institution is a long low shed. Cars and trucks, now gone, were once kept there, as were plows and carts. Anything that could be used to escape with has long since disappeared. The hoes and rakes are still there, leaning against the wall, useless. The spades are used every week to bury the dead.

Trestles have been set up in the shed, sheets of plywood laid over them. The corpses are carried out here and kept for burying days, Wednesday afternoons and Sunday mornings. Sacking and canvas are spread over the faces and chests of the corpses; the blue heavy hands and bare gnarled feet are left uncovered. Shoes, shirts and pants are always removed for someone else to wear.

Although we have been strictly forbidden to enter the shed, my sister and I spend a lot of time in here. Behind a partition we are erecting our own world. Pine cones, sticks, stones, buttons, broken glass and china are laid out in rows and circles, tiny enclosures and fences. We pretend that we are living on a prosperous farm in a village, milking cows, feeding pigeons, celebrating weddings. We make up elaborate dialogues with out Latvian uncles, aunts, cousins, friends and with our future husbands. Beate believes she will go to America and marry "Mr. Limberton." We make an enclosure of acorns for his mansion.

When the elaborate patterns are complete, we take sticks and rakes and attack them, destroying the neat rows, swirling the dust and dirt over them, stomping on them with both feet, obliterating.

"There," we sigh with satisfaction.

But then exhaustion overtakes us again. We sit still and stare. Later we tiptoe between the rows of corpses, collect and sort the buttons, pebbles, bits of glass for the next construction. We talk quietly, wiping the shards of dusty glass on our skirts.

We know most of the dead people; a lot of them are inmates we used to talk to before the Russian soldiers came, before it got so silent. Herr Schmidt gave Beate a picture of sunflowers once when he heard she had been crying because she wanted to go back to Latvia. We touch his bony fingers and hands, uncover his face and look at him.

Another day we find Hans among the corpses. He used to stride purposefully across the courtyard, then stop, paralyzed and terrified.

"He needs to know which foot he should put forward next," Frau Braun, the director's wife, told us.

We would run from skipping rope or playing hide-and-seek and pull on one of his pants legs.

"This one, this one, use this one."

That would get him going again. He would continue, a clear smile of success on his face. His feet look very much alike now. Impossible to believe they would give him such trouble choosing.

One day Frau Braun's baby is brought in, still in his little white wicker basket, a piece of gauze curtain draped over him. I lift off the white cloth and stare at the small pinched, bluish face, spread apart his tiny fingers, lift and wiggle his feet. When we hear Frau Braun coming, I hastily drop the gauze over the cradle and hide behind the partition. We hear her sobbing, lifting the baby up, crooning to it. She shuffles out when she hears someone walking by.

As soon as she is gone, I continue inspecting and rearranging the baby's tiny limbs. We know he has died of dysentery, typhoid or hunger, like all the others. We do not think about dying of disease ourselves. When I get bored playing with him, we cover the cradle and look around carefully for adults before leaving the shed. We do not want any interference with our coming here again.

Under my bed is an old wood box with my doll in it. The doll, my only toy from Latvia, is a chubby, pretty four-year old, with a porcelain face, lifelike limbs of rubber and a sturdy cloth body. Her right arm has been ripped off, and her blond hair is dirty and matted. My mother found her in a ditch where the soldiers had strewn and trampled some of our things. Expecting me to be pleased, she handed the doll to me.

I cannot stand the sight of the doll, I hate her. I feel outraged when my mother asks, "Have you played with Lienīte today? Have you fed her? Have you rocked her to sleep?" I have nothing to feed her with. Perhaps I could find something to replace the tiny tea set left in Latvia, but I do not. I feel guilty that the doll is hungry and scared, but I continue to punish her by leaving her in the dusty darkness under the bed. I am glad she is finally getting what she deserves. I myself prefer the games in the shed.

Sunday afternoons my sister and I accompany our mother to the graveyard, which is overfilled. Three long trenches have been dug in the meadow behind the cemetery; they stretch across it to the edge of the woods. The corpses are carried out on pallets, the drop cloths and sacks removed and folded for use next time. The pathetic bony bodies in stained underwear, their arms folded across their chests, are laid directly in the muddy trench. Sometimes their eyes and mouths are open. I like looking at the clods of earth hitting their faces, covering their chests, hiding them, completing something. The old men bury their fellows, smooth the clay over them.

Two of the trenches are full, the third is half filled. My mother places a bouquet of wild purple asters over the most recently buried, bends her head and closes her eyes. Her lips move. She is either praying or talking to herself. My sister and I lean against the pile of stones at the head of the trench. A rough wooden cross rises from it.

We wait patiently until she turns her attention back to us.

"Soon we will be buried here as well," she sighs. "All we can do is wait."

She lifts her thin arm and examines it, touches the white indentations where her wedding ring and watch used to be before the soldiers forced them off.

"It will be a relief, really. Nothing to be afraid of, darlings, we'll just lie down and rest with the others. So peaceful."

The trench-scarred meadow is not peaceful at all. It looks rough and unfinished: the corpses probably stir underground during the night. We stare at her.

"I hope we die while someone is still alive to bury us," she whispers.

I stretch out full length and fold my hands across my chest, my head on the pile of stones, my face turned away from my mother. When my mother keeps talking, I grasp my elbows above my head, effectively shutting my ears. I close my eyes and lie very still.

Beate has picked up a stick and is idly drawing crosses and circles within squares in the dust of the most recent grave, then obliterating them.

"I can't bear to see you so thin, precious. I cannot endure having to watch my children starve." My mother reaches to stroke my head, but at that moment I shift my position. I can't stand my mother talking like that; it reminds me of one of the times when we were almost shot. I wait for her to finish so that we can walk back to our room, stretch out on our cots, look at the ceiling and wait for darkness.

Amazing what gathering twilight can do. The last time I talked about my mother, Ingeborg told me that when she was a child her mother— lonely, unhappy in her marriage and cut off by World War II from her native country of Switzerland—started behaving strangely. She was committed to an institution for brief periods. As a little girl Ingeborg would lie in bed trembling, terrified that her mother would be taken away again. Finally her mother disappeared into an institution for good.

Ingeborg gives me two gifts, a sentence and a story. "No wonder your body craves food; it is terrified of starving," she says. Then she tells this story.

"When I was a little girl, we used to talk to a lot about the starving children in Europe. I used to take candy bars, little toys, sharpened pencils, anything small and easy to mail to school. My mother would talk in a crazy way, but she knew how to find the most useful things when I asked. Then we would put them all in a box and the Red Cross would mail them. Each class had a box. I never thought I would meet one of the starving children. You are one of the starving children."

I see the two little girls walking towards each other across the rubble-filled field by the lake. They are both blond, both about seven; their faces are hopeful but around them are darkness and devastation. An abandoned circus wagon with peeling paint is in the background, in it a hopeless dark woman imprisoned behind bars. The little girl coming from her direction offers the other, much thinner one, a bowl filled with bread and fruit. It is an act of absolute generosity.

As I am imagining this scene, I realize that the third gift Ingeborg has given me is tears. Tears have gathered in Ingeborg's large blue-gray eyes, they are flowing down her beautiful face. She is crying for me, which no one has done. Almost fifty years later I am finally able to feel. My own tears start to flow, and more words rise to my lips.

Part II

◆◆◆

• 4 •

Leaving Latvia

It was sunny the day before we were to leave our house, the sky blue and untroubled above the birches and maples. Some of the leaves were beginning to turn yellow and red, but bees still buzzed around the beds of purple and white asters and the pale yellow chrysanthemums that my mother loved. My father buried a box filled with silver flatware, goblets and the samovar, and he made my sister and me memorize the spot. We put away our dolls and toys in a cupboard that had been carried up to the attic, and my mother and Elvīra, her friend, stored clothing and linens up there too.

My sister and I were allowed to go over to "Burtnieki", the neighbors' house, to say goodbye. We held hands as we walked past the raft on the pond brimming with water lilies, where we were forbidden to play by ourselves but sometimes did, past the barn filled with fragrant hay where we had slept the summer before and across the field where Zilīte ("Little Acorn") grazed. The old white mare, whom we rode bareback, would be cared for by one of my father's parishioners while we were gone. We were both looking forward to spending the afternoon at the neighbors' house, a magic place where we had always been allowed to stay up later than at home, where open dishes of boiled poisonous mushrooms sweetened with sugar stood on the win-

37

dowsills in the summer and enticed and killed hundreds of flies, and where pots of asparagus fern flourished in the winter. Wild strawberries grew in profusion behind the house, and the loom, on which Mrs. Andersons sometimes allowed me to weave under her close supervision, was set up in the low, cool entranceway.

At dusk Beate and I returned home past the hill where a huge bonfire had blazed on John's Eve, the midsummer celebration, and where I had sat on my father's shoulders, watching dozens of fires on the other hills and listening to the singing from hill to nearby hill. The long expanse of lawn in front of the Parsonage was scarred with trenches, and we knew we would have to hide in them when the shooting started. So far we had slept in the basement on the nights when the planes roared overhead, and all the windows were covered with heavy black cloth before the lamps were lit.

The Russian front was advancing closer and closer. If we did not leave our house soon, we would be killed or maimed in the crossfire between the Nazis and Soviets. Or we would be arrested, sealed into cattle cars and deported to Siberian labor camps, the way that we had almost been before I could remember, in 1941, the Year of Terror.

But none of that seemed real to me yet. I was far more terrified of Mrs. Detlava, the new maid who had charge of my sister and me when my parents were away from home. She would swoop us up, deposit us in bed and give us her instructions.

"You girls be quiet, you better be as still as the sealed tomb after I turn out the light."

She would pinch my lower lip and pull it toward her sharply.

"If I hear one sound from you, I'll spit right in there." She would point downward into my mouth and clear her throat meaningfully.

"Remember, there has never been a better spitter than me."

Shocked but thrilled by her evil intentions, we giggled.

"The water is gathering in my mouth, girls. I'll do what I must," she would say. "I'm talking to you too, Beate, you're the rambunctious one. You're always thinking up new naughty tricks and teaching them to your little sister."

If she caught us looking at the door to the hallway longingly, she would pounce. "Don't you try tiptoeing out when my back is turned, either. If you step outside this door, you'll die. It's as simple as that. There are German hooligans, the cursed Nazis are out there, just waiting to catch Latvian children, and the Russians, those godless Communists, are not far away. And other things. Too many, I don't have to tell you."

But she listed them for us anyway. Succubi, devils, witches, magicians, vampires, werewolves, ghosts and wild boars. And Mēris, the plague, a skeleton dressed as a gentleman, in a black cape and jewels, ready to toss dice in a game of chance, and win.

"You're lucky to be inside, safe in your own beds for a while longer."

Refugees had been streaming past the house for weeks, but I did not think we would be gone for very long, certainly not forever. I had been on one trip with my parents the summer before, when I was five, and I could remember how excited I had been to go and how absolutely happy to come back to the house and the trees and the animals and my toys and my bed. I assumed that our return would be like that, that we would be back before the long sweep of daffodils burst into bloom by the bedroom windows, before the fragrance of lilacs and mock orange, which we called jasmine, scented the air on the veranda. My parents must have thought so too because my father carefully locked the door and put the key in his briefcase. He had sent another key to the neighbors with us, and he had buried yet a third with the samovar and other things.

As we made our way to the seashore, we stayed with relatives and my parents' friends, and although the adults spoke sadly of not being allowed to go to America by the Germans occupying Latvia and being worried about finding a boat that would take us to Germany, their anxiety did not seem real either. We met cousins whom we had not seen and made friends easily with other children also on their way to the coast. Going to bed early, brushing our teeth, being quiet while the adults talked were rules no longer so strictly enforced as at home. Only when the adults clustered around the radios turned very low, listening to news of the war broadcast by the BBC, which the Germans had outlawed, did we have to be absolutely still.

I remember only one incident that was ominous on our way to the seaside. The caravan of seven or so wagons was to stay on the estate of the sister of one of my mother's musical friends. But when we arrived at her large house in the country, it was deserted. The door had been forced open and partially ripped off its hinges, and it banged monotonously against the frame. Inside, the cupboards had been ransacked, clothing and broken dishes lay scattered on the floor, flies buzzed around a dark torn piece of cloth that my mother said smelled of blood.

The adults disagreed about what to do, and my mother tried to call the police in town, but the phone was dead, the receiver dangling useless from its long black cord. Had the owner gone away herself or had someone abducted her? Had the Nazis arrested her, or had the Russian partisans, unshaven men with haunted eyes who lived in the woods, dragged her away? Two partisans had come to our house the week before and had asked a lot of threatening questions, but Ōmīte, my mother's mother, had cleverly pretended that all the men were working in the field beyond the hill and would be home for dinner, even though they had gone to Riga to try to book a passage on a ship, any ship leaving Latvia.

The deserted house and courtyard made a great impression on me because they were my first experience of real disorder and displacement. The forced door especially terrified me. I could feel how exposed we would be if we stayed there, and I could not bear the monotonous way it banged, again and again, so that I was relieved when our caravan consisting of half a dozen families continued onward.

The sunlight caressed the crimson and white chrysanthemums in the abandoned courtyard. The flowers were the same colors as the Latvian flag, which is based on the white wool cape stained with blood, which a dying hero's followers carried to victory against German invaders. But I did not know that then.

The flowers are so vivid in my memory because it is the last time I remember it being sunny until long after the war, though of course it must have been. Latvia in my memory is forever associated with sunlight. When I visualize the Parsonage and grounds, the sun is always shining, and even if I am standing in the shade of the gloomy oaks, it is always a sunny day in summer or late spring. Ancient Latvians worshipped the sun and trees, which their German oppressors tried to force them to give up for Christ and the cross. They embodied the sun in stylized forms in their jewelry and praised it in folk songs and myths. Later Latvian poets celebrated the sun with words. My sister and I sang countless songs about the sun, though our family name, "Nesaule," means "no sunlight."

The last house that we stayed at belonged to my Uncle Jaša, who was a surgeon instead of a Lutheran minister like the other men in the family. Since we had to be on the ship by nightfall, we set off from there in the gray chilly afternoon. My mother was crying because her friend Elvīra had not come back and would have to be left behind, but everyone else seemed calm and resigned. My Aunt Zenta went back into the house to make sure she had not forgotten anything, and when she came out she stood on the veranda, motioning to my uncle.

"Come, lock the door," she called.

As if he had not heard her, Uncle Jaša continued sitting in the carriage, waiting for her.

"Lock the door, Jaša, we can't leave it open," Aunt Zenta repeated.

"Oh, what's the use?" he shrugged. When her voice trembled as she called him again, he got down from the carriage, put his arms around her and stroked her hair.

"It's no use locking it, precious," he said. "Someone else will stay here after we are gone. Refugees, Gypsies, partisans, the army. At least they won't break down the door if I leave it unlocked."

"But our things," she cried. "All the books and paintings. All the dishes and clothes. And Ilze's dolls. I want them safe until we come back." She started crying in earnest.

"We're not going to be back, we'll never be allowed to live here again." He continued comforting her, but he made no move to lock the door.

Finally he took out the heavy black iron key and laid it on the windowsill. "Let's leave it here for the next person," he said to her gently. "It's pointless locking up. Let them have the key if they want it. The Germans have taken our whole country, let them have the key too. And when the Russians come back in, they can all kill each other as they fight for it."

Aunt Zenta did not argue any more, and my father did not tell them how he had locked our door and the great care he had taken with our keys, so something must have changed in the few short weeks since we had left our house. Returning home was less likely, but that too did not seem real yet.

After the ship started moving, my mother and aunts took my sister and me and several cousins up on deck. We were already out of the harbor of Liepāja, and all we could see was black water and dark gray sky and a lot of fog.

Then, to our left, the outline of a tree rose out of the gloomy fog surrounding it. It was a white birch, a tree sacred to ancient Latvians, standing alone on a hillside. It was startling to see it like that, without any other trees nearby, leafless, and this made it look bereft and vulnerable.

"Look," Aunt Zenta pointed, "the last tree of Latvia. That's the very last one, try to remember it." She put her hands on my head and held them there, willing me to see.

For the first time the possibility became real that I might not be able to go back to my bed with the blue goose-down quilt and to Zilite grazing in the meadow. A wave of wrenching sadness flowed over me. I wanted to touch the tree and to hold on to it, but of course I could not. I kept my eyes on it until it disappeared into the dirty gray fog.

"Promise you'll remember it," my mother said, and I nodded.

I still dream of the tree sometimes and feel the same immense sudden sadness whenever I do, and I am reminded of it whenever I see a solitary birch, which happens more often than one would think.

My cousin told me recently that during the night, the convoy of ships we were on was bombed and that the ship closest to ours was hit. Dazed and injured people pushed into our already overcrowded space, German soldiers shouted and shoved. The survivors had to jump from their sinking ship or walk on wobbling planks in order to be taken aboard. She said that the cries of those who lost family members were terrible. Knowing that the bombs were aimed directly at us and that it was only chance that we had not been killed was terrifying.

I do not remember any of that, though I must have seen and heard it. All I remember is the wrenching loss as I watched the last birch disappear. I have relived it again and again. Behind the gray fog surrounding it was Latvia and sunlight and our house and my room with my bed in it.

The adults had assumed that once we disembarked in Germany, we would be allowed to contact friends, find a place to live and move about freely. Instead, uniformed guards with swastika armbands and guns kept us waiting on platforms for days and then ordered us into a train, which crossed Germany, took us into Poland and then back into Germany again. After about a week on the train, we were taken to a place called Lehrte.

A high barbed-wire fence surrounded the dilapidated gray barracks. Iron bars covered the dirty windows, chains and more bars secured the doors. The countryside outside the camp was flat and gray. No trees or houses broke the monotony of the deserted fields.

Inside the gates the earth was an expanse of mud. If grass had ever grown there, every blade had been trampled to death long ago. Mud and more mud stretched before us. Narrow planks had been laid here and there across it to prevent one from sinking in forever, and these too were covered with mud and slippery.

Guards in dark uniforms and high black boots hurried us along. They carried thin sticks that may have been riding crops, which they switched against their boots impatiently. Large black dogs strained on their leashes towards us. The black visors of the hats the guards wore gleamed dully.

A flag with a swastika on a red background waved in the center of the muddy space surrounded by barracks. We were made to line up here, the mud impossible to avoid, and issued tags with numbers on them. These were to be sewn on our clothes. A guard shouted in German and someone translated into Latvian that we were to wear our numbers at all times, that from now on we would be called by numbers rather than by our names, that no one would be given food without a number and that anyone caught not wearing a number would be punished.

The men and boys were lined up and marched off in one direction, and women and children in another. We were taken into a long room and ordered to undress while the guards watched through the open door. It was embarrassing and frightening. The room was bitterly cold, and there was not enough space on the wooden benches to lay down suitcases and clothes neatly. My mother and aunts tried to hide their watches under the piles of lacy slips and silk blouses, which looked pathetic and inappropriate on the rough wooden benches.

To be surrounded in a communal shower room by the naked bodies of so many women and even boys my age was unpleasant. The water, which at first was ice cold and then too hot, came down in stinging needles. But we had not washed for more than a week since leaving Latvia, so that we felt refreshed as we dried on the rough thin towels we had been issued. We were then taken to another area where the guards opened all suitcases, confiscated some money and jewelry and then sprayed the contents with an unpleasant chemical. After that, they stuck their sprayers down the front of our dresses, then the back, then up under our skirts. The chemical made our eyes and noses burn, and the sweetish sharp smell stayed on our skin and hair and in our clothes the whole time we were in Lehrte, but the spraying was repeated after every shower. The adults recognized it as the same chemical they had used to kill cockroaches at home, but which they had never aimed at a person. In the 1950s in the United States, I remembered the odor when I smelled DDT.

We were taken to a room where we would spend the next three months. About twelve feet wide and twenty-four feet long, with barred windows, it was filled with people huddled in bunk beds. The guard bolted and locked the door behind us. We were locked in. From now on we were no longer free to choose to perform the most basic actions—to eat, to wash, to get a breath of fresh air or a drink of water, to go to the lavatories outside—without the permission of the guards.

The days at Lehrte were monotonous and long. We were woken early each morning by sirens, then we dressed in the blue-gray cold and hurried outside in order to have a chance at using the latrines and the sinks. There were not enough of these, so resentment and silent shoving were common. We lined up in the square until the guards had checked off all our numbers, which could take a long time if someone was late or missing. Then we lined up again, carrying the shallow metal bowls we had been issued, and waited to be given food. It was always the same, a thin and sour gray soup made of kohlrabi and cabbage, which was ladled out both midmorning and at night. It was important to get into line quickly, as soon as the sirens sounded, because sometimes the huge cauldrons would run out of soup and those at the end of the line would get nothing. If any of the soup was ever left over, no seconds were given; it was simply passed out again at the next meal. Sometimes we were also given bread, which was either moldy or so hard that dipping it into the soup did not make it palatable. We were hungry and cold most of the time.

Lights were turned out early and we would try to go to sleep, only to be driven to distraction by bedbugs, which were undeterred by the DDT on our bodies and clothes. Round, black, swollen with blood, hundreds of them came out of the walls and the wooden posts of the bunks. The itching and pain would wake us throughout the night. Uncle Jaša refused to subject himself to the bugs; in defiance of regulations, he slept in the middle of the hard floor, his head on his suitcase.

All the methods we tried to lessen the torment failed. The adults would take turns staying awake and fanning those sleeping, but this made little difference. A more exciting method was for everyone to sit still for five minutes after the lights were turned out so as to give the bugs a chance to leave their hiding places. Then my father would light a candle and we would all swat, stamp and squash as many as we could. Even the candle was used to singe those scurrying away.

Cousin Guks had the most effective technique. Heating an implement made of a straightened safety pin, he speared the bugs, then brought them to the candle flame. They exploded with a satisfying crackling pop. Then he would blow out the candle, and we would sit still for another five minutes and repeat the procedure. The numbers of bugs did not diminish, but the hunt was exciting, and I was very sorry when the guards confiscated the candle.

We stayed in Lehrte for three months, but I remember few incidents from it. Mostly I remember the monotony and the cold and the endless mud. With the exception of the flag with the swastika, I do not remember colors other than gray. But two incidents do stand out.

I was at a barred window, watching the yard and the barbed-wire fence beyond that. It was beginning to snow; there was a light dusting on the frozen mud and dirty gray planks. It was exciting because the snow would change them to white. I was thinking about the red-breasted birds that came to feed on the rinds of bacon that were fastened to the tree branches by the dining-room windows in Latvia. They had always looked especially vivid against the snow. I wished there was something to look at here—trees, birds or animals.

An old man came out of the barracks across the yard and shuffled towards the latrines. It was startling to see him because no one was allowed outside then. He moved slowly, as if in pain, taking care to stay on the planks, which were slippery. I was impatient, I wished he would move faster before a guard saw him.

He got halfway across the yard and then stood still, looking where to step next. At that moment a guard blew a whistle, but the old man continued looking down at his feet as if paralyzed. Two guards came running through the swirling snow, brandishing their sticks and shouting. They seized him and began to beat him. It is hard for me now, in an era when everyone has seen thousands of beatings and killings on television, to explain how shocking and unnatural this was. I had never before seen anyone hit, let alone beaten; my sister and I had never been spanked or slapped, I had never seen a fistfight or a wrestling match. I stood at the window trembling, unable to take my eyes off the old man, who was pathetically trying to shield his head from the blows of the guards. Blood started flowing from his nose or maybe his mouth, and he cupped both hands over his face, bent his head further and knelt down, receiving the blows.

By this time the adults had heard the commotion and were at the windows too. They were looking at the old man being beaten, which I am now sure the guards wanted us to see. Soon my mother put her hands over my eyes, and I did not resist. She drew me and my sister away from the window and reminded us once more to be very quiet and very good, so that the guards would not get angry at us. Being very quiet and very good had an entirely different meaning here than in Latvia.

I could not stop trembling, and that evening I developed a high fever, which my Uncle Jaša diagnosed as being caused by an enlarged spleen. Later I developed another ailment that made my legs swell up to twice their size so that I could not walk, and I spent the rest of the time in my bunk. Somehow my mother got permission to bring soup to me and to the old Latvian woman who slept in the bunk bed below me.

I do not remember her name, just that she was very old. She was thin and bent over, and she looked much older than my grandmother. She had arrived in Germany months before we had. She spent most of her time standing by the barred windows, looking out at the muddy yard, craning her neck to see the gates. She was waiting for her daughter, from whom she had been separated in the crush of people getting onto an overcrowded train. She hoped that nothing bad had happened to her daughter, and she worried that the authorities were keeping them apart to torment them. She believed that as soon as her daughter arrived she would be released and together they would go live on a quiet elegant street in Vienna or Berlin, or the two of them might even go back to Latvia and live together there.

As she got sicker and more frail, she spent most of her time in bed, asking others to go look out the window for her, and the two of us got to be good friends. She knew stories and songs that she would recite in her slow quivering voice, and I would lean over my bed and look down at her face to hear her.

One afternoon I finished rereading my book of fairy tales from

Latvia, which I had memorized by then, and looked down to see if I could get her to tell me a story. All the adults were clustered around the narrow plank table at the other end of the room.

Her faded blue eyes were open and so was her mouth, and when I spoke to her, she did not respond but continued staring straight up, past me. Her body was unusually still and a fly had settled on her cheek, which she did not try to brush away. Something about that terrified me, and I screamed, so that the adults rushed over. My mother swept me into her arms and put her hands over my eyes to keep me from seeing, a gesture that became more familiar and more futile as the war went on. The last thing I saw was my grandmother kissing the old woman's cheek and then pressing her eyes closed.

I still do not know exactly what kind of place Lehrte was. The scarcity of food, the brutality of the guards, the numbers we had to wear on our clothing all suggest a concentration camp, but certainly it was not an extermination camp. After the old woman died, a bitter argument erupted between the Polish laborers who shared our room and my father and uncles. The Poles wanted to keep the body hidden for a few days instead of reporting it, so that the extra bowl of soup would still be issued and could be eaten by others. The guards discovered the body and ordered it carried out almost immediately, but the argument suggests how hungry we were.

Once when I asked my sister about Lehrte, she said that it was a place where people the Nazis did not trust were concentrated, that it was *like* a concentration camp, but was not one in actuality. When I told Ingeborg about Lehrte, she said, "It was a prison, and you were prisoners," which shocked me. "No," I said, "it was *like* a prison, but we were not prisoners."

Now I think it was a prison and we were prisoners, but it is impossible for me to find out the real meaning of so many things. A few weeks after the beating of the old man and the death of the old woman, her daughter arrived. A thin, dark-haired woman in gray-and-black-striped clothes, she came in, escorted by two guards. They allowed her to touch the pillow of the bunk bed that had once been her mother's, and she sat down on it briefly, although it had already been assigned to someone else. When they led her away between them, across the muddy planks, I could not tell whether they were helping her to walk or holding onto her to restrain her. Was she an honored guest or a prisoner about to be executed in another camp?

•5•

The Basement

We were extraordinarily lucky to receive work orders that allowed us to leave Lehrte. Uncle Jaša and his family were released first, to work in a hospital where doctors were badly needed to treat those injured in the frequent air raids. Shortly thereafter, my father and my Uncle Gustavs received work orders for the Lobethal Institution for the Mentally Defective, where they would work alongside inmates in the fields, and my mother and aunt would work in the kitchens. Everyone was overjoyed. Although the journey by trains filled with pushing, surging crowds would be hard, we believed we had experienced the worst at the hands of soldiers and guards. Lobethal was very different from Lehrte. Instead of barbed wire and endless gray mud, it was surrounded by apple orchards, gardens, rivers and lakes.

The basement under the main building of the Institution was used primarily to store food. It consisted of rooms filled with glass jars of preserves, barrels of sauerkraut and bins of potatoes, carrots and onions. It was not a good place to hide during air raids because bombs falling nearby could shatter the glass, which could then cut faces or sever veins. Even as the war went on and the basement was gradually emptied of food, people usually did not hide there because the huge building above it was thought to be a likely target.

Close to the lake was an old boathouse. Its upper story was partially demolished, but the lower level carved into the side of an embankment was secure. Pleasure boats and fishing boats had once been stored in the vast rooms below the earth. By this time all the boats were gone. The huge wooden doors shut snugly to create a haven safe from flying glass. The three huge rooms inside the boathouse basement were divided by partitions, so that each family or group of inmates had its own small area, marked with letters and numbers, more for the idea of order than for help in finding our places because usually we ran to this shelter in the dark, as the sirens wailed.

During the first few nights of the raids, we went to sleep in our own beds, hoping each night the Allied planes would not come. As the weeks wore on, we started sleeping in the boathouse basement to avoid the inevitable frantic dash across the courtyard, while sirens howled and lights flashed in the distance. We slept on thin mattresses, blankets spread on piles of hay and dingy canvas lawn chairs that had once been gaily striped. We were grateful for a place to hide during the raids.

The bales of hay that were piled against the doors of the basement did not muffle the sound of the bombs falling, sometimes far away, sometimes quite close. Everyone was very still as the bombs whistled their way to the earth. Occasionally someone would say, "Thank God," when a bomb fell near but not on the shelter, but words were rare. It was hard to know where the bomb had landed. Once we had applauded, thinking a bomb had fallen harmlessly in the lake, only to learn later that it had destroyed a wing of the village orphanage and killed some half-dozen orphans, ten- and twelve-year-old girls.

Arguments sometimes erupted in the darkness during quiet moments between planes. Someone would light a candle or a flashlight, others would object that the faint light could still somehow be seen through a crack. The hay bales caused disagreements as well. Would it be better to place them inside or outside the doors? What would be our chances of getting out of the basement if they caught on fire? Would it be better to dispense with them altogether?

But usually it was very quiet during the raids. A young inmate started whistling in the dark once, only to be hushed from all sides.

"Think they can hear him all the way up in the plane, with their engines roaring?" Pastor Braun, the director of the Institution, laughed. But the shushing continued, and the whistling stopped.

Disagreements about assigned places were quickly settled by Pastor Braun, who usually got people to trade amicably. For every person who wanted to be as far away from the doors as possible there was another who was afraid of being trapped during a fire and so was eager for a place nearer the lake.

German soldiers seldom entered the basement, just as they seldom appeared in the village. They were off fighting at the front. Once a jeep filled with men in Nazi uniforms arrived. They moved through the basement, shining flashlights into faces. People held their breaths and prayed silently that the Gestapo was not looking for them. The uniformed men asked to see papers, and Pastor Braun, who carried a ledger with him, interceded for inmates. The Nazis pulled a young dark-haired woman from a bunk, who pleaded with them. Pastor Braun spoke earnestly to an officer. But in the end they took her with them, paying no attention to his arguments or her entreaties. Originally from Vienna, she had been employed briefly in the kitchen. Her papers seemed not to be in order after all. Pastor Braun was unable to claim her as an inmate because the Institution housed only men.

Pastor Braun was accustomed to dealing with Nazi officials, but even his ability to protect had limits. The seven hundred men who lived and worked in the Institution were called mental defectives. They included the emotionally disturbed, the retarded and the neurologically damaged. Only years after the war did my mother tell us that political refugees and Jews had been hidden in their midst. Pastor Braun was periodically called to Berlin to justify the continued existence of the Institution and its inmates. More simply put, he had to convince the Nazi officials that they should not murder the people living in Lobethal. The officials saw their very existence as an affront to the creation of the master race.

Whenever Pastor Braun went to Berlin, the adults worried. So far he had been able to keep everyone alive by showing that the inmates, who worked in the fields and orchards that extended beyond the Institution, produced a great deal more food than they consumed and so were contributing to the war effort. He was ordered to keep increasingly detailed records about how much each living unit and each work group produced. He feared that a particular group of the men would be found to be less productive and therefore executed, so he had to juggle his figures. Or he could be ordered to start keeping separate records of how much food each man produced, which would endanger the oldest and frailest. And he must have been terrified that the Jews and political activists would somehow be discovered and all the inmates killed in retaliation. He himself and his staff would certainly die as well, and Lobethal would no longer shelter anyone. Pastor Braun worked on the books constantly, even with a flashlight during air raids. No one dared to object to him directly about his dim light, though some people grumbled about it in loud whispers.

My mother admired Pastor Braun and often sat next to him. He in turn seemed to enjoy her conversation as a reminder of a more elegant and carefree prewar world. I could hear their quiet voices talking in German as I fell asleep; they talked about books and music, about rowing on the lake, going to concerts and operas. Sometimes they recited poems in Russian and French, which they both knew. He did not speak of his fears for the inmates to her then, and I doubt whether my mother added to his anxieties by telling him about what the Nazis in Latvia had done to Ārijs.

Ārijs was the brother of my mother's friend Elvīra. My mother and she had gone to the Teachers' Institute together and had taught briefly in the same village. After my mother married, Elvīra came to the Parsonage regularly and she spent her summer holidays with us. I was fascinated by Elvīra because she had no family and because she seemed to know the darkest secrets. Her brother Ārijs was an axe murderer. Once his mother's favorite son and a brilliant philosophy student, Ārijs had one day taken an axe and had killed his mother.

Murder in Latvia was so rare as to be almost unimaginable. Even in 1944, when most families had been touched by the executions and deportations to Siberia during the Russian occupation of 1940–1941, when others had lost sons in war and seen neighbors arrested by the Nazis, the adults discussed a personal murder heatedly. A husband had watched his wife's lover through an uncurtained window and shot him. They speculated endlessly about this case.

Elvīra not only knew a murderer, but she had actually lived with one; he was her brother, and he had killed her mother. I waited for Elvīra to say something dramatic about this brother, but she seldom spoke of him, and then it was only to say something insignificant, like she hoped she could finish the socks she was knitting so that she could take them with her when she went to see him.

My mother would sometimes accompany Elvīra on these trips. They would spend the morning walking around the town and then visit Ārijs in the Institution. They would sit with him and watch him color or make simple drawings in the notebooks they brought him. He was always happy to see them, but often he did not seem to know who Elvīra was. He would be delighted if they brought him fruit or candy. If they brought flowers, he thanked them politely but left them where he laid them down. He spoke cheerfully to everyone they met on their walks about the grounds. Elvīra would cry on the way back into town, but then she would blow her nose, say he seemed quite well and happy, and that she would try to feel better if she could. My mother and she would have coffee and cakes in a café and return in good spirits from their outing.

It was late spring when they went to see him for the last time. Walking up the long circular drive to the Institution, they were admiring the blossoming apple trees behind the kitchen, so that at first they did not notice how empty it was. The usual carts and bicycles were not there, the director's car was gone. Perhaps they had forgotten which was visiting day or perhaps it had been changed. Under the German occupation, new rules were constantly imposed. They pulled on the massive doors, but they were locked.

They rang the bell, waited, rang again. Only then did they realize fully how silent everything was. They stepped back and looked up at the wing with barred windows. No one looked out at them through the bars, no one was on the wooden benches beneath the trees where they had so often sat with Ārijs. They climbed up on a ledge and peered in a window. They could see a corner of the reception hall and the glassed-in area for the secretaries. It was empty.

"They must have transferred everyone somewhere," my mother said, though she was far from convinced.

"Yes, I suppose so," Elvīra agreed halfheartedly.

They walked down the steps, uncertain what to do next.

"Perhaps they will know in town what has happened."

They looked back once more when they reached the gate. From this angle they could see the kitchen gardens to the side of the orchard. They were relieved to see five or six inmates, or perhaps it was orderlies, working in the gardens. They half walked, half ran towards them.

"Where is Ārijs? Where is everybody?" Elvīra shouted at them before she was near enough for them to hear. The men continued shoveling. The man leaning against a tree was an old farmer, the men working for him looked like Russian prisoners of war.

"Where is Ārijs?" Elvīra was close enough finally.

"They're dead. They are all dead," said the farmer. He looked past her.

"Dead? How can he be dead? He was fine last week."

"Everyone is dead, I just told you." He kept his eyes on the road.

"You can't be talking about my brother, my brother Ārijs. Where is he? Do you know him?"

The farmer finally looked at her, while the half-dozen prisoners continued leveling the soil.

"All the inmates are dead."

"How could they be? He wasn't even sick last week."

"I wish they would put an official notice on the door. You're the third one I've had to tell today. They gave everyone poisoned tea the day before yesterday. We've had to work without stopping to get them all buried. It's been hard work, they're exhausted." He motioned to the prisoners. "At least they made the inmates dig the trench for their own graves at the beginning of the week, otherwise I don't know what we could have done. Just covering them has been hard enough."

"He isn't talking about Ārijs, he couldn't be," Elvīra said to my mother. "They can't have killed Ārijs."

"They did," the man repeated bleakly.

"Where is the director? I want to speak to him."

"He's long gone, he left last week."

The farmer turned away from them, back to the prisoners. He pointed to a rough area of the immense trench and motioned irritably to one to grade it.

"They can't have killed Ārijs," Elvīra kept repeating that afternoon as they questioned people in town, stood in line at the mayor's office and tried to find the address of one of the secretaries who Elvīra thought might remember her. But they had killed Ārijs and all the others as well.

Elvīra never believed that her brother was dead. She returned to town again and again, she stood in lines, searched, offered bribes, petitioned. When the Russian front was getting closer and we left for the seacoast to sail to Germany, my mother took Elvīra along. By this time Elvīra talked only about Ārijs; she had to be reminded to eat, to comb her hair and to tie her shoes. She stopped strangers pulling handmade carts and demanded that they admit they had seen her brother.

Shortly before we were all to sail to Germany, Elvīra started talking about going back to the Parsonage to get my mother's wedding gown. It wasn't that far, she said, and if she walked fast she could return in plenty of time. My mother pleaded with her at first, then simply forbade her to go. Elvīra seemed to accept this, she even stopped mentioning the wedding gown, the pretext she had slyly given for her journey, which would almost certainly leave her behind the advancing Russian lines.

But the morning we were to embark, Elvīra was gone. "I'm going to get your wedding gown," she had written. "You'll need it when your daughters marry." My mother cried, she urged my father and her brothers to try to book a later passage, which she knew to be impossible. She stood by the window waiting for Elvīra until the last minute. When we sailed on one of the last ships to leave Latvia, Elvīra was not with us. She had gone back to look for her brother.

Even if my mother never told Pastor Braun about the poisoned tea, everyone in the basement had plenty of reasons to be afraid. The inmates were at constant risk from the Nazis, of course. My parents worried that the work orders we had gotten at Lehrte, the camp where we were first imprisoned, would be revoked and we would be taken back there again or sent to another, much more dangerous camp. Everyone was afraid that the Russian soldiers, notorious for their brutality, would descend on us. They would arrest the men, rape the women and shoot everyone, including the children. Everyone feared the Americans and British, who bombed the area nightly. Anyone in uniform—camp guard, policeman, pilot or soldier—was terrifying.

Every day refugees pulling carts passed the gates of the Institution. The statue of the welcoming Christ, erected by the Lutheran Board that administered Lobethal and other places for the homeless and disadvantaged, invited them in. They would be given water and soup and allowed to sleep in a designated area of the basement. The refugees had news of the front and conflicting plans for escape. They argued among themselves which area of Germany was the most likely to be held by the Germans or occupied by the Allies. But everyone knew that to fall into the hands of the Russians would be the worst.

A family consisting only of a crippled father, a twelve-year-old daughter and five-year-old boy stopped for several days. The mother had been killed in an air raid. The girl washed their clothes, hung them out to dry and then patiently fed soup to her father, who seemed dazed. I watched this family as they packed up their cart. Not having a mother seemed more terrible than anything, though several of my schoolmates had no fathers. They were away at the front or had been killed in the war.

Of the people who had left Latvia together, my Uncle Jaša and Aunt Zenta were no longer with us. They had gone to Fischbach, an area that was eventually occupied by the Americans. Now other relatives and friends scattered. The last left was Uncle Gustavs, my mother's oldest brother. Together with his wife, Hermīne, their fifteen-year-old daughter, Astrīda, and thirteen-year-old Guks, he was building a cart out of scraps of wood and metal. The number of refugees increased, the sound of guns was closer. Finishing the cart in time was unlikely. Uncle Gustavs decided to abandon all their possessions and simply start walking west. If they escaped the Russians, they might all survive, and Astrīda might not be raped.

The last of the uncles and aunts and cousins were gone.

For another day after Uncle Gustavs left, refugees continued flowing by the gates. There was a constant low rumble of guns, German planes roared overhead in the daytime, American planes flew at night. Explosions were heard nearby, bombs fell even more frequently.

And then suddenly the stream of refugees ceased. No one came down the road. Except for the ominous roar of guns, the road was silent and empty. The adults peered into the distance, listening, waiting. A half-witted boy was the last one to run past. He looked over his shoulder as he ran. He would not stop to answer questions.

The afternoon was overcast, gray and chilly for late spring. It looked like darkness would fall long before evening. We met in the courtyard on our way to the basement.

"Pray God that we will be safe," my mother said as Pastor Braun passed us, leading a group of inmates to their shelter.

"He will let his light shine on us," he replied confidently.

"I am sorry you stayed behind for my sake," Ōmīte said. "I have had my life, but the girls have not."

"Shush, now," my mother soothed her mother. "We would never leave you, you know that. We have always been together."

"They won't do anything to an old woman. But I wish you had taken the girls and gone."

"We'll never abandon you. We will be together, whatever happens."

"Forgive me for all the times I've been angry with you," Ōmīte said. In a rare gesture, she embraced my mother and kissed her. Usually the two did not touch, and Ōmīte's face did not light up when she saw my mother, as it did whenever one of her sons entered the room. Now, as if embarrassed at her own emotion, Ōmīte bent down, caressed my forehead, smoothed my hair. I held my mother's hand firmly.

"We will be all right, nothing bad will happen," my mother said. "We'll just go into the basement, get under our blankets and go to sleep. When we wake up, maybe the Americans will be here. But if not, we will still be all right. And we will be together."

"Yes, don't be scared," Ōmīte said. "We will be all right, and we will be together," she repeated.

I was glad we had not gone away as my uncles had and left Ōmīte alone. Ōmīte would be so sad without us, she would be very frightened now, she would cry and no one would comfort her. I could not stand to imagine her so abandoned. And I myself felt secure. I knew that no matter what happened, my mother and father and sister would never leave me either, just as they had not left Ōmīte.

I pulled on my mother's hand. "Smile, please," I begged. In Latvia I had sometimes asked my mother to smile when she looked abstracted and sad, but I felt much greater urgency to see her happy and attentive now. Both my mother and my grandmother smiled.

Papa was hurrying out of the main building with another suitcase. Our possessions would all be stowed in the basement.

He was stumbling towards us, the suitcase much too heavy for him, but I could see that something else was terribly wrong.

He was crying.

Although he was struggling to control himself, there were tears in his eyes and a wild, broken sob escaped him. "They'll kill us. We are going to die." He dropped the suitcase and reached towards my mother.

"Not in front of the girls," my mother and Ōmīte said simultaneously.

"If they don't shoot us, they'll separate us, they'll deport us to torture camps in Siberia," he whispered. My mother let go of my hand to comfort him.

It was the first time I had seen my father cry. I was painfully sorry for him, I would do anything to help him. But my sympathy was lost in a wave of pure terror. Now I knew my father could not protect us, and something terrible was going to happen after all.

"Shush now, let's not frighten the girls." Ōmīte's voice was firm.

With fierce effort, my father steadied himself. "Only God can protect us now. Let us pray," he said.

The five of us formed a circle in the deserted yard. "Our Father, which art in heaven . . ."

When we finished, my mother said, "We will be all right. Or at least it will all be over quickly," she added as an afterthought.

"We are in God's hands, he will protect us," Ōmīte said.

But this time I did not believe her.

Another siren sounded, the guns seemed much closer. A cold rain was beginning to fall, the sky to the east was very dark. We hurried into the basement.

We woke before it was light, as someone was pushing the doors open. Heavy steps sounded, angry voices cursed in a foreign language, lights were flashed into faces.

"*Krievi*, the Russians," my mother whispered.

Darkness hid the faces of the soldiers themselves, who were searching the basement. They seized one of the inmates and shoved him out the door.

"*Uhri, Uhri*," the soldiers shouted. "*Uhri*!" They were looking for watches.

They shone a flashlight into Papa's face, then over his hands and arm. They pulled off his watch. Dark fingers pointed at his wedding ring. When he had trouble getting it off his finger, one of the soldiers made a chopping motion as he laughed. I could see his cruel face, the hollows exaggerated by the flickering lights. The slanted eyes held no mirth. He looked impassively as my father struggled to get off the ring. Finally my father got it past his knuckle and handed it meekly to the soldier.

"*Uhri*,"—watches—"*Uhri*," the soldiers continued through the basement. They dumped the contents of a few suitcases on the ground, kicked them with their boots and stamped on them. Then they made their way past the partition.

"Is it all over? Are they finished? Are they going to leave now and never come back?" I whispered to my mother.

"They're gone for now, but they will be back. It will be all right if we are very quiet, so that they do not notice us. You must not speak and you must not cry, otherwise they will be angry."

"Did you understand everything they said?" Ōmīte asked.

"No. Some of them are Mongolians, I think," my mother said.

"Dear God, preserve us," Ōmīte replied.

Almost immediately the soldiers returned and started shining lights in faces again. Uncle Gustavs and his family had been forced to return during the night. The road leading to safety had been blocked by Russian tanks. My sister and I had been strictly warned to tell no one that they had tried to escape or something terrible would happen to them. Maybe someone else had told the soldiers; I was sure that my sister and I had not. Uncle Gustavs and Guks were the first to be shoved with guns to the doors of the basement. Then other men were pushed to the doors.

"They are going to shoot them, oh my God, they are going to shoot them," one of the women screamed. A soldier hit her with the butt of his gun.

Two soldiers pulled Papa from his mattress. When he tried to touch my mother's hand, either to hold on or to say goodbye, a soldier kicked him from behind. It was too dark to see clearly, but I could hear him staggering. I wished as hard as I could that they would not hurt him, that he would not have to cry.

"Are they going to shoot him?" I tugged on my mother's arm.

"Shush," Mama said. "You have to be very quiet or they'll be furious. I don't think they will shoot everybody. Don't say anything." She put her hand over my mouth.

The soldiers were searching the basement, tossing bundles from corners, pushing all the men to the door. "Our Father, which art in heaven," Pastor Braun began, and others joined in. A shout from the soldiers silenced everybody.

The men were made to line up in twos. Uncle Gustavs and Guks made a pair; Pastor Braun was holding Hans, one of the inmates, by the hand; but Papa was pushed to the front of the line, away from them. The last thing I saw was that he was walking alone. I held myself rigid, concentrating my whole being into willing that they would not make him cry.

◆ 6 ◆

Hilda

Hilda was a young, scrawny, freckled, red-haired German woman who worked as a secretary in the Lobethal Home. Her husband was away, fighting at the front. She told everyone how worried she was because his letters did not arrive regularly. She spoke freely about her fears and her hopes to anyone who would listen. People laughed at her indulgently for her lack of reserve. She had hoped to get pregnant when her husband had been home for three days' leave, but one could never predict how things like that turned out, she said. She was afraid that her husband would die and that nothing of him would be left. When the Russians came, she had not seen her husband for almost a year.

After the soldiers had taken away all the men, they continued their search for valuables. They ordered all the suitcases opened and their contents dumped on the floor. They inspected women's clothing and patted women's bodies. My mother had hidden her wedding ring in her shoe, but the soldiers seemed to know about that. They ordered her and other women to remove their shoes and overcoats. When Hilda fumbled with her buttons, they slapped her and screamed at her. Then two soldiers started to pull her behind a partition.

"No," she cried. She fell on her knees on the muddy floor and raised her arms as if praying. "No, no, no," she pleaded.

But the soldiers were unyielding. They only dragged her more roughly, so that her knees scraped along the rough cement floor. Momentarily safe, the other women looked away. If the soldiers took Hilda, they would leave them alone for now. If Hilda resisted too much, the soldiers might choose one of them.

Ōmīte whispered something to Hilda, who nodded. Hilda struggled to her feet, pulled up her skirt and stuck out her stomach obscenely. It was flat and smooth under her thick gray cotton underpants. She tried to push her belly out even further, she patted it with her free hand, then rubbed it in frantic circling motions. The soldiers stopped and consulted among themselves. Then they fiercely pulled Hilda towards the partition.

But the pause gave hope to others. This part of the Russian army was made up of soldiers from Mongolia and though their masculine traditions encouraged them to rape, they seemed to have an unclearly defined respect for mothers. Hilda's attempt to convince them that she was pregnant failed, but later in the morning this scene was repeated with another woman, a refugee who had arrived only a few days before. This woman, about seven months' pregnant, was not raped. After she raised her skirt and pulled down her pants to expose her full, blue-veined stomach, she was left alone in the middle of the floor. She stood there, her face flushed with shame, and then tiptoed back to her seat.

The soldiers, so far, had also not taken behind the partition any women with children. I had at first been told to hold Astrīda's hand and to pretend that my cousin was my mother, but that plan had to be abandoned when I refused to let go of my mother. Astrīda, face smeared with soot and head covered with a gray scarf, was now holding my sister's hand. Every time the soldiers came closer I was terrified that Astrīda would be led away and that it would be my fault if she were.

"What are they doing to Hilda?" I whispered to my mother.

"Shush. Don't say anything. Don't cry. Shush."

I could hear Hilda moaning, then the grunts, laughter and jeering of the soldiers. Then more grunts. Grinning soldiers crowded around the partition. Hilda shrieked a couple of times, thuds followed, and she subsided to a whimper. Finally she made no sound.

"Is she dead?" I whispered again, but this time my mother only put her hand over my mouth and shook her head. Would they kill her with an umbrella, I wanted to know, but dared not ask. The previous evening I had heard the pregnant refugee talking about Russian soldiers who had somehow stuck an umbrella into a woman, then opened it, and so killed her. I could not understand how they had done that—had they forced the umbrella into her mouth or her bottom? I trembled as I tried to visualize it.

After a lot of scuffling and grunting, the soldiers pushed Hilda out. She was clutching her coat tightly around her waist; her face and neck were flushed a deep red. Her thick brown cotton stockings were bunched around her thin ankles, her legs were blue. She looked ashamed.

When she had gingerly made her way back to her seat, the women moved closer together, away from her, and drew their skirts around themselves more tightly. Hilda kept her eyes on the floor, as if she were the one who had done something terrible. The other women glanced at each other furtively. Who would be next? No one said anything.

And then Hilda started to whimper. She rocked back and forth; her whimpers seemed to hold all the pain in the world. Again and again and again, the wordless timid sounds of anguish continued. The other women sat frozen. The soldiers watching us did not seem to hear. No one did anything. The crying continued. It would never stop. We would have to listen to it forever.

Suddenly Ōmīte stood up. Looking defiantly into the faces of the soldiers keeping us prisoner, she made her way across the muddy soiled floor, willing them not to interfere with her. Her progress seemed unnaturally slow, as everyone watched to see whether the soldiers would seize her. When she reached Hilda, the German women drew even further away.

Ōmīte sat down next to Hilda, took her hands in hers and started gently rubbing them, then she massaged her shoulders and neck. When Hilda finally went limp, Ōmīte put her arms around her. She held her, stroking her hair, as if she were a small child, with the same kind of tenderness she showed to my sister and me. Hilda whimpered a while longer, then gradually quietened. The soldiers leaned against the partition, surveying us. I could feel Astrīda tremble next to me. I, too, registered each movement a soldier made.

All the other women without children were eventually dragged behind the partition. They begged, cried, implored, prayed. They struggled until slaps and blows stopped them. They pleaded pregnancy, claimed sickness, feigned madness, showed nausea, clung to posts, fell to their knees, called for their mothers, prayed to God. Nothing helped. Grunts, laughter, thuds, slaps, cries of pain and more grunts continued.

Once the soldiers pushed a woman down on the floor in front of the partition and tore at her clothes. A soldier fell on her, grunting and rooting. My mother tried to keep me from seeing, but it was too late. In a flash, I understood it all—the pleas of the women, the grunts of the soldiers, the way they could use an umbrella to kill a woman. The terror of every woman and girl there was also my own.

The soldiers spent the day circling us, threatening us, stirring our muddied possessions with their guns, searching for valuables, kicking mattresses and chairs in frustration at not finding more. They shoved or hit anyone who was in their way. Every time new soldiers arrived, we held our breath. Would they rape girls? Would they have no qualms about raping women with children? How many times would they rape the same woman? So far the soldiers had not taken the old women or the very young girls, but could that, would that last as the long day wore on? Would they rape my mother? My sister? Me?

I struggled to control my tears, to sit absolutely still and to conceal my trembling, so they would not notice me.

During one of the brief intervals when some soldiers were behind the partition and others had left the basement, Aunt Hermīne decided that her daughter, Astrīda, was not safe with either my sister or me pretending to be her children. I had not been able to sit in Astrīda's lap longer than a few seconds without straining towards my mother, and Beate tried to hold onto Astrīda and my mother simultaneously. It would be easy for the soldiers to find out who our mother really was if they tried.

Aunt Hermīne and my mother pulled up one of the straw-filled mattresses, and Astrīda lay down on the cement floor. They laid the mattress over her, then piled pillows and coats on top of that. We half sat, half lay on the mattress. We could feel Astrīda moving helplessly beneath us, and we tried to lean forward and to shift our positions repeatedly in order to give her some respite from our weight. Once while two soldiers were looking straight at us, Astrīda moved quite violently. Aunt Hermīne and my mother both yawned and stretched.

The soldiers regarded us suspiciously, but finally turned back to the partition where another woman was moaning in pain.

Meanwhile Hilda, sitting with Ōmīte, had a dazed expression on her face. Then she began to speak. "I'll kill myself, I'll kill myself," she repeated monotonously.

"Shush, precious," Ōmīte would say, but she did not really seem to expect her to stop. She patted Hilda's hand, while Hilda continued her litany.

Whenever the soldiers looked away, I would tug on my mother's skirt.

"Smile," I would whisper, "please smile." My mother forced herself to smile.

"Tell me everything will be all right, tell me the soldiers will go away."

"Everything will be all right, the soldiers will go away. But you have to be very quiet. Don't make them angry," my mother would whisper automatically.

"Smile, please." My mother would again compose her face in a smile like a grimace and hold it for a second or two. During these brief moments I felt immeasurably better; maybe everything would be all right after all. But a heavy weight of sadness and fear settled over me as soon as my mother's face became apprehensive again.

During other brief intervals my mother would whisper to my sister and me, "You will be all right if you pray. Recite 'Our Father, which art in heaven.' Do it *very* quietly, but keep repeating 'Our Father' to yourself. You'll be safe if you repeat that."

As the soldiers circled, I recited the prayer to myself, wishing as hard as I could that they would not touch us, that they would go away. It was difficult to concentrate on the words of the prayer while simultaneously wishing for something else, but I could just manage it. I repeated the prayer again and again, I recited the words obsessively all through the rainy afternoon and into the night.

The following morning at dawn, the women and children in the basement were roused and led outside. By then we were glad to go. We thought we could not bear more of what had happened to us in the basement during the previous day and night. We did not know yet that we would have to stay in the basement for days. Those who had wished for death were glad: Perhaps now we would finally all be shot.

It was still chilly, it was still drizzling. Guns still rumbled in the distance, a plane droned overhead. An explosion and momentary silence followed. But the Russian soldiers were not concerned. They were secure in their possession of this area. The lake was dark, almost black, the ground soggy with rain.

Women and children were lined up in a half-circle facing an old, perfectly formed oak tree. Its branches could have shielded us from the cold drizzle, if only we had been allowed to shelter under them. We looked at each other questioningly. If they were going to shoot us, why were we lined up like this? I thought that before they shot you, they made you dig your own grave first. They had done that to Ārijs, they had done that to the people executed during the Russian occupation of Latvia. I had heard the adults talking about it around the dining table in Latvia, late at night. How did they think they were going to get us all shot and buried, lined up like this? I could not ask my mother because the soldiers were looking at us. They would get angry if I spoke.

The soldiers huddled under the oak tree, passing around a bottle. Most of them had tied women's raincoats and scarves over their heads and shoulders and even around their hips to protect them from the cold drizzle. It was too early to see any of the bright reds and yellows of the clothing they had taken away from women against the dark outlines of tanks. We shivered; the rain was getting colder, seeping down our backs and numbing our hands and feet. No one spoke.

Suddenly we heard whistling—loud, firm, melodious. Someone was whistling "Nearer, My God, to Thee." Pastor Braun appeared on the walk from the main building and for a moment we felt elated. He would save us from the Russian soldiers as he had saved so many from the Nazis. He had come to free us, he would make the soldiers leave us alone, he would take us to safety.

But as he entered the half-circle, we saw that his hands were tied behind his back, that soldiers with guns surrounded him. He in turn saw the waiting women, the frightened children, the solitary oak and the drinking soldiers. The meaning must have been clear to him then if it had not been earlier. He finished whistling the verse without dropping a note.

The soldiers pointed him towards the oak. He stepped forward resolutely, then paused next to my mother. "*Jubilate*," he said directly to her, "rejoice, it's Ascension Day."

"*Jubilate*," she replied and stretched her hand towards him, but a soldier stepped between them. Pastor Braun seemed to understand her gesture.

"*Jubilate*." He nodded.

I saw that my mother's face was covered with tears under the kerchief she had pulled over her forehead to make herself look older.

Pastor Braun started whistling again, just as firmly. He whistled "Nearer, My God, to Thee" while the soldiers found a white handkerchief and tied it around his eyes. He whistled while they pushed him against the tree and formed a line themselves. One of the soldiers shouted at him, probably to tell him to shut up, but he was speaking in Russian and in any case the handkerchief blinded Pastor Braun, so he continued whistling. He whistled while one of the soldiers, an officer perhaps, raised his fist threateningly and cursed us. Pastor Braun almost got through the second verse before the soldiers fired and his whistling ceased midline.

I stopped praying after I saw what they did to Pastor Braun. Prayer seemed pointless. No one was listening, no one was helping, no one would. I did not realize then that I would never again regain my simple faith. The picture that used to hang over my bed in Latvia, which showed an angel guiding children safely over a broken bridge and away from a violent storm, would come to seem sentimental and false. I would feel cut off and inadequate whenever my family prayed together. Some tie had unraveled without my understanding, though I did not know the extent of my loss.

But when I saw my mother's lips moving in prayer, I pulled on her and whispered, "Smile, please."

Pastor Braun's body was left in the rain at the base of the oak tree, and we were herded back into the basement. We shivered with cold. It was hard to believe that the soldiers had only been here for a little over twenty-four hours.

No one knew what they had done to the other men. I tried not to think about my father, and I was furious when the women speculated in whispers about the men. They might say that my father had been shot. Why did they not know that as long as they did not speak, he was all right? How dare they whisper? Why didn't my mother stop them?

The German women had always made it clear that my mother was different. They were spiteful in assigning the hardest tasks in the kitchen to her, and they tried to blame her when something was lost or stolen. My mother was unaccustomed to the hard physical work expected of her, which she found even more difficult to do under hostile, watchful eyes. One night my sister and I had been awakened by my mother sobbing about the petty cruelties of the other women, while my father tried hard to comfort her. We lay still, afraid to show that we were awake. Each time I begged my mother to smile, I knew she could just as easily start sobbing. But she did not. She smiled every single time I asked her.

Ōmīte had not had to work in the kitchen. She spent the days mending underwear and socks for the inmates and keeping an eye on my sister and me. The German women would have regarded her with suspicion simply because she was Latvian, but Ōmīte had also earned their enmity by actions. One afternoon word spread among the children in the courtyard that someone would die and that Germany would win the war. We formed a circle and skipped around chanting, "Shithead Roosevelt is now dead, shithead Roosevelt is now dead!" I joined in happily. Ōmīte rushed out, grabbed me by the arm and scolded me right in front of everybody: "Don't ever hope that anyone will die." She started to say something else about Germany losing the war, but stopped herself. She made me stay inside for the rest of the day. Now Ōmīte was taking care of Hilda, who was somehow condemned simply for being the first to be raped, while the other women drew away.

But my grandmother and mother also had an advantage. Since they had lived in Russia, they could understand Russian, and so they were able to provide bits of information. Pastor Braun had been shot because the Russians said he was a Nazi collaborator. No, the soldiers so far had not mentioned shooting the other men. No, we would not be allowed to leave the basement soon, but a high-ranking officer was expected and maybe he could control the soldiers.

The long gray afternoon drew to a close. It was still raining, the soldiers were still clustered by the partition, women and girls still huddled—waiting, trembling. Astrīda moved convulsively under the mattress.

The soldiers seized an eleven- or twelve-year-old girl and started dragging her away from her mother. They had judged her too young before. Her mother, with graying hair and shapeless body, stood up and tried to convince the soldiers to take her instead, but they laughed and shoved her back. They tightened their grip on the girl. She struggled, at the same time looking expectantly to the circle of women for protection.

At that moment Hilda came to life. She stopped mumbling to herself, jumped up and caught the arm of a soldier. She swiveled her hips and laughed into his face in a way that he saw as provocative, but which sounded mocking. The soldier dug his elbow into the side of his comrade and said something that made them both roar with laughter. They let go of the girl and led Hilda behind the partition. A lot of hooting and applauding followed.

When Hilda returned later, the other women glared at her with hate and condemnation. Only the mother of the frightened girl started to say something, but thought better of it. Hilda returned to her seat next to Ōmīte, while the other women seemed to form a circle that excluded her. Hilda was taken behind the partition several more times.

Finally darkness fell, and no new soldiers appeared. The same ones had been coming in and out of the basement, and they were finally growing subdued. The always dim lights were not working, but the soldiers no longer shone their flashlights into our faces. There was nothing else for them to find. Gradually they started drifting away to the main building to eat and sleep.

The temporary lull was broken by sudden shouted orders. This time the soldiers were choosing older women, those they had left alone before. They motioned to Ōmīte, then to my Aunt Hermīne. Ōmīte murmured reassurances, quickly touched my cheek and Beate's and then stopped to button Hilda's coat. My mother sat very still, her fingernails digging into my hand.

When a half-dozen older women were lined up, the soldiers opened the basement door and started prodding them out into the soaking rain.

"Savages," my mother said out loud. With rigid body, I waited for the shots, but none came. A soldier put his head inside the door and said something to the others.

My mother's body gradually relaxed, she loosened her hold of my hand, then absentmindedly lifted it up to her lips and kissed it.

"Ōmīte will be back. They're only taking her to the big house. They want her and the others to peel potatoes and cook sauerkraut. She'll be back."

We sat still, half listening for shots anyway. The rumble of guns continued but no shots were fired close by. Maybe Ōmīte would come back after the soldiers had finished supper.

We had not eaten or drunk anything all day. The absence of food was probably a blessing because the soldiers did not allow anyone to go to the makeshift lavatories just outside. We were afraid to use the buckets behind one of the partitions as we did during the air raids. The soldiers would certainly attack anyone partially unclothed. We were soiled with urine, hungry, thirsty, cold and sick with exhaustion.

I shut my eyes, but all I could see was Ōmīte, alone, walking up towards the main building in the cold rain, and my father, also alone, walking far ahead of Ōmīte. They both looked so scared and lonely, I longed to touch them, but of course I could not. An image of the soldiers shoving my father toward the oak tree, the way they had Pastor Braun, kept returning obsessively each time I shut my eyes, so I stared at Hilda instead. Reciting "Our Father" no longer helped because I could not concentrate and the words had lost all meaning. I sat still, registering in my stomach and chest every movement each soldier made.

The few soldiers who had stayed behind to guard us were lounging on mattresses they had driven women from. They were passing around cigarettes and bottles of vodka. Their harsh laughter was quieter; maybe they would finally fall asleep.

Mrs. Franz, a very old German woman with wrinkled, liver-spotted hands who used an elaborately carved walking stick, crossed herself. She patted a pillow behind her, trying to arrange it in a more comfortable position. She undid a few hairpins and shook her thin gray hair, the way Ōmīte did before sleep. Then Mrs. Franz put her gnarled hands to her mouth and started removing her false teeth.

A soldier leapt on her. The upper plate was in his hand, and he was forcing his fingers into Mrs. Franz's mouth for the lower one. She screamed in pain, at the same time groping ineffectually for the teeth the soldier was holding at arm's length.

As the lower plate gave and the soldier was about to put both plates in his pocket, my mother lunged at him. The fury my mother had held in while the soldiers took away her husband and her mother and her wedding ring gave her strength. For an instant it looked as if she was going to bite him, sink her teeth into his neck, rip his flesh. Surprised, the soldiers shoved her away.

She took a deep breath and controlled herself. Then she started talking. She grimaced, she gestured, she pointed towards Mrs. Franz's mouth, she motioned towards her own. The soldier with the teeth listened to her briefly; he had not expected any of the women to speak Russian. Then he spoke roughly once more, shoved the teeth deeper into his pocket and shook his fist at her. He was very angry. We learned later that he had said his mother in Russia did not have a single tooth, while this old German bitch had rows. This too was part of the respect the soldiers had for mothers.

My mother tried once more to get him to see that false teeth were made for a particular configuration of the mouth, that they would not do the old woman in Russia any good, but that the old woman here would not be able to eat without them. The soldier did not want to hear more. He raised his arm threateningly, as if to strike her.

When my mother said something else, he slapped her, then pushed her against the cot and hit her hard in the face with his fist. The other soldiers immediately surrounded her. I leapt at one of them and tried to pull him away by holding onto his leg, kicking, pummeling and trying to bite. I saw the soldier's surprised furious face and then I felt the barrel of the gun jabbed into my chest.

The pain was searing, so that I fell backwards, and though I struggled, I could not stand up again. The soldiers dragged my mother out the door. She was screaming, and they were calling her names whose ugliness was clear even though the language was strange. They took her away, into the rainy darkness. I thought I heard their steps moving off into the direction of the old oak, and I tried to get up to follow, but fell. Then it got very dark.

It was getting light. It was still drizzling, the sky was still gray, but the guns were quieter. Hilda was sitting by herself, her coat unbuttoned again. She was mumbling again, "I'll kill myself, I'll kill myself, I'll kill myself." Her monotonous voice went on and on. It was very cold, unnatural for late spring.

"Where is Mama?" I asked. "Did they shoot her?"

"Maybe she'll be back," my sister said.

"When? I want her. Let's go look for her." But the pain in my chest kept me where I was.

Beate pulled the heavy blanket more tightly over us both, it made a little nest of warmth. "Maybe it will be all right," she said doubtfully.

I wanted to ask her to smile, perhaps she would do that for me, but I knew it would mean nothing. We moved as close to each other under the blanket as we could while still keeping our eyes on the door. We were longing for our mother to come back. I had never, ever wanted anything so much in my life. I would never, ever ask for anything else again, if only she would come back.

Instead, new soldiers began to arrive.

•7•

Mothers and Daughters

My mother did come back. She came back the following morning, escorted by a Russian officer. The soldiers had taken her outside to shoot her. I do not know what the charge was, or if they needed one, but some formalities about shooting civilians must have existed because they did not take her directly to the open area by the oak. They half dragged her, half pushed her to the main building, where soldiers, prostitutes and a few officers were spending the night. She had a glimpse of Ōmīte working in the kitchen.

They took her into a hallway and kept her waiting there for most of the night. Shouts and singing came from the dining room and reception hall. She knew some of the songs so she started humming one—something, anything to make the soldier guarding her see that she was human. She tried to talk him into letting her go, but he ordered her sharply to hold her tongue.

She was taken to Pastor Braun's study. All the mirrors in the reception hall had been smashed, all the paintings on the walls were slashed. The bathroom door was wide open and two soldiers were playing with the taps, turning them off and on. A third was washing his feet in the toilet. Through another door that had been left ajar, she could see a soldier moving on top of a naked woman.

The woman's wide-open eyes looked past the soldier to the blank wall ahead.

Most of the soldiers in this unit were Mongolian peasants for whom mirrors, running water and electricity were new. My mother had known people like them during her childhood in Siberia. She used to talk about them loving and caressing their horses but striking their women and about their wearing heavy dark clothing during the summer, which they said kept out the heat. Another story she told was about a peasant who kept trying to bring daylight into his windowless hut in a bucket. She knew their language, but otherwise she did not have much in common with them.

She was left in Pastor Braun's study and made to wait again. A young soldier prodded her when she tried to sit down, but otherwise ignored her. The shouts of the soldiers grew louder, they were drinking more and more vodka. The drunker they got, the more dangerous they would be.

Finally a senior officer arrived. He was accompanied by the soldier who had taken the old woman's teeth. Aggrieved and angry, the soldier accused my mother of attacking the conquering army. He was indignant his comrades had not shot her on the spot.

My mother began talking. It is one of the things I most admire about her, that at this moment she could talk, that she knew the language and that she knew what to say.

She was also helped by a fortuitous circumstance. The officer was city-bred and educated, so that the false teeth appeared to him in a different light. But even more than that, he had lived near Omsk, as had my mother as a child. They knew some of the same streets, some of the same shops, some of the same people. He had gone to the same school as my mother's brothers. He did not hold my mother's Russian past against her, even though she and her parents had fled the country following the Revolution, and they had been members of the landowning class standing in the way of economic justice. Instead, the officer and she speculated about what had happened to some of the teachers at the school, and he told her that the mill her parents had built was still in operation. Both of them spoke with longing of the flowering meadows and dark forests.

He ordered the soldiers to release her. My mother knew that her safety would last only as long as the walk through the doors, so she persuaded him to help her further. He allowed her to find Ōmīte and

Aunt Hermīne, who were dozing in the kitchen, and then escorted them himself.

"The conditions in the basement are terrible," my mother told him, "rape, looting, brutality."

"That's against the regulations," he said. Whether he believed her or not, he agreed to take us elsewhere. A different unit of soldiers was occupying the orphanage and it might be safer there. He took all of us, including our cousin Astrīda and Aunt Hermīne, along the lake to the village orphanage.

At least, that is what my mother once told me happened while she was gone, and I try to believe her. I remember walking on the sandy path with my mother and a Russian officer. When I try to visualize the reunion with my mother and my grandmother, I can remember very little, though it must have been overwhelmingly joyous. All I can see is the moment when she came through the basement door. Her face was flushed, she drew her coat tightly around herself and she dropped her eyes. She looked ashamed, the way that Hilda had, though perhaps I am only imagining it.

We are in the dining hall of the orphanage, where the Russian officer has brought us. It is not a real shelter since it is above ground, but it feels enclosed because the shattered windows are boarded up and the guns and planes have receded. There are only women and girls here, more girls than in the basement. The girls are dressed alike, in dark blue uniforms with white collars and black pinafores. A few are my age, about seven, but most are older. Three elderly nuns are on a bench in front of them; they are reciting the rosary. The girls are sitting close together, quietly.

There are not as many soldiers here, but otherwise it looks the same. The floor is littered with mud-smeared clothes and papers. Shards of crystal and china crunch under their muddy black boots. The soldiers stomp on faces in photographs taken at weddings and christenings. The girls draw into themselves, just like the women in the basement, but there is no partition. My mother whispers that these soldiers are not Mongolians, and perhaps that is another difference.

The women and girls stare at us, we do not belong here either, but they make room for us on one of the benches. We sit down and spread the old blanket over our legs. We wait. The soldiers come in and out, they talk and gesture with their guns, their boots are exactly the same. But they allow us to have water from a bucket with a common cup, and they do not interfere with anyone going to the bathroom to the side. The officer has given my mother a loaf of bread and we devour it. I can feel the orphans watching us hungrily.

We are overwhelmingly tired, we have never been so exhausted. We try to make ourselves comfortable on the hard bench, but there is no back to lean against. I close my eyes and rest my head against my mother. I am no longer trembling. It is more peaceful here.

But then the door bursts open and yet more soldiers push into the room. They are the same as the soldiers in the basement, Mongolians. I would recognize the slanted eyes, the dark glistening skin and the high cheekbones anywhere. They survey the huddled women briefly, then stare at the orphan girls. The nuns spread their arms in front of them. Their white hoods flutter. A soldier takes a step forward, then stops.

The soldiers inspect those of us on the other benches. Dark hands with blackened fingernails reach towards us; they grab a woman by the hair in order to get a better look at her face. She shrinks away from the soldier, she tries to knot herself up, but he yanks her face towards him with dirty hands. He presses his knee into her lap to straighten her, so that they can decide whether she is the one they want.

"God will punish you," says a nun. Her face is impassive; only her hood trembles. The soldiers do not seem to hear nor would they understand her if they did. They pull the woman, who is trying to stay doubled up, towards the door.

And then something miraculous happens. Another woman, who looks like the sister of the one who has been seized, steps to the piano in the corner of the room. She seats herself, opens it, begins to play. A melody fills the air. She is playing "Die Lorelei."

> "I don't know what it means
> that I am so sad
> A fairy tale from old times
> haunts my mind . . ."

It is a lovely, plaintive melody, strangely appropriate.
Startled, the soldiers turn towards her. They have not expected this.

Their grip on the other sister lightens; one of them lets his hands drop altogether. They stand frozen in the middle of the room, listening to the music. The woman at the piano finishes the first verse and starts another.

Their eyes on the playing woman, the soldiers release her sister. They follow her hands on the piano, they listen intently, they move into the melody themselves.

The young woman left standing in the middle of the floor takes a slow, tentative step backwards, away from the soldiers. They glance at her without interest, they do not try to stop her. Their eyes are on the hands making the music. Slowly, slowly, afraid to startle them, the victim creeps back to her seat. She has gained a few minutes of reprieve—is it too much to hope that she has escaped altogether? She draws into herself again, folds herself up. They will have to force her to straighten anew.

Her sister keeps playing. She plays "Die Lorelei" several times, and when she notices their attention wandering, she begins a waltz. She plays waltzes, mazurkas, marches and hymns. The soldiers grow tired of listening standing up, so one by one they drop to the floor. They form a circle around the woman at the piano. Their chins rest on their knees, their faces are rapt with attention, they watch the woman's hands gliding over the keys.

Other soldiers come bursting in, ready for violence, but the melodies filling the air and the mesmerized faces of the other soldiers stop them. They stand uncertainly for a few minutes, they lay down their guns, they rest on the ground. They take off their helmets, they loosen the collars of their uniforms, their bodies become pliant, they sway gently together.

The woman plays and plays, and the soldiers listen. When she tires, she nods to her sister, who slides onto the piano bench next to her. Together they play a duet, moving easily into the double melodies they must have practiced as girls. They do not allow the music to cease for an instant. Music can stay anger and hate.

When the exhausted woman gets up, her sister takes over and continues playing. A soldier grasps the tired woman's elbow and jams her fingers back on the keys; he looks angry at the discordant chords. But her sister goes on playing until he understands that the music will continue, so he lets the tired woman go back to her seat. Her sister plays until she can no more, and then another woman glides across the room and onto the piano bench. Chopin and Mozart flow through the room; the soldiers are quiet.

My mother takes her turn playing. She plays a Russian folk song, and the soldiers nudge each other delightedly. They shout at her to play it again. The soldiers who took her from the basement may be in the circle by the piano, their dark skins and impassive faces are so alike. I am afraid to meet their gaze, so that I cannot tell them apart, but if they are, they do not interfere with my mother's playing. They groan when she stops, but subside when another woman plays "Nearer, My God, to Thee."

While the women are able to play, while the soldiers are willing to listen, we are safer than we have been. The women play all the melodies their mothers made them practice as girls. They play until twilight descends.

When the soldiers begin to grow bored and restless, they wander away in twos and threes, looking for someplace else to go. The rain has diminished to an intermittent drizzle, but it is still cold. Only a few soldiers remain in the dining hall, and when darkness comes, even the last two leave. It would be a good time to sleep. Though I am repeatedly startled into wide-awake terror because I believe I hear soldiers returning, I doze for much of the night.

The morning of the next day is gray and cold once more. When the soldiers, guns unslung, push their way into the room, all the silent women and girls are awake already. They order us outside.

We are made to line up in twos. I hold my mother's hand, my sister holds my grandmother's. The soldiers are furious again, they are different from what they were like at twilight. They prod us with their guns, they curse us, they shove anyone they think is in the wrong place. It is very important to be very quiet and very compliant so that they do not notice us and get angry. Beate reaches towards our mother's hand, but a soldier pushes her roughly against Ōmīte.

In the chill drizzle, we are made to walk towards the lake, then along the lake path, between the slender white birches. Their new light green leaves look vulnerable. No one knows where they are taking us. I look back once. The three nuns are in the line, but the orphan girls have been left behind in the hall, alone, with other soldiers. We have to keep our eyes on the sandy path. We step over gnarled roots, and the wet grasses brush against us as we walk. We sense rather than see where we are being taken. The basement is just ahead of us, the clearing with the old oak is beyond that. We have come full circle.

Putting one foot in front of the other, we keep our eyes on the ground. The soldiers order us to stop, there is some confusion ahead. My mother listens intently to their shouts, then she turns to her mother.

"They are lining us up to shoot us, did you hear?" she whispers.

"I couldn't tell," Ōmīte whispers back, but she does not contradict my mother.

"Come," says my mother suddenly. "Let's go up to the front of the line. If they're going to shoot us, let us be the first ones. Nothing can save us now. And I can't bear having to watch more people die." Her voice is beyond weariness. "Let's go past the others." She starts pulling me by the arms.

She wants me to be shot, I think.

"No, no, I don't want to go." I dig my heels into the sandy soil of the path. There are perhaps twenty women ahead of us. They will have to shoot them first.

"Yes, we must. Let's go," my mother says firmly. She pulls me by the hand. "Come on. It will be too terrible to have to watch all of them die."

But I struggle. "I won't. I won't. I don't want to." I pull towards the back of the line, I want to be the very last one. I try to hold onto a slender low branch of a birch tree. The young leaves rip and crumble in my hand as my mother yanks me forward, hard. I grab at another branch.

My mother gives up struggling with me and tries to coax me instead.

"Come, precious, it won't hurt. We'll just hold hands, they'll put something over our eyes. But if they don't, you must shut your eyes as tight as you can. Squeeze them shut and don't open them for anything. Keep them closed, and then you won't feel anything. It won't hurt, precious, I promise. Come with me."

"No."

I do not move.

My mother is angry again. "You have to come, we can't stand here and watch the others being shot." She makes another attempt to take me by the hand and pull me forward.

Not knowing I will feel guilty for these words the rest of my life, I say, "I want to see it, I want to see them die."

I am furious. "I will not go."

A soldier yells at us to be quiet, and the two of us stand silent and trembling with rage. It is impossible to see what is happening ahead of us in the clearing, it is something terrible, but my fury at my mother knows no bounds. I want to be as far away from her as possible, and at the same time I am holding onto her hand so tightly they would have to chop off my hand for me to let go.

Shots ring out ahead. Soldiers motion us forward. They prod us with their guns because we are not moving quickly enough for them. I am afraid that my mother is going to try to pull me to the front of the line again, but she does not. Suddenly she seems exhausted and totally powerless. She bends down and strokes my cheek, she turns around and kisses my sister's hair.

"Remember to shut your eyes," she says, "and keep them shut. It won't hurt. And remember to say 'Our Father' while you are waiting. It won't hurt, and you will go to heaven. I promise you'll go to heaven, precious. Just think about how beautiful it is there, full of angels and lovely light. Come, let's start. 'Our Father, which art in heaven . . .'"

The line, which has been inching along, suddenly jerks forward. We step into the space left by the women ahead of us. We are coming into the clearing, we are back by the old oak.

I expect to be stood against the oak, where they made Pastor Braun stand, so it takes a while to realize that we are being shoved into a half-circle of observers again. My mother tries to cover my eyes, she does not want me to see what is under the oak.

A soldier pulls my mother away again. This time she does not fight and neither do I. I have expected this.

The soldier yanks me out of the line. He puts his hands on my throat and makes strangling motions. This moment is as terrifying as the soldiers taking away my mother, as terrifying as struggling with her, but somehow this fear is even sharper and clearer. My heart seems about to burst, I cannot get my breath. I can neither scream nor pray. I cannot shut my eyes. I feel myself losing control; warm urine runs over my legs and splashes on the soldier's muddy boots. The shame I feel becomes part of the moment.

I know he has every right to kill me.

The soldier looks down at his wet boots, curses, tightens his hands around my neck and then flings me away from him. I expect to hit the tree, I would welcome being senseless, but my mother is between the oak and the soldier, and I fall against my mother's legs instead. She raises me against her and squeezes me so tight my shoulders hurt.

The soldier puts his hands on my neck and again demonstrates strangling motions. He barks at my mother to translate.

He is finally out of my line of vision, so I can see what is under the tree. Lying on the ground is Heidi, the girl who sits next to me in school. Heidi's face is blue and puffy, but her body looks almost the same. Her feet are bare and she is wearing no coat, only a short-sleeved dress with tiny sprigs of blue flowers. The bit of petticoat that shows is muddy. Her clothes and hair are soaked; she must have been lying here for a long time. She seems heavier somehow.

Next to Heidi is her mother, Mrs. Heimlich. A rag is tied across her mother's eyes. There is a dark hole in her cheek and there are two or three dark holes in her chest. She too is barefoot. Her dress is pushed up above her hips, there is a dark stain between her legs.

My mother is translating, her voice shakes. "He says that if anyone else tries to commit murder or suicide, she will be shot, and that we will all be shot too. He says that this mother strangled her daughter and then tried to kill herself, but that they stopped her in time. They have shot her as an example of what will happen if anyone else tries to kill herself."

She pauses and the soldier shouts some more.

"He says we have to understand that they do not like killing. He says that if anyone tries to kill anyone, they will shoot all of us. We will all die."

When my mother finishes speaking, she tries to cover my eyes again, and I let her. I have seen it. I will see it again and again. When I close my eyes I see Heidi's puffy face and heavy body, and her mother's face turned away from her. It is as if they are engraved somewhere behind my eyes.

I try to understand that Heidi's mother has strangled her, just as the soldier has demonstrated on my neck, where I can still feel the imprint of his hands. She must have done it harder, or Heidi would be alive. I try to imagine it, but I can't. Later the soldiers must have brought her mother out here and stood her against the oak like they did Pastor Braun. They have done something else to her before they shot her. They have punished her.

I bury my face in my mother's skirt and cling to her as tight as I can. She does not free herself with one of those subtle movements that I know. She holds me tightly against her on one side, my sister on the other. Then she lets my sister go, she takes both her hands and presses my face against her stomach so hard I cannot breathe, as if to erase the sight of the dead mother and dead daughter.

I feel my mother's warmth, but there is something terrifying about being so enclosed by her. What will she do next, what will she try to force me to do? When she lets me go, I rub my eyes hard with my fists, but Heidi and her mother are there in the blackness and the showers of sparks I make as I grind my fists against my lids. I know I have seen them somewhere before and that I will continue seeing them forever.

A dream flashes by me. It has been almost two years since I dreamt it, sleeping under my blue goose-down quilt in my bed in Latvia. My mother used to comfort me dozens of times about this dream. I used to worry then only about her being sad and distant.

Now the dream seems much more terrifying. I believe it has been an omen, that it has somehow foretold her pulling me forward, but that I have failed to heed.

In the dream I am walking on a sandy path lined with birches, I am going away from the Parsonage in Latvia, towards the woods. It is a clear blue summer day, I am completely happy. My mother, her white linen dress glistening in the sun, is on the road ahead of me. The path curves to the left, so that I lose sight of her and have to run to catch up. She is moving quickly towards the dark pines beyond the birches, so I run faster to keep up with her.

In the sad light under the pines, my mother's dress is suddenly black. I realize she is trying to run away from me, she does not want me with her. I long to reach her, but she eludes me. She clambers into the fork of a crippled tree, leaving me below. When I manage to catch the hem of her dress, I see that all her clothes have changed, they are all black. She is wearing a man's black laced shoes rather than the light strappy white sandals she had on the path.

I stretch out my arms for her to lift me up, but stop, terrified. Her skin is wrinkled, her face cruel and knowing, her fingers bony and sharp. She motions to me invitingly. She has transformed herself, she is a witch, my real mother is lost. I scream myself awake.

I used to ask my mother to turn on the light to see that she hadn't changed into something evil. She used to promise me that she would never change, that she would always be there, that she was herself. I used to believe she would always protect me, I was certain she would never harm me. Just as in the dream, I cling to my mother even though I fear her.

I look at the two figures below the oak again. Heidi's eyes are open, she is staring unflinchingly into the rain. Her mother is turned away from her; she would be looking beyond the lake, if she were not blinded by the cloth. Mother and daughter are only a few feet away from each other, their fingers reach towards each other, but they do not touch.

We stand watching the rain fall on the corpses. Even the soldiers are silent.

My mother leans down and whispers, "Are you all right, precious?"

I nod. I would like to tell her I'm not, I would like to ask her when and where I have seen the dead mother and daughter before. Why do I know that all this has happened before, why am I certain that it will happen again and again?

But I do not say anything. I nod and pretend that I am all right. I ask my mother to smile, and she does. I pretend that makes me happy, I hold onto her hand, I close my eyes, but the gray cold stays inside me.

The corpses lay there for several days in the rain. Someone threw an old horse blanket over them, to hide Heidi's open eyes and her mother's face turned towards the lake, away from her. Their bare feet, vulnerable and almost black, were visible beneath the coarse gray cloth.

We were taken back to the basement and kept there for several more days. The women whispered among themselves about what Mrs. Heimlich had done. Somehow a motive had to be found, and one was. She supposedly received news that her husband had been killed at the front, and so, too desperate to live, she killed her daughter and planned to take poison herself, but the soldiers interrupted her to execute her. This did not comfort me; it made it seem worse. If my father did not come back, what would my mother do?

Hilda continued to rock back and forth. "I'll kill myself, I'll kill myself, I'll kill myself." The other women began speaking to her to tell her that she was not allowed to: it would be her fault if we were all killed. My mother tried to talk another Russian officer into letting us leave, this time because we were Latvian, not German. He said that we would be put on a train and sent back to Latvia. Our country, he explained, had been liberated because it was occupied by the Russians. From that point we pretended we were German. On the rare occasions that we spoke to each other, we used only German. It was another necessary pretense.

"Smile," I kept saying in German to my mother. When she did, I pretended that I was all right. But Hilda, the other raped women, the orphan girls left in the hands of the soldiers, the plaintive melodies on the piano would haunt me.

I could also not speak about what was severed between my mother and me that morning and neither could she. The whole universe was motherless during the war and remained that way for me long afterwards.

◆ 8 ◆

The Aftermath

My mother was taken away by the soldiers again, this time because a meal she had been ordered to supervise was unsatisfactory. The hungry women in the kitchen had eaten most of the meat, and the soldiers held my mother responsible. We were all taken outside again to be shot, but a different officer ordered us to be taken back inside. The violence and chaos in the basement continued.

But the story grows repetitious.

Gradually things changed. Fewer soldiers entered the basement, fewer stayed. There was nothing more for them to find. Finally one morning, about ten days after the soldiers had first arrived, only women and children remained. We had been taken outside earlier that morning to watch as three soldiers were shot for violating the order against killing civilians. They were evidently the same who had shot Heidi's mother, though they looked like all the rest. It was the last execution we were forced to witness.

Afterwards the soldiers drifted away. It took us a while to realize that no one was standing watch over us so that we would not leave the basement. No one was cursing or threatening us. We sat still in the desolate space for several hours before we surmised that evidently we were free to go.

We walked down the lake path in the direction of the village, then crossed the fields to an abandoned farm. The soldiers were probably still in the village, so that going there was dangerous. One of the women in the basement had come from the woods, where she had seen a strange signaling station, about a day's walk from Lobethal. She wished she could have stayed there forever. Behind the huge mirrors and searchlights were buildings full of food and supplies. She had eaten canned meat and thick sweetened milk and had carried some with her.

My mother and Aunt Hermīne speculated about trying to find this place, but finally decided against it. It was too far away for us to walk. Ōmīte was exhausted, Astrīda was flushed and feverish, her skin gray from the ashes and dust with which she had tried to disguise herself, and I felt weak because of the pain in my chest. Even if we did get there, the station might be occupied or looted by the soldiers, or both. And my father and uncle and cousin would never find us if we went too far. If they were still alive and if they were released, they would look for us in Lobethal. If they could not find us, they might return to Latvia, and we would never see them again.

For several days we walked furtively from one abandoned farm to another. We made makeshift beds out of any old clothes we could find, so that we could all huddle together in the same space in the corner of a room furthest away from the doors and windows. We looked for food, but except for a few raw potatoes and beets, we did not find much.

Sleeping was hardest in these early days and for months afterwards. I would stretch out, close my eyes, count to a hundred and back, as my mother had told me to do, but I would still be awake when I finished. I could feel soldiers creeping towards us. When she asked me if I had said "Our Father," I nodded and counted to a hundred a second time instead. As I felt myself drifting off to sleep, I would jerk myself awake because I thought that with my eyes closed I would not hear the approaching soldiers. Or I would doze off, only to be startled wide awake, my heart pounding because I felt soldiers' hands fastening around my throat. Everyone else was usually awake too, listening in silence, praying that the far-distant trucks would continue on their way, past us. I would give up trying to sleep and watch the moonlight shining into uncurtained windows and over the bare floors, over my sister and mother and grandmother. Each was lying very still, pretending to sleep, in order not to disturb the others.

Finally there did not seem to be much point in wandering about the countryside like this, and we decided to go back to Lobethal. Food had been stored there, and my father and the others might be there, or at least we might get news of them. The soldiers might still be there too, but we had nowhere else to go.

The road from the gate was empty, but the ditches were littered with bleached and misshapen photographs, empty gasoline cans, ripped clothing, single shoes. The windows of the main building were smashed, the doors off their hinges, the locks broken. The sun was very bright; flies and insects buzzed on the littered veranda. It was all very familiar, unsurprising, even right somehow.

We moved slowly through the rooms, afraid of what we might see next. Everything that could be smashed had been, but we found no corpses. The kitchen was empty, the floor littered with broken cups and bowls. Flour had been scattered in a fine film over everything. No one was there, but someone had wiped clean the top of one of the huge institutional stoves and lined up a few pots.

We made our way to the basement. We were anticipating the jellied meat and the sweet preserves, we were ravenously hungry. But when we opened the door to the main storage room, we saw that everything there too had been smashed. The stench of rotting food mixed with excrement rose to meet us. We held our breaths, covering our nostrils and mouths with our hands. Shards of glass were embedded in the foul slippery mess, and we tried to avoid stepping into the deepest parts.

Except for the saüerkraut, the drunken soldiers had destroyed everything. The wooden barrels where the sauerkraut had been stored were licked clean. Nothing was left for us to eat.

The stairs creaked behind us and we froze in terror. It should not have made much difference when we were killed, but we were constantly afraid anyway. We stood still, looking guiltily at each other, breathing the foul air, our hearts pounding. The steps came closer.

When the door was pushed aside, it was only Frau Braun, the dead director's wife. Her face was haggard, her eyes red, her clothes hung loosely about her. She was wearing what looked like one of Pastor Braun's jackets over a shapeless summer dress. Her hair was limp, her dark eyes enormous. She bore little resemblance to the fashionable woman she had been just a few weeks ago. Then, wearing strings of pearls and a smart suit with padded shoulders, an alligator bag held firmly in her hand, she had sat confidently next to her husband when they set off to see the officials in Berlin.

She shook her head, anticipating our questions. "There's nothing to eat here. But they have carrots, over behind the barns. They are boiling them now."

I turned to go, I was halfway up the stairs, running past Frau Braun.

"Would we be welcome?" my mother asked, and I stopped, afraid of what Frau Braun would say. She had always been cool towards my mother, perhaps because she disliked Pastor Braun's evident attraction to her.

Frau Braun hesitated, then said kindly, "Everyone is welcome. This is Lobethal, we welcome the homeless here."

Then she looked directly at my mother. "I am glad you have come back," she said, "it's much safer for you here."

"Thank you," my mother said, her voice trembling, "thank you for your great kindness."

"And we also need you here. You can help us clean all this up." Frau Braun gestured at the layer of rotting food and filth. It did not seem possible this basement could ever be immaculate and orderly again, let alone filled with food and supplies.

"Carrots," I said. I was worried that there would be none left if we waited. I also hoped that Frau Braun would come with us, so we would not be driven away by the people who had them. I knew they were not ours and we had no right to them.

"Come," Frau Braun said, "I'll show you where." She brushed past me, then took my hand. "It isn't very far."

Later that afternoon we walked what seemed like endless miles to the village hall. Here too the windows were shattered and most had been boarded up, but a few unshaven, tired men stared out through the cracks. More men looked out between the bars in the second-floor windows. A Russian soldier sat tilted back in a chair in the entrance, his gun resting on his knees. He stretched lazily and squinted at us in the afternoon sun, but he made no attempt to drive my mother and my sister away.

My mother talked to a few of the men closest, then called up to those staring out of the second-story windows. After a commotion, a wait and another commotion, my father appeared in the window above us. My Uncle Gustavs and Cousin Guks were behind him. Thinner, with blue circles under their eyes, they looked tired past the point of exhaustion.

"Are you alive? Are you all right?" my mother called.

"It's been terrible," said my father.

"I'm sorry. Have you had anything to eat?" my mother asked.

"We are all right, Valda. We are still alive." My mother's brother interrupted whatever else my father was going to say. "Are you all right yourself? Where is Hermine? Is Astrida all right?"

My mother cupped her hands again. "Yes, we are all right. Hermine and Astrida too." Her voice was lifeless.

We stood silent, looking at each other, too far away to talk or to touch.

"They took my wedding ring." My father raised his hand and pointed to the bare finger where the ring had been. He seemed to have forgotten that we had all seen him struggling to remove the ring while the soldier laughed.

"Later a soldier ordered me outside, away from the others. I thought he was going to shoot me. But he only made me take off all my clothes in the lavatory and he took them. He took my boots too, I am barefoot." He gestured towards his feet, as if we could see them.

My mother reached her arms towards him to comfort him. I could see the white indentations on my mother's fingers and wrist. She did not say anything about her own missing gold wedding band and other rings, and he did not ask. Something much greater than possessions had been taken from them both.

"We will be released soon," said Uncle Gustavs, "maybe tomorrow. All they are waiting for is another list of Nazi officers to check us against, and there isn't anyone like that here." The men crowding around the windows were either old or they were very young boys who had somehow escaped the final conscriptions at the end of the war.

"Will you be all right?" my mother asked my father.

"Yes." His voice shook a little, and I was afraid that he was going to cry, but he did not. "They wanted to shoot me earlier, but Pastor Braun intervened. He saved me. I am grateful to God and to Pastor Braun."

"Yes," my mother said, listlessly.

We stood about for a while longer, gazing up. There wasn't much else to say, and we were afraid to make the soldier angry by staying too long. We waved goodbye and started back to Lobethal.

I had been longing to see my father again, and when he came to the window, my heart leapt wildly with joy. Now, walking back to the Institution, nobody said anything. My mother's face was sad, and I did not ask her to smile. Rather than being happy as I had expected to be, I felt sad. A permanent gray film spread over everything.

My parents were reunited. We all worked very hard to clean up the chaos and filth. We carried buckets of foul-smelling garbage to the back of the house, swept up broken glass and picked up the litter that lined the roadsides. We watched the adults board up windows, boil whatever soiled clothing still looked usable, scald the surfaces in the kitchen and scour the few unbroken dishes. A huge fire blazed outside on which we piled everything that could not be salvaged. A few of the inmates were already sick with dysentery and typhoid, so the cleaning must have been part of a futile attempt to check the spread of the disease as well as a way to reestablish order.

One by one the rooms were cleared. Our family shared a single room, by choice rather than by necessity, since many rooms on either side stood bare and empty. Later, when Ōmite got sick with dysentery, she moved into one of these rooms because she feared infecting us. When we heard trucks or tanks at night, we listened together.

Everyone slept badly. People went about exhausted, ashen-faced, their eyes rimmed with red. But during the day, we worked. The only hope lay in trying to restore order.

Maybe my parents talked to my sister and me, maybe they talked to each other about what had happened, but I cannot remember them saying anything at all. I see them now, silent, working instead of speaking, my mother in a coarse gray dress, down on her hands and knees, scouring the floors with sharp sand in the absence of soap, my father dragging broken furniture and stained mattresses towards the pyre in the backyard. I stayed where I could watch my mother. But I was afraid to get too close to her.

I remember others talking, though; in fact, only the stories remain vivid from this period. People told them as we stood leaning on brooms and rakes around the pile of broken, excrement-smeared furniture and watched it burn. Or we sat in the sun on rough gray blankets or burlap, the ruins of the church and a wing of the bombed orphanage in the distance behind us. The stories seemed inordinately funny. Women lifted their aprons and wiped the tears that had gathered from laughing too hard, the few men repeated punchlines and burst into raucous laughter.

One story was about high-ranking Russian officers, including generals, giving a formal ball in one of the mansions they had commandeered in Berlin. Common soldiers and prostitutes—that is, the starving German women who followed them—were not even allowed into the ballroom; the dance was going to be much too elegant for them. The orchestra struck up a polonaise, the lights strung on trees glistened in the garden, the tables groaned with food. At first some beautiful German women arrived. They too were camp followers, but they were friends of the officers, not of the common soldiers. These women were well dressed and well fed. They wore evening gowns and light summer wraps, flowers and jewels adorned their hair, they talked charmingly of music and art. Only German women knew what real elegance was, only they had taste.

Next came the fat Russian women, wives of the officers. The Russian women were coarsely painted, their hair was tightly curled, but they were wearing satin and silk nightgowns—yes, nightgowns. They had been allowed to choose whatever they wanted from the warehouses full of finery that had been taken away from civilians and this is what they had chosen, nightgowns. No self-respecting German woman would be seen outside her bedroom in one of those. Weren't the Russian women stupid, fat, uneducated, inferior, dumb? "Charming, charming," a Russian general had murmured. In spite of his power and privilege, he was an ignorant bumpkin too. "Charming, charming," we squealed hysterically.

Another story was about a Russian soldier who had stopped an old woman on the street and had made her give up the man's overcoat she was wearing. Soldiers did this all the time; we had all seen them point to boots, coats, shoes, anything they wanted, now that no one had any jewelry left. The old woman cried that she was cold, she begged to be allowed to keep her coat, she would freeze to death without it. But the soldier was unmoved. The old woman got down on her knees and kissed the soldier's hand, then his foot. She begged him to remember his mother and at least to exchange coats. The soldier, drunk and impatient, took the old woman's coat, but in a sentimental gesture he flung his stinking, tattered army jacket on the ground for the old woman.

And guess what? The old woman was really very clever, she knew what she was doing. The sleeves and pockets of the filthy jacket were lined with hundreds and hundreds of gold watches. The greedy soldier had been too drunk to remember his treasure. The watches would keep the old woman well fed and warmly clothed; she could trade them one by one. She could eat whatever she wanted for the rest of her life, she could stay warm and snug in her house forever. But the cruel soldier would wake up with a terrible hangover the following morning and would he be sorry! He would search for the old woman but would never find her. Finally the soldier would have to report for duty, but he would have no army coat, so he would be punished. He would be shot, as he deserved. As he was waiting for the bullets to tear him apart, he would cry aloud and beg forgiveness for looting and robbing and raping and beating and killing.

The pleasure of this story was further enhanced by an incident that took place a few weeks later. The soldiers ordered us all into the dining hall at the Institute to watch a film about the victory of the Russians over the Germans. A sheet was tacked onto a wall, and we sat on benches facing it, while my mother translated as an officer spoke about Russians liberating many countries, for which we should all be grateful. He told us that the Russians had been minimally assisted by the Allies in their great victory as we would see, but that we should get down and kiss the earth because we were now in Russian hands.

Finally they turned out the lights and the screen lit up. Tanks and trucks filled with American soldiers rolled down city streets, women and children offered flowers and waved flags. I had never seen a movie before, I thought it was magic. This was better than the tiny people who I had once believed lived inside radios. It was possible to sit here and see something that had happened earlier somewhere far away. I was entranced. The cameras shifted to a square filled with soldiers expecting the historic meeting of General Eisenhower and General Zhukov in Berlin. A stern voice spoke of the significance of this moment, the victorious Allied forces coming together in Berlin. Eisenhower walked towards Zhukov with a determined step; the military band played. Zhukov came towards him eagerly, his arms extended in welcome.

"*Uhri, Uhri,*"—watches, watches—someone shouted from the back of the dining room. The timing was exactly right, the mocking imitation of the Russian accent perfect. Zhukov was after Eisenhower's watch. The audience exploded with laughter.

The projectionist turned off the film and turned on the lights. Soldiers with guns pushed between the tables and benches looking for the culprit. In front of the blank screen, the officer stood scolding. We managed to stifle our laughter.

Finally the lights were turned off again and the film was shown from the beginning. The soldiers were lined up in the square again, flags waved, the band played the welcoming march. Zhukov stretched out his arms expectantly.

"*Uhri, Uhri,*" came a shout from a different part of the room.

"*Uhri, Uhri,*" a voice like the one that had spoken earlier replied.

We laughed and could not stop when the soldiers turned on the lights again. They dragged a few inmates to their feet. By slapping one of them, the soldiers finally succeeded in getting everyone in the audience to sit straight-faced.

They turned off the lights again. Shouts of "*Uhri, Uhri*" erupted as soon as the first Russian soldier appeared on the screen. This time they turned on the lights and did not try to show the film again. Over the shouts of the soldiers, we filed out, snickering. The common laughter almost made up for not seeing the rest of the movie. For several days afterwards all anyone had to say was "*Uhri, Uhri,*" and we would collapse with laughter.

Other stories had to do with food, especially with the difficulties and deceptions in finding it. A man secretly traded his wife's wedding ring for two cans of butter on the black market. He had been offered a taste of it from a can he had been allowed to select himself. The butter was indescribably delicious—creamy, fresh, cool, sweet, glistening. But when he got home and opened the can, it held gritty mashed potatoes. He opened the second can and that too was filled with the same inedible mess. And for this he had given his wife's wedding ring.

Another man was offered a pork roast, so he dug up all his family treasure that he had buried earlier and took it to the railroad station where he was to meet his contact, a man with dark skin and darker eyes. They exchanged suitcases surreptitiously, and the man started for home happy, his mouth watering for the pork roast he would have for dinner. But when he set his suitcase down on the next platform, a thin trickle of blood seeped out, as he had feared it would. A Russian soldier noticed it and ordered him to open the suitcase. The man begged and tried to bribe the Russian to split whatever the suitcase contained, and the soldier finally agreed. But when they opened it, no roast or ham greeted their eyes. Inside was the corpse of a small child, carved into chunks, and the severed head, with the eyes wide open, staring at them.

I spent a lot of time thinking about these stories, inventing variants and new endings. I would somehow get to Latvia and dig up the silver samovar and spoons my father had buried next to the day lilies and irises at the Parsonage. I would only stop to pick up another pair of boots for my father, which looked like the ones I imagined my mother's Uncle Žanis wearing in the dark forests of Russia. These boots would bring my father power and happiness. I would hurry back to Germany and successfully trade all the treasure because I would know not to accept anything sight unseen. Or I would walk into the woods and find the signaling station filled with cans of meat and sweetened milk. I would somehow convince a soldier to give back my mother's and father's wedding rings, and my parents would be happy again. All the uncles and aunts would gather once more for a huge meal. Or I would meet the old woman who had the soldier's coat, and if I was very good, she would give me some of the watches and jewels. My mother would be overjoyed, she would kiss me and say, "Thank you, precious." Everything would be the way it was in Latvia, only better.

These stories and my daydreams underlined what was happening in Lobethal and elsewhere. As the supply of carrots dwindled, people told fewer stories, they grew grimmer, we laughed less at our conquerors. Starvation began in earnest.

Hilda wandered around muttering, her already slender body now thin to transparency. She was pregnant. The fetus clamped onto her frame, his cruel Mongolian eyes narrowed even further, seemed visible under her clothes, sucking nourishment out of her, pulling her downwards, strangling her. Ōmīte had tried to keep an eye on her, and my mother and Frau Braun took over when my grandmother got sick. But one night Hilda drowned herself in the lake, just as she had threatened to do.

I used to dream about her during the years I was married. I would see her thrashing about in the dark water, struggling not to be pulled under by the monstrous fetus that would not let her go. She tried to speak, to call for help, to explain herself, to scream, but no words would come. No one could hear her. I woke in terror at four each morning during those long years, but I tried to forget about it during the day. The war had not been so bad, no one in my family had been killed, as others had. I was a failure because I could not forget about it. During the long gray years I stayed married, I kept dreaming about Hilda because there was no one who had the courage to hear, no one I trusted enough to tell. There was no one with whom I could talk in bed.

♦ 9 ♦

Escape

Every Wednesday and every Sunday, my mother, my sister and I went to watch the mass burials. Of the seven hundred inmates in Lobethal, over four hundred died of starvation, typhoid and dysentery. My mother would say that soon we would be buried there too, and although I hated her saying that, there was no reason to believe otherwise. We were deep in Russian-occupied territory, we were dazed by what had happened to us and we were starving. Everyone around us was starving too. There was nothing to do but wait.

Lobethal was about fifty miles from Berlin, but it might as well have been on the moon. Cars and motorcycles had been confiscated or were rusting away useless for lack of parts. Gasoline was not available. Horses had been requisitioned or killed for food. Roads were heavily patrolled by soldiers, bridges were guarded. While in the early weeks of the occupation we had walked long distances looking for food, we no longer had the strength to do so. We waited.

In the early days after the war, Berlin was not the closed, divided city it became later. The Berlin Wall had not been built, and it was possible to go from the sectors occupied by the Russians to those held by the British. Even so, there was no particular reason to go to Berlin. We heard that the city was in ruins and that it was filled with thousands of starving, homeless people. At least in Lobethal we had a place to stay. We passed through Berlin on our way to Lobethal. During an air raid, we had been ordered out of a shelter. The owners pushed us out into the street in the middle of the raid, and we had to lie on the ground at the base of a building, covering our heads with our arms. So we already knew what it was like to be homeless there.

Guks, my fourteen-year-old cousin, had been to Berlin recently. He occasionally worked for a carpenter in the next village. Anyone who knew how to repair anything was in great demand, although materials were scarce. Money was useless, but the carpenter paid Guks by letting him eat the midday meal with his family and by an occasional present of food. The carpenter spent as much time on scavenging and bartering for materials as he did on repairs to the bombed and vandalized houses.

In October, six months after the Russians arrived, the carpenter heard that someone had nails to trade in Berlin. The carpenter knew a man who owned a garage and who still had a truck, more or less in working order. The carpenter also had enough cigarettes and jewelry to be used as bribes and payments. He took Guks with him to Berlin to help load whatever was going to be traded. Once there, he sent Guks off to amuse himself until dark. The carpenter was going to spend the afternoon with a woman who had once been a writer. Together with her two daughters this woman had been kept for days in a basement by a unit of Russian soldiers and had been repeatedly raped. The carpenter said it had knocked the snobbishness out of her, that in order to stay drunk she would now do anything. He had a bottle of vodka and some canned meat to give her.

Guks spent the afternoon wandering about the city, looking at the bombed buildings, avoiding groups of soldiers. Finally, tired, he sat down on a park bench to rest and dozed off. He woke to women's voices speaking Latvian. They sounded very familiar. At first he thought it might even be his mother and sister; their dialect was certainly from Alūksne, the district where his family had lived.

Sitting on the next bench were two young women, dazzling creatures, well dressed and well fed. Their faces were bright with makeup and with enjoyment. They were giggling and speaking loudly in Latvian, but they did not seem afraid that someone would overhear them and send them back to Latvia.

Guks might not have started talking to them had they not done something typically Latvian. Since there are so few Latvians, we tend to assume that no one else can understand us. So the sisters started discussing him. What, they wondered, was such a darling boy doing wearing such awful clothes? Should they take him home and undress him? What would he do if they put him into the bathtub and soaped him up, washed his face and ears and neck? Would he mind it if they lathered up his chest? What about his other parts?

"Yes, he would," Guks said. He liked them, but he did not want them to get away with thinking that he didn't know they had been talking about him. "Oh, this is terrible," they blushed and shrieked, but they were delighted really. They had not seen other Latvians in so long.

They took him back to their apartment, which was filled with exquisite china, beautiful clothes and more food than Guks could believe existed anywhere in the world. They fed him an enormous meal and persuaded him to choose a new shirt and tie from a cupboard full of men's clothes. They teased him about the bath, but assured him that this time they wouldn't wash him because their clients would start arriving as soon as it got dark, so they had to get ready themselves. But just wait till next time; they would scrub him until he was pink and shiny and smooth, and he would never be the same after that. Guks blushed and laughed and was flattered.

They told him a little about themselves and questioned him about his family. They were from Alūksne, just as Guks had thought, and they had worked in a factory until the end of the war. They decided then that rape would be inevitable when the soldiers came in, so they had, as they put it, placed themselves under the protection of officers. They had many such officers protecting them now: it was better than being raped by a crowd of common soldiers, and they had more luxuries than anybody else in Berlin.

When Guks told them his last name, they emitted more shrieks of delight. They knew Aunt Hermīne, Guks's mother; she had lived just a few doors from their mother. But they had lost contact with her after she married a straightlaced Lutheran minister. They themselves would have been bored to death by someone like that. But, of course, Hermīne was respectable and religious herself and liked sitting in church, listening to sermons rather than enjoying life. They had seen Guks's father in the pulpit once, he had been awfully grim, but that was at a funeral, so perhaps that explained it. They didn't go to church much otherwise. So, really, they were old friends, sort of. They kissed Guks and ruffled his hair.

When Guks told them about the starvation and hopelessness in Lobethal, they were horrified. How terrible, you must leave there at once, they cried, and they patted his cheek. You must come to Berlin, something better will happen here, they promised vaguely.

But then the oldest sister, Marta, remembered hearing that Latvians were indeed arriving in Berlin. One of the officers had told her that a camp for the displaced and homeless had been established in another part of town. He said that too many people had arrived who could not be admitted, people with the wrong papers and the wrong politics had to be kept out, and screening them was a very hard job. But quite a few Latvians were already in the camp, which provided food and shelter. Marta gave Guks directions how to get there.

They made a parcel with canned meat and jam for him to take back and sent him off full, happy and smeared with lipstick. They made him promise that he would come visit them again when he was safe in Berlin. He'd be older then and they could give him that bath without robbing the cradle. They could see that he really wanted to have it.

Guks's return caused great excitement. The can of meat he brought back was opened and we were each given a small slice late at night. Once more the adults, though diminished in number, sat around a table, whispering about what to do. Should we try to leave? What dangers would we encounter? What were the chances of first getting to Berlin and then into the camp? A year ago in Latvia they had also planned like this, and it had not turned out well. Then Guks was considered one of the children, and he had spent a lot of time playing with my sister and me while the adults talked. He had greatly impressed us by sucking out raw eggs and swinging dangerously from the barn rafters. Now he was accepted as an adult and was crucial in the plan for escape.

The adults speculated in whispers. Was there even any point in trying to get to Berlin? Which Latvians were being admitted to the camp and what might their politics be like? Maybe only collaborators with the Russians during the earlier occupation of Latvia in 1940 were being accepted. Perhaps we would be admitted only to be turned over to the Russians again and sent back to occupied Latvia to be executed for having tried to escape in the first place. Or the gates might be shut against us and we would be left to wander the streets, unable to get back to Lobethal. At least here we had a place to stay as winter approached.

And how were we going to get to Berlin? Who would drive us there and how could we possibly pay someone enough to take such a risk? Could we evade the patrols on the roads? Was there any point in trying when all it might mean would be that we died sooner than we would in Lobethal? It may have been this last argument against going that actually convinced them to try. We were dying of starvation anyway, so we might as well try to escape. At least it would all be over sooner. No one except Guks could have been very optimistic.

The whole family pooled resources. My father and Uncle Gustavs had both buried on the grounds of Lobethal the heavy silver crosses they used to wear over their black ministerial robes during services. My mother had also buried some gold teaspoons that belonged to Ōmīte, saved from another war. Her family had carried them all the way across Russia as they escaped after World War I. If food had been available on the black market, these would have been traded away long ago. Now it seemed providential they had not.

Every detail of the plan must have posed dangers. Just finding a safe time to go into the woods carrying a shovel, to locate the exact spot again, to find it undisturbed, to dig up the crosses and spoons, to carry them back without being stopped must have been risky. They also had to find someone they could trust, someone willing to accept these things as full payment, someone who would keep quiet about the plan even if he did not undertake it.

They had to find a truck that was running and which would not break down on the way and someone to drive it who had access to gasoline and who knew the whole system of patrols, sentries and bribes. And who could guarantee that such an enterprising person would not simply take the valuables offered as payment and then turn around and betray us to the Russian soldiers? Even if that did not happen and we miraculously got past all the sentries, would we finally be admitted into the camp?

Such plans would have been difficult to make even if everyone had been in good health and spirits. My parents were defeated, exhausted and emaciated. Both of them had experienced war as children, both had been scarred by that. But they successfully made all the essential arrangements. Less than a week after Guks had been promised another meal and a bath too, we were ready to go.

✦ ✦ ✦

We again had to make preparations to die. We asked each other's forgiveness for past wrongs and embraced formally, just as before the Russian soldiers arrived. Then everyone prayed together, looking so united as they bowed their heads. I pretended I was praying too as I waited for them to finish. I no longer asked my mother to smile either. I knew, however, the most important things: I must not speak and I must not cry. I would make others angry if I did. It was essential to be compliant and to pretend to be all right.

After midnight we tiptoed down the hallway and out the back door, without anybody seeing us. It was a clear, cold, moonlit autumn night. We hurried towards the woods. We did not have much to carry, only small bundles of clothes.

I was reminded once again to be very quiet. If soldiers stopped us, my mother would do all the talking. Once we got on the truck that would take us to Berlin, the driver would speak to the sentries. If I were questioned directly, especially if I were separated from everyone else, I should show no response whatsoever, even if the soldiers hurt me. The driver would be telling different stories to each sentry, and to contradict him could be fatal.

We got to the woods without being stopped. It was a relief to be away from the road, where we had been so exposed in the moonlight, which was nevertheless necessary as the driver would try to pass a particular crossroads with his lights off. We sat down at the very edge of the woods, our feet in a dry ditch. If anyone approached, we were to run into the woods and hide.

We waited for quite a while. Though I knew what we were doing was very dangerous, I was also excited, impatient to have a ride in the truck, and curious to see what another place looked like. Maybe we would get far away from soldiers.

Finally we heard a faint sound in the distance and scrambled into the woods. A truck without lights was coming down the sandy road. It slowed when it got close to us, stopped, backed up slightly.

"That's him," my mother whispered.

The driver conferred in hurried whispers with the men, and we climbed in quickly. The back gate was raised, the canvas flaps lowered, and we were on our way.

Sitting on the wooden truck bed we remained alert. Every time the truck slowed, every time it lurched to a stop, we tensed ourselves for the flap to be raised, and for all of us to be dragged outside. Once the driver spoke softly with several others, but we could not make out the words. In a little while we were allowed to continue.

Then the truck stopped again. Steps crunched on the roadside gravel as someone came around to the back. A Russian soldier lifted the canvas and shone his flashlight from face to face. He said something in Russian, then in German. We all sat very still, pretending we could neither hear nor speak. After more hushed discussion and an even longer silence, the driver got back into the truck and started up. A jeep carrying two soldiers holding guns followed us for several miles, then turned back.

Dawn was breaking when we got to Berlin. The driver let us out on a deserted street, which he judged to be near the receiving center. He would not take us closer for fear of being questioned by the British, nor would he agree to come back later in case we were not admitted. He had carried out his part of the agreement and would take no further risks. We were on our own.

We sat down on the pavement near our bundles while my father went to look for the center. He came back soon to tell us that we could walk there easily. Everything was going smoothly.

But when we rounded the last corner by the center, we saw a line of people a block long stretching in front of us. The closed gate suddenly seemed miles away. Hundreds of refugees, many waiting since yesterday and even the day before, were ahead of us. Disappointed, we trudged to the end of the line. Later, hundreds of others would line up behind us.

Rumors of all kinds circulated. Only Estonians and Hungarians would be admitted, Latvians might as well get out of line right now. Only people who had left their countries between certain dates would be accepted, those who had left even a day earlier or later would be turned away. Only those from areas occupied by the British had a chance, those from elsewhere were out of luck; the British would not anger their Russian allies by taking in people from their territory and therefore rightfully their subjects. No one without passports and birth certificates would be allowed in. This last rumor made it seem hopeless since all our papers had been lost during the looting.

When the gate was finally opened in midmorning, the line moved more slowly than any in which we, accustomed as we now were to standing in line, had ever waited. People stood on tiptoe to see, they questioned everyone who was turned back in order to estimate their own chances. Anyone who tried to push ahead was berated by others.

The only hope for staying alive was to be admitted to the camp.

We stood on the cold pavement all day. The line slowly inched forward. Occasionally someone rejected would walk past us, ashamed of being found worthless. We tried to discover and define how that person was different from us. In the late afternoon a young Latvian couple with a small baby decided to leave because it seemed futile. They had been in line since the day before, but they had to meet someone on the outskirts of Berlin who would not wait for them a minute past five. At least they would have a roof over their heads in the winter. They comforted themselves that the chances for admission were not good for Latvians anyway; they had heard of very few being let in.

Fresh rumors started circulating that the British officers would close the gates any minute since it was about the same time that they had done so the day before. We continued waiting, watching the soldiers. They would stand up, stretch, talk among themselves or one of them would even leave, but they would eventually continue working. They questioned the men, wrote down their answers, conferred, made decisions. No one knew what the rules were. Telling the truth might condemn us to homelessness, or save us.

That evening, as a cold rain began to fall, we were the last family admitted to the receiving camp. I do not know how my father and Uncle Gustavs were even able to speak by then. We had stood all day, without water or food. We had to tell the truth, and we were then judged by mysterious, arbitrary standards. These soldiers too could have decided that we were not worth feeding. And we had nowhere to go if we had been found unworthy.

An officer motioned us into the camp, past the table where others were being questioned. After we entered, two soldiers got up and pushed the wrought-iron gate shut, then secured it with a lock and chain.

A murmur like a moan rose from the hundreds of people behind us. "Please, let us in." "Please, don't close the gate." "What time will you open tomorrow?" "Will you open tomorrow?" "Please, let us in too." "Please."

I could feel the despair and anger behind me. I was afraid to turn around and look at all the others being kept out. A seven-year-old

Estonian boy and his grandmother had been in line right behind us. The boy did not have any parents, his face had lit up when we were called forward. I did not want to see their faces now. But it was also as if all of the people who were still starving in Lobethal were lined up outside the gate too. I could feel the disappointment of the hundreds in the outer darkness, their murmurs followed me, their anger burned my back as we walked to the dining hall of the camp.

The following is one of my favorite memories, I think of it often. We were taken to the dining room, which at one time must have been a ballroom or banquet hall in the palatial private house the British had requisitioned. The parquet floors gleamed, the crystal chandeliers glistened. Long white tables, which in memory seem covered with damask but which must have been only plain scoured wood, were arranged on the warmer side of the room, away from the windows. We stood in another line, but just briefly this time. Our shabby clothing, our boils, our sticklike limbs did not matter. We were hungry and they fed us.

We were given warm strong tea with sugar and canned milk, soft white bread, hard thick slabs of margarine and great spoonfuls of raspberry jam. My father said a prayer. Ōmīte wiped her eyes as she ate. We praised everything again and again, though actually the flavors were very strange. The tea I remembered from Latvia was hot and clear and flavored with camomile or mint; the bread was heavy and coarse and dark; the butter was rich and soft. But I still think of this as the most wonderful meal of my life. I often dream of the room, especially the way the chandeliers were reflected in the windows, shutting out the cold, rainy night, and all of us safe, sitting together around a table.

I have since read that raspberry jam in wartime Britain was rumored to consist of saccharine, food coloring and flecks of sawdust for the pips, and I wonder whether that was what we ate. The British had food rationing themselves until 1950, yet they gave us of what little they had themselves. They took us in, fed us, housed us and accepted responsibility for us. Like the day itself, which included waiting and then guilt about others left outside the gate, their generosity was not perfect. It was human and flawed but real and consistent, and it saved us.

Part III

◆◆◆

Part III

·10·

Waiting

Life in the camps meant waiting. Three times a day we stood in line for food, which was monotonous but blessedly available. The gray tasteless pea soup served at each meal was nicknamed the Green Terror. The pale dry bread was made of an unfamiliar grain, corn, which was called *kukurūza* in Latvian, while the British soldiers guarding the camp called it *maize,* a word that meant bread in Latvian. Sometimes there were scrambled eggs made from canned powder, and milk reconstituted from sticky white dust that came in large blue cans labeled KLIM (milk spelled backwards!). For a week each child was given a square of chocolate from faraway England—so sweet, so aromatic, so delicious—but the practice was stopped without explanation. No one had fruit, cheese, vegetables, meat, fish, cookies, candy or pastries. People spoke longingly of what they would eat if only they could.

Before going to sleep, my sister and I whispered together about the thin buttery crêpes filled with veal and mushrooms or smeared thickly with strawberry jam and cream, which we ate in Latvia. We were gawky girls with limbs so thin that we stood out even among the inmates of the camp. "Here come the two threads," boys would shout when they saw us coming. But our boils had disappeared, our skin was less pale, our hair seemed ready to glint in the sunlight. We were hungry again; we were going to live.

During my five years in D.P. camps, from the time that I was seven until I was twelve, I spent thousands of hours waiting in line, while the authorities decided what I could have, where I could go, what I deserved. To complain or to try to change anything was useless because that would only anger the authorities. It was disgraceful not to be thankful for everything. The lessons I had learned during the terror of the Russian soldiers—that I should neither cry nor speak, that I should be quiet and compliant, and that I could only wait rather than act—were reinforced over and over again.

We were all waiting. We waited for food, clothing, medication. We waited for days when we were allowed outside the gates for a few hours to walk in the surrounding woods or down the dusty roads to half-empty German villages. We waited for a chance to leave the camps, to go back to Latvia or failing that, to emigrate to another country. When opportunities to depart finally opened up, we waited again for others to decide whether we were good enough, whether we deserved to go where we wished. We were all waiting for a chance to have a real life.

Standing in line we talked. Adults spoke longingly of real coffee, since even the watery liquid brewed from burnt chicory was not regularly available. They talked of the cigarettes they had smoked, of times they had had so many in their possession that they left them carelessly in crystal containers on their coffee tables or carried them about in slender silver cases and casually offered them to friends and acquaintances. They described the French cognacs served to friends and the bottles of wine stored in their cellars. They recalled apple orchards, raspberry stands, wild strawberries, trout, mushrooms, all theirs once for the taking, in Latvia, at home.

They spoke of trading and contriving. Some still had gold rings, watches, cufflinks and jewels, which they could barter on the black market for food and clothing. Trading with the surrounding German communities was illegal and dangerous, beatings and robberies were frequent, but people risked it anyway.

Everyone was delighted when Mr. Jansons started acting as a go-between. In Camp Montgomery he had his first great success. He acquired a dozen tiny pink piglets from a nearby German farmer and delivered them to the lucky families with valuables to give in return.

This camp, unlike the four earlier camps where I had lived, consisted of barracks rather than Quonset huts. Under most floors were dirt crawl spaces that could be used for storage. Trapdoors opened directly from some of the rooms into these dark snug places, like underground caves, where the pigs lived. Spoiled food from the kitchens, peels and greens from the beets available occasionally, scavenging in the countryside and Mr. Jansons's further skills in trading fed the pigs; they grew and fattened. We speculated about the ways in which the owners might share the bounty, but we also enjoyed watching the little pigs—a hopeful sign of the future—thrive for their own sake.

But one morning a troop of British soldiers descended on the camp with guns, ropes and sticks. They went from door to door, questioning everyone, systematically searching for trapdoors. They drafted several translators to speak to the dozen or so different nationalities in the camp. Among them was my mother, who translated into Latvian what a Hungarian actress who knew English translated into Russian. The soldiers claimed that the pigs made the barracks unsanitary, that their smell was unpleasant, that the dirt would lead to disease and even the death of children.

No one was convinced. By this time all the pigs had names, minutely discussed personalities and secure places in the families owning them. They were not only future pork roasts and crackling bacon, but family pets on whom a lot of affection had been lavished.

Hindered by scolding women and jeering men, the soldiers lowered themselves into the cramped crawl spaces. They groped about in the darkness for the slippery pigs, many of whom had indeed been kept almost as clean as the children. Shouting directions to one another, with resolutely pleasant faces, the soldiers tried to capture the squealing pigs, who playfully evaded them. Gradually they developed a method. A perspiring man held a small pig flat on its back while another tried to tie the short legs flailing the air. Finally they heaved the trussed piglet into a waiting truck.

At first I was terrified of the soldiers, who seemed to have the right to do whatever they pleased, but gradually I relaxed into comforting solidarity with the other observers. Those not immediately concerned with intervening on behalf of their particular pig—because she was so good, so clean, so quiet and so smart—stood around watching and laughing at the British.

A young soldier, red-faced with exertion, dragged Mrs. Saulitis's piglet, Pārsliņa ("Little Snowflake"), outside. Mrs. Saulītis, whose name meant "sunlight," followed, alternately telling the soldiers that they should be ashamed of themselves and go find a real war to fight and calling on Pārsliņa, held awkwardly and at arm's length, to escape. The red-haired sergeant with the moustache lost his footing and stumbled against the young soldier just hard enough to make him drop Pārsliņa, who landed upside down, too shocked even to squeal. She righted herself almost immediately, flew into Mrs. Saulītis's outstretched arms and buried her head in her bosom. Mrs. Saulītis stroked Pārsliņa's head, murmured lovingly into her ear, kissed her and held on tight.

An unequal tug of war began. The soldiers tried to get a grasp on Pārsliņa's smooth pink hindquarters, but their delicacy forbid them to grab Pārsliņa around the middle or the shoulders, which were snug between Mrs. Saulītis's large warm breasts. We shouted encouragement to Pārsliņa and to Mrs. Saulītis and laughed derisively at the efforts of the soldiers. When the red-haired soldier yanked Pārsliņa by the tail, we booed, and Pārsliņa squealed pathetically. Mrs. Saulītis gave the soldiers a venomous look and soothed and patted Pārsliņa protectively.

I was overcome with admiration for her. What courage Mrs. Saulītis had! How lucky Pārsliņa was to have a protector like her! How loved Pārsliņa must feel even as she was being attacked!

The soldiers tried to reason with Mrs. Saulītis.

"Tell her she will catch a disease from her pig."

"No," said Mrs. Saulītis, "Pārsliņa is very healthy, she has no germs. I too am very healthy, as they can see. They can examine me if they like." On the edge of the crowd a few young men tittered, whistled, applauded and stamped their feet. Mrs. Saulītis threw them a disapproving glance.

Captain Vilciņš was called in next. He was the president of the elected administrative board, on which my father also regularly served, which helped the British soldiers in running the camp. Dashing in his long leather coat left from the days when he used to win riding competitions all over Europe, Captain Vilciņš arrived from a meeting devoted to decisions about allocating space, setting up schedules for the work everyone had to do in the kitchens, settling disputes and planning community activities. Two other board members hov-

ered behind him while he told Mrs. Saulītis to obey orders. Mrs. Saulītis refused.

Finally the British camp commandant himself was called.

"Tell that woman she is a public nuisance. If she does not let go of
that pig, I will have her arrested and transported to the Russian sector of Berlin. She'll get herself sent back to Latvia if she isn't careful,"
Lieutenant Sutherland said briskly.

At this Mrs. Saulītis finally yielded. She kissed Pārsliņa and laid her
gently in the arms of the red-haired sergeant, who guiltily tiptoed with
her to the truck. He set her down tenderly. Relieved, the other soldiers
slammed shut the doors of their trucks and jeeps. They left, a cloud
of fine dust rising behind them.

A story started circulating immediately that a Lithuanian woman
had managed to save her pig by putting it in a dress and covering its
head with a scarf. She cried that her little girl was near dying with a
mysterious fever and spots, and the soldiers backed out, convinced
that she was tenderly bending over a feverish child rather than a pig
to be roasted on Lithuanian Independence Day. Those Lithuanians,
they're so brave and they know what they are doing, in spite of most
of them being Catholics, said the Latvians. The Estonians, on the
other hand, claimed that the Latvians, resourceful schemers and man-
agers, had contrived to hide some pigs in the woods because the camp
administration favored them with advance information. But in any
case, no pig—brushed, washed, wearing a ribbon or led on a leash for
an airing—ever made an appearance in Camp Montgomery again.

I left the crowd speculating about any surviving pigs and followed
Mrs. Saulītis towards her room, which she shared with two other families. I was afraid to get close enough to her to see the ineradicable
pain I had learned to expect on my mother's face, but I felt compelled
to trail behind her anyway. I wanted to cheer up Mrs. Saulītis for the
loss of Pārslina.

Mrs. Saulītis walked more and more slowly, so that I had to stop in
order to stay unobserved. I heard a low murmuring sound. Was Mrs.
Saulītis crying? I was useless to help her. But no, those were not sobs.
Mrs. Saulītis was clearing her throat, she was humming to herself, she
was singing solely for her own pleasure as she walked towards the
gray barracks. I was amazed to hear a woman singing happily like that
by herself, for herself. Even in Latvia, my mother's songs had held

longing and pain. Now she did not sing at all. But Mrs. Saulītis was singing, swaying a little as she walked.

> *"Es meitiņa kā rozīte,*
> *Kā sarkana zemenīte,*
> *Pienu ēdu, pienu dzēru,*
> *Pienā muti nomazgāju.*
>
> *I'm a little girl like a little rose,*
> *Like a small red strawberry,*
> *I eat milk, I drink milk,*
> *And I bathe my face in milk."*

When the song was finished, she passed her hands over her hips in a satisfied caressing way that left me breathless with admiration. She glanced languorously over her shoulder, noticed me, stopped.

"What are you doing, tiptoeing behind me like a mouse? Come up here at least and keep me company."

She held out her hand for me to grasp.

Just like that.

We walked in silence until I gathered enough courage to say, "I'm truly sorry about Pārsliņa. I'm sorry they took her away from you."

"Yes, so am I."

"I liked her. She was a wonderful pig."

"Yes, she was. Very good looking, very sensitive, but cheerful. An unusual pig."

"Was she smart?" I wanted to know.

"Oh yes, very intelligent, almost an intellectual. A wonderful pig." Mrs. Saulītis searched for the right word. "Unique. Truly unique."

"I'm sorry," I repeated, "please don't be sad." I was embarrassed as soon as I had said something so personal. But she did not seem to mind.

She gently squeezed my hand. "I'm all right, precious," she said. "I'm sorry to lose her, but it can't be helped. These things happen."

Precious! It had been a long time since anyone had called me that. I looked up at Mrs. Saulītis's face. Her clear blue-green eyes were not filled with tears; she wasn't holding back sobs while smiling. She was not pretending.

"Well," said Mrs. Saulītis after a pause, "what did you think of me? I gave those soldiers a good fight, didn't I? I bet they won't forget me in a hurry."

"I thought you were wonderful."

"Did you?" Mrs. Saulitis, delighted, laughed out loud. "Actually, I think so too. I know some of them will toss and turn and dream about me tonight. And those board members are lucky I didn't tell everybody what I know about them, dry old sticks that they are. I'll tell *you* some other time."

At her door she let go of my hand and gave me a quick hug. Vitality from her rich auburn hair and soft white skin warmed my dry skin and limp hair.

"Yes," Mrs. Saulitis said, "I bet that sergeant can't get me out of his mind right now, I'm engraved on his heart. Who knows, something good may come, even from this. Poor dear Pārsliņa, though. I can't bear to think what they'll do to her."

Early each morning my mother left the room we shared with another family to go to her teaching and translating tasks. As soon as she was gone I ran to meet Mrs. Saulitis by the bulletin board near the kitchens, where lists were posted of those to be moved to other camps. I knew that any day I too could be ordered to get on a waiting truck again.

Families in some other Displaced Persons' camps were luckier. They were taken from receiving centers, such as the British center in Berlin, directly to camps where they were allowed to stay for the next four or five years. They could explore the area, learn its resources and contrive small comforts in their rooms. They could plant vegetable gardens and raise chickens and geese hidden from the authorities, who seemed to look the other way from creatures smaller than pigs. More important, uncles and aunts and cousins and grandparents could all stay together. Everyone could make friends and count on seeing those friends again.

But our family happened to be in a group that the British moved from camp to camp as private quarters were gradually returned to civilians, as soldiers were demobilized and as the number of units was reduced for easier administration. During the five years we moved a dozen times or so. Sometimes a few rooms in the army barracks, quonset huts or commandeered private apartments were pleasant, but even those looked bleak because the bomb-shattered windows were boarded up and did not admit much light. Bunks and bundles were pushed against windows as well because space was at a premium. Rooms were divided and subdivided by blankets, sheets, tarps, plywood, cardboard, anything that could be used to create the illusion of privacy. Movement was difficult unless one went sideways. Conversations were conducted in whispers. Arguments were subsumed under the pretense that they had not been heard. Politeness and self-control were essential.

Sometimes Ōmīte was with us, at other times she was with one of her sons in other camps. I believed, rightly, that as soon as we were really settled in the space assigned to us, as soon as I had made friends, a notice would be put up that we were to be taken to yet another camp. The next cluster of ugly barracks surrounded by barbed wire would be even bleaker because it was unfamiliar.

Which morning would Mrs. Saulītis be taken away? How soon would the next loss come?

But in the interlude, there was pleasure. Almost everywhere I had lived, I had watched women start gardens. They saved and traded seeds from radishes, carrots and cucumbers, they transplanted wild strawberries from the surrounding fields, they dug up tiny pink and white English daisies and coarse purple asters, which grew in thick clumps along the deserted roads. Sweet peas flowered under the windows of the crowded barracks and were brought in to scent the rooms. For the first time, June peas ripened, and Mrs. Saulītis made a beautiful green-and-white soup from evaporated milk and peas, which bore no resemblance to the gray-green liquid served in the dining halls. She handed me a full bowl and talked with me while I ate.

Captain Vilciņš, who had studied in Paris, ran the camp administrative board with decisiveness and style. He ordered two barracks torn down and a fountain constructed on the cement base of a latrine. Holding a slender cane, his white silk scarf fluttering in the breeze, he stood resolutely at attention while his instructions were carried out. His plan was that flags of all the nationalities in the camp would fly, trees would grow overnight and people would stroll in the shady plaza in the evenings. We would soon enough forget the greater crowding in the barracks necessitated by this civic improvement. We should overlook the trampled grass in the square and the lowly origins of the glistening fountain. But even during the dedication of the Heroes Plaza, marked by interminable speeches, the water sputtered, then died, as if calling attention to its source. We spent our evenings in the open space on the other side of the camp and avoided the plaza, which was quickly renamed Latrine Walk.

But the fountain was flowing freely this morning. I could see the needles of water as I ran, relieved, towards Mrs. Saulitis's door. Neither of our names had been on the lists, and a new one probably would not appear until Tuesday, four whole long days away. Colors of the rainbow sparkled in the spray, the ground was less pitted and dusty.

I would have spent every waking minute with Mrs. Saulitis, if only my mother and Mrs. Saulitis herself had permitted. As it was, Mrs. Saulitis allowed me more time than I dared hope for. I expected to be sent away every time I knocked, and I was thrilled when I was invited in.

Mrs. Saulitis let me dig and weed under her window, which overlooked Captain Vilciņš's fountain. She showed me how to dig up wild pink roses without damaging the roots, to wrap them tenderly in a piece of burlap, to carry them to camp and plant them again. One day she set me to transplanting a whole row of English daisies.

"They will always be there, even after you are gone," Mrs. Saulitis told me.

"But I won't be here to see them. Will I be here to see them?" Perhaps Mrs. Saulitis knew something.

"Well, maybe you won't be. But the daisies will be happy to have a good place to grow, in such a safe sunny corner. They will be grateful to you for having planted them. They'll flourish after you're gone. And you will have made the world more beautiful."

So saying, she gave me a real gift, a lifelong love of flowers and gardening, which has gotten me through many difficult times.

But then I did not know the value of what I had been given. "But I want to stay here, I don't ever want to move again," I said.

"I know, precious," Mrs. Saulitis said, "but this isn't a real life. We can't live like this forever. Everyone needs a home, work to do, a future to plan and look forward to."

I kept my head down and continued digging ineffectually at the base of a clump of grass with a small trowel, Mrs. Saulitis's only tool. I didn't like the way the conversation was going; I had heard it all before.

The men asked, "What's the point of living? Here we are, lawyers, economists, engineers, architects, politicians, with nothing to do. All we can do is wait. Our training is useless, we're idle ourselves."

And my mother would say bitterly, "Artists without paints and canvas, farmers without land and animals, carpenters without tools and materials, musicians without instruments. How can our lives have any meaning? But at least your father and I can keep busy."

I did not like it that my parents were never at home, but I had heard others speak enviously of them for having work to do. My father delivered sermons, presided at funerals and weddings, comforted the grieving, organized Bible discussions and youth groups, served on the administrative boards and sometimes even left the camps to go to church conferences. He also taught religion, specifically Lutheran religion, a required subject in grade school, and he lectured on theology and philosophy in high school.

My mother was never home either. She taught Latvian and German, which were required in grade school, French and Latin in high school. She had offered to teach Russian as well, but the memories of Russian atrocities were much too new, and no one wanted to learn it. She worked well into the evening hours as a translator in the camp administrative office. Some nights she accompanied my father to family celebrations and church functions.

"It's hard living like this," Mrs. Saulitis said, "hard, but not hopeless." She drew out the silver cigarette case engraved with lilies she always carried, checked her reflection in it and reapplied her dark red, almost black lipstick. She ran her hand approvingly through her wavy auburn hair.

She smiled at me. "Who knows," she said, "something good may happen today. Anyway, we might as well look nice while we wait."

Something good did happen. Mrs. Saulitis got a room of her own, an unheard-of arrangement in the camp where two or three families crowded together in a single room. Her husband, to whom she never referred, had disappeared during the war, so it wasn't even as if she were about to be reunited with him. The new arrangement caused much criticism of the administrative board members, who maintained a discreet silence.

Mrs. Saulitis had been observed teetering in her high-heeled patent-leather shoes while walking to the woods with one of the British soldiers, the one who had pulled Pārsliṇa by the tail. She had been seen on her return to the camp, leaning on his arm, looking a little flushed but quite self-possessed, her high heels sinking into the ground, while the red-haired sergeant bent over her solicitously. People sniffed and nodded significantly when she walked by, though no one said anything.

Couples did marry and women had babies in the camps, but sexual activity seemed nonexistent, and possibly for the vast majority it was. People were recovering from malnutrition and the immediate effects of the war, and they were mourning those who had been killed or from whom they had been separated. Depression must have been common, but no one knew the word or the concept. Theories of post-traumatic stress were decades in the future. Young courting couples did go off to walk in the woods when the gates were opened. Bands of boys, grinning in anticipation, followed to see what they could see, so such erotic adventures must have been fraught with the danger of being interrupted and embarrassed. But Mrs. Saulitis could not have had marriage on her mind.

After Mrs. Saulitis moved into her own room, the sergeant arrived on Saturday afternoons, packages in his hands. I lined up with other children silently watching him. Mrs. Saulītis always took a long time answering the door, while he straightened his tie, fiddled with his moustache and pretended not to see us. He did not leave until late at night and had even been observed climbing into his jeep on Sunday morning. A thick new olive green wool blanket covered Mrs. Saulitis's window at night.

While we planted wild poppies, Mrs. Saulītis told me about her love affair with the sergeant. I adored being taken into her confidence. The war had not robbed her of sensuality and romantic possibilities, as it had my mother. Only Mrs. Saulītis's life held drama and excitement. She gardened in a flowered silk kimono, which fell open, revealing a black satin bra straining over her firm white breasts. She commented on which of the men would really like to have a better look, who had tried to come into her room late at night and who was dying of jealousy right now because she was in love with the sergeant. Mr. Ķiploks, a highly respected member of the church board *and* the camp board *and* a married man, had threatened to slash his wrists because he was so in love with her. She had to run to get him a drink of water to calm him down. She was afraid that he would be dead by the time she got back from the pump by the kitchen, but he was just sitting there, looking at his watch and tapping his foot impatiently so that he could begin his dramatic performance again as soon as she got back. He did not know that she had seen him through the window, so he had no idea she knew that he wasn't as desperate as he said he was. Men were interesting, of course, but they were not to be trusted, Mrs. Saulitis said. They might seem passionately in love and faithful, but were actually skittish like healthy young colts.

But the sergeant loved her, she believed he did. He begged her to go to England with him, but she was holding out for America. He was heartbroken she had refused him, and in fact had even brought her a bottle of Coca-Cola. This, she explained, was a superbly delicious drink of complex and subtle flavors, indescribable really, but if she were forced to say what it resembled, she would have to say it was a cross between ambrosia and some exotic French liqueur. It made one feel quite different—freer, more powerful, more hopeful. She wished I would get a chance to taste it sometime. She would have saved me a sip, but the sergeant, who loved her to distraction, had insisted she drink it to the last drop. She showed me the short thick green glass bottle, which stood on her window ledge and was the envy of passersby.

Another time Mrs. Saulitis showed me a pair of nylon stockings, the first nylon stockings anyone had seen, anywhere. She held them up to the light and spread her fingers inside to demonstrate how sheer they were. Everyone else in the camp wore much-darned wool and cotton stockings. I had seen silk stockings at celebrations, but they were nothing compared to nylon. My sister and the older girls, with whom she now spent all of her time, stopped to chat with Mrs. Saulitis too and asked to see her stockings, which she obligingly produced.

Mrs. Saulitis also taught me my first words of English: "thank you," "please" and "I love you." But the most glamorous were to come. Mrs. Saulitis explained the upper-class British custom of leaving London to go to beautiful country houses and gardens for weekends.

"Weekend, weekend, holiday—you have to learn to say that. You'll need to understand that when your own lover offers to take you out into the country. Or someday, when you live in a house with a beautiful garden of your own, you can say that when you invite your guests."

On Saturday mornings, before she started getting ready for the sergeant, Mrs. Saulitis sat on a tree stump and sunned herself.

"Weekend, weekend, holiday," she smiled and waved to anyone coming by.

"Weekend, weekend, holiday," people mimicked behind her back, but she did not care. Soon everyone in the camp was saying, "Weekend, weekend, holiday."

Mrs. Saulitis laughed good-naturedly. "They may disapprove," she said, "but see how they imitate me? Just like my husband's mother."

"What happened to her?" I asked. What I really wanted to know was what happened to Mrs. Saulitis's husband.

"Oh, her! She's back in Latvia. She may be in a Russian prison for all I know, though I don't wish that even on her, smelly old lizard that she was. She didn't want to leave her house and farm and barns and stores. She said she'd rather die than give up what she had spent her whole life accumulating, so she stayed behind to be killed."

"What about Mr. Saulitis? Did he stay behind too?"

"Who? She was a widow."

"No, Mr. Saulitis. Your Mr. Saulitis."

"Oh, my husband, you mean. The less said about him the better. He joined the German army as fast as he could. He said he wanted to be on the winning side, but he really wanted the chance to beat up Gypsies and Jews. He used to rave against them often enough. Thank God, he didn't get to do much of that. He was killed soon after he joined."

I did not understand. My parents spoke with admiration of Latvians who hid Jews from the Gestapo or who bicycled furiously to warn Gypsies that a German convoy was coming down the road. They spoke of Nazis and Communists with equal indignation. Latvians themselves were imprisoned by the Gestapo in Salaspils or taken to other concentration camps in Poland. I had thought all Latvians stood firm against the Nazis.

"Wasn't he Latvian?" I asked.

"Yes, he was. And he wasn't the only one like that either. Where do you think that shifty-eyed Mr. Ziemelis got his scar? He tells everyone now that it's from dueling when he was at the university, but I heard he was cut by broken glass when he and other bullies vandalized a Jewish jewelry store."

This conversation, and others like it, would haunt me years later as I studied photographs of the faces of concentration-camp victims. Being Latvian did not exempt me from responsibility and guilt.

But now I went on to questions that seemed more immediate.

"Aren't you sorry he's dead? Didn't you love him?" And when Mrs. Saulitis did not answer, surprised at my own boldness, I persisted, "Why did you marry him then?"

Mrs. Saulitis considered the question carefully. "No, I didn't love him. My parents got me to marry him."

"Why?"

"They wanted to keep the property together; my father's farm adjoined his mother's. So that when Helmuts started walking over on Sunday afternoons, they were very pleased. They sent me to bring him his tea, they seated me next to him whenever he stayed to supper. When he asked my father for my hand, of course he said yes."

"What did you say?"

"Well, I was only seventeen. I'm not an intellectual like your mother, I was brought up to be married. And Helmuts was handsome then, with his ruddy skin and broad shoulders. He looked so masterful, standing there with his straight back and in his polished black boots, that I felt quite ready to faint. It wasn't until later, when he turned every conversation into an argument, when he got furious or wheedling when someone disagreed with him, that I didn't like him anymore. When his mother refused to deed him the farm, he got even worse. He bragged about pulling an old Jew's beard, and I was with him once when he forced a Gypsy wagon off the road. He started waking me up and keeping me awake every night, shouting at me for not having any children to raise as good Nazis."

Mrs. Saulitis's cheerfulness was lost for once. I saw that she was crying and making no attempt to hide her tears. "No, I was glad to see him go into the army before he started beating me regularly. I didn't grieve when I heard he wasn't coming back."

After a while she wiped her eyes. "It's all right, precious," she said. "So you see, for me something good did come from the war. At least I have to try to think so. I thought I would be doing all that hard work on the farm from dawn to dark and putting up with Helmuts every night for the rest of my life. But the war changed that for me, even though I can't go back home."

She squeezed my hand. "Come," she said, "I found a small weed-choked peony bush in the shade behind the storage sheds. Let's go see if we can give it a better place to live."

A few weeks later, we had to move again while Mrs. Saulitis was to stay behind in the room she had gotten through the intercession of the sergeant.

I went about as if in a trance, speaking to no one, not hearing when anyone spoke to me. As at every other point of great stress, I got sick. I developed a high fever and was carried into a waiting truck. I do not remember the move itself, I do not recall saying goodbye to Mrs. Saulitis.

In the new camp I slept on a straw mattress in the warmest corner of the room, which my mother had made great efforts to secure. She took my temperature and urged me to drink cup after cup of hot water. My father sat with me, his cool hand on my forehead. Even Beate postponed going out to join the group of older girls in the camp.

Beate, far more sociable than I, had a passionate interest in becoming a member of these groups wherever she lived. She was popular and was quickly chosen as one of the leaders. Usually she did not care that they drove away me or anyone else younger with derisive shouts. She herself told me firmly that I could not tag along. But now Beate sat with me, reading to me, urging me to get better.

Eventually my fever dropped. I got out of bed and went to school again. I did not mention Mrs. Saulitis. I do not remember speaking about her to anyone.

But in the next camp, I systematically began to seek out other women without children of their own. They taught me darning, knitting, embroidering, mending, solitaire, palm-reading, whatever they knew. I was obsessive about securing their attention. Once I was friends with two such women simultaneously: thin, precise, never-married Miss Tieviņš and gentle, sad, widowed Mrs. Dumpītis. For some reason these two women hated each other on sight, and keeping both relationships going took exquisite tact and constant worry, but somehow I managed it. But no one else had Mrs. Saulitis's warmth or sense of possibilities.

• 11 •

"The Riches of the Heart"

School was the one reliable anchor for me. In every camp national groups organized their own schools, so that children could catch up with what we had missed during the war and be ready for the future. Even first graders went to school six days a week, from early morning to noon. Enough homework was assigned to keep us indoors till twilight and beyond. Adults questioned any child seen playing outdoors and freely offered advice about the necessity of completed homework, good grades and readiness for the future.

Standards were uniformly high and discipline strict. When a teacher entered or left a room, we stood at attention until given permission to do otherwise. No physical punishment was ever used, but being stood in the corner was so shameful that only a few of the wildest boys had survived it. We were constantly admonished to sit ramrod-straight on crates or on benches without backs. Pens and pencils were scarce, though later there were slates and chalk and even paper. An abacus and a blackboard were moved from room to room. There were a few cheaply reproduced paperbacks, and teachers read aloud from books loaned by various inmates.

Most learning was by rote. As soon as we could write, we took down information from the teachers' dictation, to be memorized and reproduced later. We memorized multiplication tables, case endings, elements, trees, stars, cloud formations, occasions for using punctuation marks, names of characters in novels and stories. At least once a week we were tested on our ability to copy correctly a literary passage dictated to us. Capitals, commas, long marks and division of words into syllables were expected to be perfect. Each Monday we had to recite a poem we had memorized, word perfect and "with appropriate feeling."

I studied hard. My parents had both excelled in school, winning prizes and honors, and they expected Beate and me to do well as a matter of course. When we got fives, that is, the highest grades, we received no comment, but fours were cause for dismay and disappointment. A three was a disgrace. A two, a failing grade, would mean being kept back a year, to study with smaller children. Even death would be preferable. It was unthinkable not to do an assignment.

I was terrified of the teachers and of failing, but I also loved studying. We were constantly told of the importance of learning. The most frequently quoted lines—"The riches of the heart do not rust"—were from a poem by Kārlis Skalbe. This was interpreted to mean that one could lose all one's material possessions in looting and wars, one could lose one's family, friends and country, but that knowledge was a precious, everlasting possession. I did not question this. Here at last was something positive and permanent. I knew that if I tried hard enough, I could master almost anything, and this gave me real satisfaction and a sense of control.

Talking, whispering, passing notes or throwing spitballs erupted after teachers left the room, but was highly unusual if they only turned away. Most wild behavior took place on the way to and from school, and only boys and older girls seemed to engage in it. I concentrated on getting perfect grades and on being very quiet and very good.

So I was very surprised one morning when I saw girls from the fourth grade jeer and mock Galīna, who sat next to me in the front row and who also got all fives.

"*Sūdīga krieviete*, shitty Russian," they shouted.

Galīna did not look back, but walked on quickly, with head bent.

Ērika, the tallest girl in my class, pulled on my black pinafore. "Wait," she said, "you walk back here with us. Don't you dare walk with that shitty Russian."

"Comrade Galīna, comrade Galīna," someone lisped mockingly.

"But she's Latvian," I brought out timidly. Galīna had just won a prize for the best Latvian composition, and she sounded exactly like everyone else when she recited.

"That's what you think. Her father's a Russian, he's a leftist. He's a filthy Russian Communist and Jew."

"But her father's dead," I pointed out.

"Doesn't matter. Jews sucked Latvia dry," Ērika said.

"Jews catch Christian children. They put them in barrels full of spikes and roll them down hills," someone else volunteered.

A chant began.

"*Žīdiņš, jūdiņš, kamparsūdiņš* little Jew, little Judas, little camphor shit."

"No," said Ausma, far more bold than I. "My mother will make me stay indoors if someone tells her we were shouting that. She scolded Mrs. Pļaviņš just for humming,

> '*Lietiņš līst, saulīte spīd,*
> *vecam žīdam tupeles plīst,*
> *the rain rains, the sun shines,*
> *the old Jew's slippers burst.*'"

Mrs. Pļaviņš hadn't even sung all the words, Ausma said, but her mother had been furious anyway.

"Oh, good, let's not sing that," I happily agreed with Ausma.

"Well, anyone know any rhymes in Russian?"

I kept quiet about the verses I had recited to the Russian soldiers.

"All right, everybody, you better find some," Ērika ordered.

I saw Ausma beginning to drift off to one side, so I pulled my arm out of the crook of Ērika's elbow.

"Isn't it awful what they are saying?" I asked when I caught up with her. "Are you going to bring in dirty Russian words?"

"No, I will not. And some of the others won't either."

"Good for you. It isn't fair. Galīna is a Latvian, she is nice, she is smart, they can't do that to her," I tripped over my own words.

"No," said Ausma calmly, "she *is* a dirty Russian and a nasty Jew. Her mother is Latvian, but Galīna was born in Moscow."

A wave of even greater protectiveness rose in me. Galīna was like my mother, who was Latvian but had also been born in Russia, and so was different from others.

"But it isn't ladylike to screech like that," Ausma said primly. "Everybody in camp can see us. I'm not going to behave like a fish-wife just because Ērika says so. It isn't polite."

The threatened taunts did not materialize, perhaps because Ērika had to move, perhaps because school was almost over for the year. Everyone was more interested in the activities planned for the summer.

Most Latvians in the camps were well-educated professionals who taught what they knew. Choirs, plays, gymnastics, book discussions, chess tournaments, lectures and crafts classes took place constantly. Children watched volleyball, basketball and soccer games. We were taken on nature hikes and told stories as we sat by campfires. Girls were taught to darn and hem, to knit Latvian mittens with intricate patterns, to embroider pillow covers on burlap with tiny cross-stitches in traditional designs.

Galina and I spent the free hours of one whole summer together. Camp Seedorf, located by a seldom-traveled highway, had strict rules against going into the village. Men and boys had been beaten by Germans, so walking in the woods and playing on bridges and railroad tracks were forbidden. But no one cared if Galina and I crossed the ditch to the meadow. A cement foundation of a farmhouse was still standing, and a few moldy lilac bushes shielded the barracks from view.

We spent countless hours lying on a blanket spread in the sun on the fragrant grass. We read everything we could get our hands on. I liked books about living on farms, planting and harvesting, storing grain and hay in barns for the long winter ahead and transforming barren soil into fertile land. I also liked stories, many of them translated from other languages, about roaming through forests with wolves, flying away with wild geese or living alone on a desert island. These books, their covers protected by brown wrapping paper, could be borrowed from school a day at a time and had to be read immediately.

Best of all, though, were the books that we had been strictly forbidden to touch. Galina brought one about Genghis Khan warming his feet in the bloody insides of still-breathing female captives, and we took turns reading it aloud to each other. Under my skirt, I smuggled out a thick volume of Catholic saints stories, which my mother had found in a ditch outside the camp. My father had called it mostly superstition and my mother had criticized the naïveté of its style and the crudity of its emotions, and both had agreed that it contained much material suitable only for adults. It was slow going because the leaves were water-marked and curled, so that the best passages were often unintelligible. In addition, it was in German, necessitating laborious searches through the German dictionary, which my mother had lent us on the assumption we were memorizing vocabulary lists for school. When anyone approached, we had to stop reading, even if we were right in the middle of a passage about Roman soldiers' removing a woman's clothes in order to flay her.

But usually no one bothered us. We talked about the stories we had read, and if they had sad endings, I invented happy ones. We plaited wreaths of clover and cornflowers, watched frogs and insects in the ditch and pretended that we were living anywhere but in the camp.

One afternoon as we were lying in the tall grass, enveloped in the fragrance of red clover and mint, watching the glistening dragonflies, a truck screeched to a halt and several soldiers got out. The driver and another soldier leapt over the ditch, put on pleasant expressions like masks and strode towards us. All smiles and affability, they started to question us.

I knew better than to reply. I had been told dozens of times that if the Russians found out my family was in the camp, they would demand that the British turn us over, to be taken back to Latvia. We would be imprisoned, tortured by having our nails pulled out, our knees broken, our hair singed off. Finally we would be shot.

The soldier spoke in Russian first, then switched to German.

"Come, come now, we know you girls can speak German," he said. Maybe he had noticed the dictionary, in plain view on top of the blanket.

"Who else is living in that camp there? Any Latvians? Lithuanians? Estonians?"

I felt my heart stop; he must know something. I concentrated on an ant crawling over my bare toes.

"How many people in the camp? Are all the buildings occupied?"

Undiscouraged by our silence, he switched tactics. "I'll give you something very special if you tell me."

He returned to the cab and produced two large orange-colored fruit, a kind we had never seen. He tossed one into the air, then the other. He juggled with them skillfully.

"At least answer me if you girls can speak German?"

"Yes, we can," Galina said and held out her hand for one.

"Are there any Poles hiding there, any Hungarians? I know you girls are not the filthy Germans, I could see that right away. I'll give you each an orange if you tell me where you are from."

"Let's tell them we're Estonians," Galina whispered.

"No, we can't even speak it. He'll know we're not."

"What language is that? Is that Polish? Are there many Poles in the camp?"

"Yes," Galina said. She kept her eyes on the fruit.

"Who else?"

"Russians," Galina said, "lots of them."

"Good. That's exactly what I wanted to know."

He handed an orange to each of us. "You're good girls, I can see that. Life must be hard in that camp, eh?"

We curtsied our thanks. "Let's run," Galina whispered, and we did, as fast as our legs would carry us, leaving even the blanket to be retrieved later. From the safety of the latrine, we watched the soldiers counting barracks, measuring, conferring, smoking.

"You shouldn't have said that." Clutching my orange, I self-righteously reproved her. "They will seize all the Poles." I didn't care at all what happened to the Russians.

"I hope they do," Galina whispered fiercely. "Dirty Poles, dirty Germans, dirty Russians, I wish I had told them to take all you dirty Latvians too."

"Oh, no, Galina, don't say that."

"Oh, yes. I hope they line up all of you and shoot you. I hate everybody."

"Galina, please."

"I'll say anything I want. I hope they strip you naked before they shoot you, you're one of the filthy Latvians, all of you always sticking together. I hate you," Galina shouted at me.

The words were bitter, but the orange, like Mrs. Saulitis's bottle of Coca-Cola, was indescribably delicious. My mother praised me for bringing it back to be shared. She talked about eating oranges, long ago in Riga, the year before she got married. Crusty white bread, aromatic black coffee with thick sweet cream and buttery cheese had accompanied them. She had shared this meal with my father. He had told a funny story that had made her laugh.

Now she cut the skin, peeled it back carefully, divided the orange into sections. The flesh had a slightly reddish tinge, the white seeds were slippery and bitter, the sweet flesh burst against my teeth. I vowed to myself that someday I would have oranges, whole ones, whenever I wanted.

I was glad that my mother, preoccupied as soon as the meal was over, did not question me closely.

"Yes, yes," she nodded absentmindedly when I explained that some soldiers had just pulled up and given oranges to Galina and me.

After that, whenever I heard a truck approaching on the near-deserted road, whenever a new notice was posted, whenever I saw Galina pretending not to see me, I worried that all the Poles would be rounded up, handcuffed and turned over to Russian soldiers. But nothing like that happened.

Gradually the memory of the soldiers' cajoling and Galina's anger faded, but the fragrance and taste of the orange, the way the skin slid off to reveal the fruit, the way it offered itself up in sections and my mother's happy look remained.

My mother was seldom with us, but when she was, she was tired or sad. I would watch her getting ready for the christenings and weddings at which my father officiated. She sighed as she inspected her one good dark blue wool dress, its seat shiny with wear. She held up to the light and studied the folds, thin to transparency, of her two different sets of white collars and cuffs, one of linen, the other of lace, then sighed again as she fastened one on.

Sometimes she briefly included me.

"Here, hold this mirror," she said. I concentrated on keeping steady the three-inch-long shard of what had once been part of a large perfect oval.

She pulled back her hair and twisted it competently but severely at the nape of her neck. Something about that silent gesture always made me feel sad. I wanted to fling myself into her arms and cry and let her comfort me, but I did not. I knew that something had been damaged between us, but nothing about how to heal the wound.

My mother's hair seemed coarser and frizzier, the skin on her hands somehow flatter and less distinct than when she used to tuck me into bed in Latvia.

My mother fastened her amber pendant, her only ornament from Latvia, at her throat and sighed. I would have liked to hear again the story of how my parents found this dark rich translucent jewel in the sand of the Baltic Sea, how my father had it polished and strung on silver for her the year they married, when they were completely happy. But I did not ask.

My mother rubbed the nicks and scratches on its surface. She was probably thinking of the boots of the soldiers scarring the amber rather than the waves of the Baltic Sea gently polishing it for hundreds of years. I wished I could still ask her to smile, but instead I forced my own face into a smile.

"When will you be back?"

When she did not reply, I persisted. "Who else will be at the party?"

"Oh, nobody special."

"Will any of my teachers be there? Will they do anything unusual?" I had been scandalized by hearing that Miss Lazda, the fifth-grade teacher, had been seen smoking a cigarette behind the communal kitchen. I would have liked to tell my mother about it, then perhaps she in turn would tell me another secret about the teachers and we could discuss them.

"I expect it will all be the same as usual," she said dryly. "Go get the matches and light one."

I let the wooden match burn down just far enough, blew on it to cool it and handed it to my mother, who darkened her eyebrows with it.

"Will Captain Vilciņš be there?"

"Yes. He always is. I said it would all be the same."

"Will he sit next to you? Will he kiss your hand?" Mrs. Saulitis, in spite of her love for the sergeant, had speculated about romantic possibilities with Captain Vilciņš. His manly figure and perfect manners would make him a wonderful lover. I longed for my mother to confide that although Captain Vilciņš was honorable and too noble to declare himself, he admired her from afar, that she still had great power over him and other men. I wanted her to have the radiance she had possessed in Latvia as she wheeled her bicycle away from the orchard, brought back wild strawberries, inspired music.

"Captain Vilciņš may sit next to me," my mother said in the same tone she would have used to agree that it might rain tomorrow.

Out of questions, I watched her.

"Have you done your homework?" she finally asked.

"Yes."

"Have you got your poem memorized?"

"I know it, really I do."

"Better look it over one more time. Studying is important. Remember, no one can take away the riches of the heart."

"Yes."

"Well," she sighed, checking her image in the mirror one more time, "education is the only thing to put our trust in." She paused and gestured vaguely around the room and at her own face.

"The rest of it is completely hopeless," she said.

But sometimes my mother became quite animated. She had a new interest that took a lot of her energy: disturbed and suicidal people, or, as everyone called them then, crazy people. She visited them, entered their lives, listened to their stories, which others dismissed or thought inexplicable, justified their views and their behavior, worried about them, looked out for them.

The first of these was Vilma, a slender, pale, clumsy fifteen-year-old, who came to my mother's notice because she neither spoke nor responded to anyone in school. Slowly, patiently my mother got Vilma to talk, then to confide in her. Vilma's mother had said that she wished Vilma had never been born; the mother preferred her younger brother, a lively, blond eight-year-old. But Vilma's mother was dead, buried under the rubble in Dresden. Vilma's grandmother, a stern, willful old woman in charge of the two children, continued the preferential treatment of Vilitis and scolded Vilma. Vilma's father had not been heard from since he was ordered onto a truck to dig trenches for Russian soldiers, but my mother assured Vilma that her father would return. She swore to Vilma that her father loved her with all his heart.

When Vilma started threatening suicide, my mother often spent the night with her to see that she came to no harm. My mother did not share the then-universal opinion that people who openly threatened suicide never killed themselves. Later Vilma started disappearing after leaving notes addressed to my mother. She had gone into the woods to hang herself, to the river to drown herself, to the railroad trestle to fling herself down on the sharp stones below. Wild with anxiety, my mother got the governing board to send out search parties and she accompanied them herself. Later she brought Vilma back to our room, covered her with a shawl, chafed her hands, tried to get her to drink something warm and begged her to promise that she would not try to kill herself again.

When Vilma was finally taken to an asylum in Bremen, and was forgotten by her grandmother, my mother went to considerable trouble to visit her. For the next thirty years, across two continents, she kept up contact with Vilma. She sent her packages for Christmas, Easter and birthdays, and wrote her regular letters. She tried to make sense of the dozens of scrawled, mostly incoherent pages Vilma sent in return. When Vilma became pregnant by a married orderly in the Bremen institution, my mother comforted her when he did not marry her as he had promised he would. She added the baby, a fragile pale little creature, to her list of those to care for, and sincerely mourned with Vilma when the little girl died.

Mr. Banderis was another of my mother's people. Tall, trembling and so thin that everyone laughed that he would be invisible if he only turned sideways, Mr. Banderis often sat with her. He collected wildflowers and pressed and arranged them in a Bible; or he laboriously printed letters to public figures. Mostly he wanted to talk to my mother about whom he should sacrifice himself to. Should he offer to marry Princess Margaret when she got older, even though he personally did not think she was so very beautiful? He would be glad to do it, so that the British nation would not have the disgrace of their princess being an old maid. The British had been very nice to him, so he stood ready for anything required. Should he offer to marry the Duchess of Windsor, so that they could have their old king back? Mr. Banderis would try his best to overlook how skinny the duchess was.

Mr. Banderis's entire family had been deported to Siberia, and he bitterly blamed himself for not having been home so that he would have been taken with them. He worried about them freezing, barefoot in the ice and snow; he knew they were starving.

My mother coaxed him to eat, but he finally quit eating altogether and had to be institutionalized. The last time she heard from him was when he wanted her to translate and mail a letter to President Truman. He thought it a shame that the president had a homely daughter, but there was no reason for her to be a lonely old maid too when Mr. Banderis was standing ready to sacrifice himself. He would marry her, he would work hard to make her happy, he would save America from the disgrace of a president's daughter without a husband.

In addition to Vilma and Mr. Banderis, my mother had another half-dozen people in whom she took an interest. My sister and I did not like most of them, and we were annoyed by their presence and her attentions to them.

"Here comes another one of her admirers," Beate whispered one day when she saw Mr. Banderis leaning into the wind as he made his way across the square surrounded by barracks. She moved closer and took my hand.

"Stupid, stupid, stupid Mr. Banderis," I whispered.

"And stupid, stupid, stupid her," Beate said.

"Shush, don't call her that," I murmured, watching my mother running towards him, taking him by the elbow and solicitously helping him inside. But I wished the wind would flatten them both.

"And he's not crazy, he's just pretending anyway," Beate added.

"Vilma is too, she is just making it up," I asserted.

My sister and I shared the common opinion that disturbed people were shamming and that they should simply pull themselves together and "quit being crazy." After all, what had happened to them was not so bad. Others had had it worse.

Complaining about anything in the camps was unacceptable; self-control and discipline were required. Illness, lack of meaningful work, hopelessness about the future were all to be borne stoically. We should be grateful to be alive, and pride should keep us from showing the conquering Russians that they had defeated our spirit along with taking our country.

After all, thousands of Latvians were deported, tortured or executed during the Year of Terror, that is, the Russian occupation of 1940–41; thousands more arrested during the German occupation, which was followed by the final Russian occupation in 1944. (Russian troops would not leave Latvia until 1994, and large numbers of retired military personnel and other Russians are still living there today.)

Like a bell tolling, news arrived every few months of relatives and friends. Sniegs, that talented but tormented musician, had been deported. Maybe he was digging ditches or sawing wood in some remote frozen hard-labor camp in Siberia rather than composing religious songs filled with erotic longing. Not a vigorous man, he might be dead already; if not, he would certainly be broken by the harsh conditions. Were he to survive, he would not make music again. His hands would be ruined and his spirit crushed, if not by torture, then by hard work.

Elvīra was dead too. She had been caught in the crossfire between Russian and German troops a few kilometers from the Parsonage, before she got my mother's wedding gown. My mother prayed that she was at peace at last, no longer tormented about her beloved brother poisoned by the Nazis.

All the uncles and aunts left in Latvia were gone too. My father was from a large family, one of six. He had lost his brothers and sisters once again, as he had at age seven when they were dispersed by the death of their parents. Oscars had been sentenced to hard labor in a prison camp in Siberia, Anniņa had disappeared without a trace, Lilija was very sick and not expected to live. Letters addressed to Vilis were returned unopened. Milda was no longer allowed to live in Riga but had been ordered to do hard physical work on a collective farm. If she received letters from abroad, she would be arrested or shot.

I told myself not to think about these uncles and aunts whom I had known so briefly but vividly. To cry about them meant I was engaging in self-pity and whining. Aunt Milda with her purple silk dresses and red shoes with very high heels, which I admired, and Uncle Oscars, who was my favorite because he knew how to wiggle his ears—both were gone and should be forgotten. So should cousins and neighbors and friends.

I would lie in bed, listening to my parents whisper about them. I tried to push away recurring images of dark blood drying around bullet holes in Oscars's and Milda's faces and chests. I scolded myself for repeatedly thinking of them. Even though they were alive, my parents were afraid to write to them for fear of further reprisals against them. I would never see them again, I should make myself forget them. I was sure there was something wrong with me because I could not.

Solemn ceremonies were held in the camps every June 14th, the day of mass arrests of Latvians by Russians in 1941. Flags at half-mast, commemorative wreaths, speeches and solemn music marked the day. Everyone vowed to remember the deported, tortured and executed. We vowed never to forget Latvia, a small defenseless beautiful country of white birches and fragrant pines, which had been invaded, brutalized, oppressed, lost.

Compared to others, Vilma and Mr. Banderis had nothing to complain about. Compared to others, I, especially, should be happy and grateful all the time. My family had been lucky, we had had a charmed life, we had made miraculous escapes. But when my father said that he was deeply grateful to God for protecting us and guiding us to safety, I felt mute choking fury.

Even before I was old enough to remember, my parents had been on a list to be deported to Siberia during the Year of Terror. But a woman from my father's congregation who had seen the lists for the next day's arrests walked across the dark fields and waded a creek to warn us. My parents hid with Beate and me in the woods. They returned home a month later when the German army drove the Russians out and occupied Latvia themselves.

But no matter how hard I tried, I failed to control my dreams by willpower. I dreamt of black boots striking cobblestoned streets in the middle of the night, trucks screeching to a halt in front of houses darkened for sleep, cattle trains waiting for mothers and daughters and husbands and wives, all torn away from each other. That was what had happened to others in my family, to Latvians, Jews, Gypsies, socialists, to all enlightened and independent people throughout Europe. I despised myself for not feeling happy all the time, but at least I did not whine and complain like Vilma and the rest of my mother's charges. I could take some small pride in that.

Still, some of my mother's passionate interest grew secretly inside me. I felt that my mother's charges knew something that no one else did—that they were living in a more authentic reality—and that their knowledge was important. They had admitted terrible truths to themselves, which the rest of us worked hard to deny.

My mother herself stayed true to the damaged and suffering. For the next thirty years she regularly stopped to talk to disturbed, drunk and homeless people in libraries and on the streets. Nothing of their distress or behavior surprised her. She conversed intimately with them and occasionally gave them small presents and money, in spite of solemn warnings from others against such generosity. Only years later did it occur to me that her solicitude to Vilma, the daughter who was not loved as much as the son, or to Mr. Banderis, the man who had lost everything and everyone important to him, was a way for my mother to express her own pain. I wished then, too late, that I had been able to give my mother the same kind of attention and love she gave them.

In addition to my mother's charges, there were plenty of other signs that all was not well. Bitter ironic jokes about D.P.'s were common. Many people were silent and lethargic. Drunkenness was rare because of the scarcity of liquor, but there were occasional alcoholic outbursts by men weeping and wishing for death. Once a father viciously beat his eight-year-old son with nettles on his bare legs before women and men came running to pull him away. A mute, shell-shocked young man, deaf to the orders of the British sentries to stop, was shot and killed as he desperately continued running. And for months on end, brutally tortured cats and squirrels appeared hanging on fence posts, too often to be the work of only one person.

A twelve-year-old boy named Kārlis, one of the most beautiful boys I have ever seen, with black wavy hair, gray dreamy eyes, skin like marble and cheeks like roses marred only by a few sprouting coarse hairs, started cornering girls behind the latrines and on the edge of the camp, pulling down their pants, gagging them, choking them, attempting rape. I was able to outrun him, but I knew he was clever. He hid behind corners and crouched at the bottom of the kitchen steps at twilight. It was only a matter of time before he caught me.

Telling my mother was out of the question, so I told my sister. Beate promptly consulted her group of older girls, who usually whispered together, taunted boys and laughingly ran away with long strides. They held a formal meeting at which they sentenced Kārlis to appropriate punishment. They captured him in a meadow across the road from the camp and pinned him down. Beate and her friend Irisa held cow dung over his face until he swore he would never try to catch me again. After this, he left me alone. But the vigorous screening process for emigration did not single him out, and he went to Canada, where he later murdered a ten-year-old girl.

· 12 ·

America for Women

Gradually emigration opportunities opened up. England, Canada and Australia began admitting young single workers, mostly for jobs their own people did not want to do. Families were separated once again. My cousin Astrida, at age eighteen, went to Canada by herself, to work as a maid. She married a young Latvian warehouse worker there a few months later. Except for her Canadian employers, no one else attended her wedding at the registry office, and she went back to washing dishes and making beds the following morning. Another cousin left to work in the coal mines in England.

When the United States opened its doors, it was again only to the most desirable workers, that is, the young and vigorous, those unencumbered by children, illness and old people. Ōmite, who had finally rejoined our family, was not allowed to emigrate with us, since America would admit only one dependent per worker. Once more Ōmite urged everyone to go, saying she had had her life. But we had not abandoned her even when the Russian soldiers were coming, so how could we leave her now?

The future in the camps looked meaningless and bleak, and my parents struggled silently with the guilt of even thinking of leaving Ōmite behind. Finally Uncle Jaša and Aunt Zenta, who had only one daughter, went to the United States, and they immediately began the difficult process of arranging for her to join them. With no guarantee of success, this development was nevertheless hopeful, and it left my parents free to attempt to emigrate themselves.

Actually, no one used the word "emigration". People spoke of "continued exile," which was what going to America meant. Most Latvians longed to return to Latvia, they daydreamed about the time when Latvia would once more be free of Russian occupation, and they mourned leaving Europe for another continent because that made the return to Latvia less likely. To this day "exile" rather than "emigration" is the prevailing word in American Latvian communities.

Before being allowed to go to America, everyone had to have a sponsor who would guarantee that the newcomers would have a job and a place to live so that we would not become public wards. Thorough political screening followed to weed out Nazis and Communists and those belonging to front organizations for either party. Repeated mental and physical examinations were also required.

The tension in the camps became close to unbearable. Having to separate from family and friends yet again was part of the anxiety, and so were the various tests that we were undergoing, most often without being told the results. Reading and math ability, teeth, eyes, ears, skin and bodily cavities were checked and checked again, and again. A dark spot on a lung or partial deafness in one ear meant the person was condemned to the camps forever.

"We treated our horses with more dignity," said Captain Vilciņš.

A cartoon of an astonished camel appeared on the camp bulletin board with the caption, "It is easier for a camel to enter the gates of heaven than for a D.P. to get into the United States of America."

In my family everyone tested positive for TB, which was rampant in the camps and was grounds for exclusion from the United States. We had X-rays next, without being told what they revealed. Then the loudspeaker called only me back for more X-rays, then more. More silence followed. During the day I worried that it would be my fault if my family had to stay in the camps after everyone else had been allowed to leave. At night I dreamt that they had all gone off and abandoned me, as Vilma's grandmother did her.

In groups and individually, we were asked whether we knew that the United States was a democracy and whether we approved of democracy. We were asked whether we were insane, homosexual, alcoholic, criminal or immoral.

"Are any of you prostitutes here?" the sober-faced official at the head of the table asked a room full of people. Andrejs, a boy in Beate's class, gave her and me such a sharp nudge from behind that we exclaimed and jumped up startled, like eager volunteers. The official frowned at us, and my mother told us that we had disgraced ourselves. "You've spilled the chamber pot in public by not controlling yourselves," she said. Nothing about getting to America was a joking matter.

A Lutheran congregation in Indianapolis had agreed to sponsor my family, and we were going through all the examinations in the hope that we would be able to settle there, although that place was only a name to us, when a complication arrived in the form of a letter from Brazil. A Lutheran congregation was willing to offer my father a position as an assistant pastor as soon as he had learned sufficient Portuguese.

Naturally, that was where he wanted to go. America held out no promise to him of being able to practice his profession. Like lawyers and other professionals coming from the camps, he would have to do unskilled manual labor there, which might or might not lead to something better in the future.

My mother had been absent or abstracted for so much of the time that she had not seemed like a real force. But when America began fading as a possibility and Brazil threatened, she suddenly came to life. Open conflict between my parents was very unusual because they always made a point not to argue in front of my sister and me. But the conflict between them quickly intensified.

"It's a great opportunity for me," my father said. "I will be in the pulpit instead of digging ditches or loading trucks."

"You'll have to dig ditches anyway if you don't learn Portuguese."

"I'll learn it, don't worry. I'll start as soon as I can get a dictionary. And some peace," he added with a significant glance.

"I'm not going to Brazil," my mother asserted. "I'm not going, and I'm not letting my daughters go."

"Why not? What do you have against it? They can go to school there, just like anywhere else."

"School? What kind of school are they going to go to in Brazil? Where are we going to get the money to send them to school?"

"I'm sure the church will arrange something, some school for ministers' daughters, even if I can't."

"I don't want my daughters going to any school for ministers' daughters, a charity school, where they will have to clean pews and wash altar cloths and learn to be grateful for being allowed to work the skin off their fingers. I don't want them to be trained to serve and flatter ministers, like in *Jane Eyre*. I will not let them be part of some rector's spiritual harem. My daughters are going to the university."

"The university? What do you think, that we're going to be millionaires? We're in a camp, we don't have a penny, we're not going to turn rich the minute we step on dry land in America."

"They're smart and they study hard."

"Yes, of course, and they're pretty. They'll learn a little Portuguese in Brazil, they'll work in some office for a few years and then they'll marry."

"Pretty? Marry?" My mother laughed bitterly. "They need education. That's the only hope there is. And in America there is education for women. They can get scholarships and go to a university. They can have a better life. They're smart, they're my daughters."

"But I'm telling you, they can do that in Brazil."

"No, in Brazil education is for the rich only. I don't want to live where only the rich have a chance. Besides, women aren't educated in Brazil, they're not even allowed out on the streets alone. The Brazilians probably shave the heads of any women they suspect might be unfaithful. What kind of a life is that for a woman?"

Even a representative of public opinion was brought in to try to sway her. Captain Vilciņš, his leather coat crackling from the cold, kissed her hand, looked meaningfully into her eyes and then talked long and earnestly about the opportunities my father would have in Brazil.

She did not yield. Only in America would my sister and I have a chance for an education.

"See, Captain Vilciņš says too that Brazil is a great opportunity for me," my father said.

"What does he know? He's just another of the whiskered old snake-men who run everything around here. Look what happened to his

Heroes Plaza." She motioned derisively in front of her, though Latrine Walk was in a camp five moves ago for us and for him.

"He's a man of the world, he's lived all over Europe."

"I don't care. We've all seen enough of Europe ourselves, the darker side anyway."

"But you used to listen to him. You used to say he was a sophisticated man. You used to respect his opinion."

Something in me desperately wanted my mother to acquiesce when my father said that. My mother's resistance seemed connected to her marred beauty, the scattered age spots on her hands, her impatience as she inspected her image in the broken mirror. If only she yielded, I could continue to create romantic fantasies about her singing with pianist Sniegs, smiling at Pastor Braun, laughing with soft delight as she and my father found amber in the white sands on the shores of the Baltic Sea. I would not have to mourn her lost sensuality and happiness. Maybe I would not have to struggle with my own conflicts in the future.

"I know what I'm doing," my mother said firmly. "I refuse to go to Brazil, and I am not letting my daughters go. Captain Vilciņš can try to charm me into compliance, others can tie me up and carry me onto the boat, but I will not get off in Brazil."

"But life in America will be harder."

She put her arms around my sister and me in a gesture of solidarity. It was thrilling. I was suddenly elated that she had not given in after all.

"We three are going to America, where women can be educated," she said. "That's the place *we* choose to live."

Single-handed, with her husband and public opinion against her, she won. Without newspapers or recent books, she had a clear-eyed view, from which she refused to deviate, of the class system and machismo of Brazil. She had absolute faith in the educational opportunities for women in America.

The conflict between my parents was the last real barrier to leaving the camps. Shortly thereafter we were found fully acceptable to enter the United States. I was interviewed several more times, selected to be the official one-millionth D.P. allowed to emigrate, to participate in publicity and to recite something from memory in a foreign language to American journalists, as I had to British officials visiting the camps.

I dreaded the task. I got sick, as I so often had at times of unbearable tension, which delayed our departure for a month. I felt guilty, but secretly I was very relieved. I was as terrified of reciting to yet more strangers as I had been of the Russian soldiers. Nor did I dare tell anyone that I did not want to leave the camps. They were familiar, and they offered moments of solidarity with others and the possibility that someone like Mrs. Saulitis might mother me again. But to say that out loud would mean I was ungrateful.

Finally, after I recovered, for the last time wearing tags with our numbers pinned to our clothes, we sailed from Bremerhaven for the United States of America, where my mother believed education and autonomy were possible for women.

I thought the war was over, the camps were behind me and that life in America would be an entirely new beginning. I believed that the past could no longer affect me. The instant I arrived in America, I would forget everything bad that had happened. The gray film over everything would lift. I would be happy, I would be free.

I would remember only happy things from the camps. The flower-bed under Mrs. Saulitis's window, of course, the time everyone in the camps was wearing shiny patent-leather dancing shoes sent from America which looked so comical on the muddy paths, the purple wool jackets. My mother had first choice once in selecting blankets for each of us, and she returned with beautiful rose and purple tightly woven wool. She saved the cigarette rations that she, my father and even my grandmother were issued, and arranged with a German seamstress to make winter jackets for Beate and me. They were lined with white silk from a parachute and fastened with large black frogs. They were new, they had never been worn by anyone before, they were made especially for us. They were glorious jackets.

The adults were wonderful as they roused themselves from lethargy to make so many things possible for us. The plays were the best part, especially a performance of *Twelfth Night* when I was ten. Professional actors, young amateurs and an eminent director collaborated. A simple trellis entwined with flowers on a platform at the end of the dining hall was Illyria. The Clown sang and played the *kokle*, a traditional Latvian stringed instrument similar to a zither; the air was full of music. The words did the rest, as magical in Latvian as in English. I was entranced, and I believed that the events had really happened, even when people told me that only in a make-believe story could Orsino be such a fool as not to know right away that Cesario was really a woman. Even now I can clearly see Viola and Sebastian, identifiably twins by their costumes of dyed cotton, which from the distance looked like dark green velvet. Their gender did not matter to me. I loved the part where Sebastian and Viola are reunited, and I was sorry that brother and sister could not be together forever, just by themselves, rather than marrying other people. The two figures so alike, dark-haired and slender both, dressed in deepest green, were mirror images of each other. I used to imagine a brother like that for myself, someone smiling and loving who would make me laugh. With him I would not feel the inexplicable heavy sadness that oppressed me, that I was ashamed of and which only studying and excelling in school could keep from overwhelming me.

Sebastian and Viola believed they had been separated forever, but they were reunited, after all. They meet in another country, after chaos and darkness and storms. They hold hands, they tell each other their stories, they find happiness again. They were also in my far distant future, although I did not know it yet.

• 13 •

Learning America

Summer 1950. Mrs. Čigāns is an expert on America, she has been here for three months. Pastor McCormick relies on her to meet newly arriving D.P.'s at the train station. She unerringly picks us out of the crowd in the cavernous old building. The platform on which the train arrives from New York is like dozens of other platforms on which we have waited.

"Welcome," Mrs. Čigāns says to us. There are only four of us now: my mother, my father and my sister are here, but Ōmīte has had to stay behind in Germany. I miss her and worry that she is crying because she is lonely and abandoned, even though I know she may join us later.

"Welcome," Mrs. Čigāns repeats. "Welcome to America," she says. She looks a little disappointed when she sees us close up but is too kind to say so.

Her name means Gypsy, but she looks American. She strides ahead boldly, her clothes like nothing we have seen. She is wearing a dress of some strange aqua material, neither cotton nor linen, with a circle-cut full skirt. Her waist is nipped by a wide black belt that seems to be made out of rubber, her black hair is pinned up in hornlike rolls away from her face. Her legs are shapely and strong, and black hairs curl provocatively over the white bobby socks thrust into high-heeled black patent-leather shoes. She stops waving the scarf she has been using to attract our attention and expertly knots it so that two rabbit ears nod above her forehead. She takes out a compact and checks her bright red lipstick.

"Now, girls," she says as soon as we are settled in a taxi, "you will have to watch out, this isn't safe little Germany, oh no." She laughs and inspects her glistening red nails. "Oh no, not at all. See that light? You have to move fast when it's green and never start to cross the street when it's yellow, don't even *think* about it."

A siren sounds in the distance, very faint but growing louder, familiar, ominous.

"Yes," she says. "When you hear that, run as fast as you can and jump on the sidewalk. If you are scared, stay close to the buildings, away from the street until you get used to it. But always hop on the sidewalk as quick as you can, otherwise the police will drive right over you, they'll flatten you like you were made of wet clay, they won't stop to take you to the hospital or cemetery. Things move fast here in America, so you have to hurry up."

The ambulance screeches by the halted taxi. "See what I mean?"

Beate and I put our heads together and whisper.

"And another thing," Mrs. Čigāns says, "don't think you can talk to each other in Latvian, you can't. They don't like it, the Americans. You always have to speak English. You are inside the melting pot," she adds mysteriously.

We are silent. After a pause Mrs. Čigāns smiles at us. "Don't worry, you'll learn. It isn't that difficult. *They* all speak it, don't they?"

In the hotel lobby she continues to teach her own hard-learned lessons. A television set is in the center of comfortable chairs and sofas. It is one of the very first in Indianapolis; even Pastor McCormick does not have one yet. If only it were turned on, we would really see something then, Mrs. Čigāns says.

In the restaurant she points to a stack of small colorful boxes. Cornflakes. Tea in bags. Jell-O with tiny square pieces of fruit in it. Bottles of Coca-Cola. She knows just what deserves comment.

In the middle of the vast room is a table laden with chicken, sliced ham, hard-boiled eggs, white rolls, applesauce, butter, jam.

"You can have anything you want, and go back as often as you like until you can't eat anything more. So just help yourself. See where the plates are in the metal racks?"

In the center of the table is a hollowed melon filled with sliced apples, oranges, strawberries, grapes, more melon. A row of small glass dishes is arranged next to it.

"*Melone*," my mother says.

"Melon," Mrs. Čigāns echoes. "See, you are speaking English already. We'll come back later, after we eat all the other things. There will be enough."

But when we come back, the sliced fruit is gone, the melon boat is empty except for a little liquid in the bottom.

"Take it easy, take it easy," Mrs. Čigāns says. "That's one thing you have to learn to say. Take it easy."

She looks around the room. An elderly couple is silently eating chicken and mashed potatoes at a table by the window. Two full glass dishes of fruit are in front of them, waiting for their attention.

Mrs. Čigāns marches over, picks up the fruit dishes from the startled couple's table, returns and sets them down briskly by her own plate. My mother looks at her disapprovingly.

"Oh, no, I don't think that's . . ."

Mrs. Čigāns reassures her. "In America you can do anything you want. All you have to do is say *excuse me*. Come now, girls, practice it. Say *excuse me*."

We try to do as she says.

Nat King Cole sings "Mona Lisa" on all three Indianapolis radio stations. What kind of a king is he? Perhaps he is English; nobody mentions he is black. Beate spends a lot of her time glued to the tiny radio in one of the bedrooms in Pastor McCormick's house. She memorizes the words and sings along.

Pastor McCormick's congregation has been shrinking recently because the church is located on the near north side of Indianapolis. Middle-class whites are moving further north, blacks are moving in, some poor whites called "hillbillies" are staying. The Pastor says he has worked tirelessly to bring over new white people from the camps in Germany, although he has run into some opposition. Ladies in flower-trimmed hats and immaculate gloves move a little further into the pew when my parents and I come in.

Pastor McCormick's four-bedroom house on a quiet elm-lined street is full of Latvians. We are sleeping in the bedrooms, hallways, basement and attic. We are used to being so crowded—it seems almost natural, though it is disappointing after American movies have promised wealth and space.

This Sunday everyone is worried because the Pastor has just given Mrs. Čigāns a bill for food and lodging. She had foolishly assumed that everything was free until she found a job. The camps had been full of wonderful stories about the reception in America. One family had been taken to their own apartment, the cupboards full of dishes, the refrigerator full of food, the closets full of clothes. A ladies' committee had stood ready to give everyone English lessons. Another family had been told to choose whatever they needed at a supermarket, then driven to a department store for clothes. Take whatever you need, the welcoming committee had said, this is America, the streets are made of gold. No one has yet heard the other stories of middle-aged former professors working in the cotton fields of Mississippi and being threatened with jail and deportation if they tried to leave. Mrs. Eglitis has not yet gone insane after being denied a doctor when the baby could not be born. "Our cows don't have such trouble," the plantation owner said. "She's not such good stock as I thought."

So Mrs. Čigāns's bill for a thousand dollars for a three-month stay is a shock. Middle-class homes in Indianapolis are selling for only twelve times that. Mrs. Čigāns cried, afraid she would never make her way in this country, but the Pastor was kind. He told her that she could take years to pay. She said that she was grateful. We are all grateful, it is the only emotion we allow ourselves. But our anxiety is evident because we whisper even as we speak in Latvian about the frightening future, about how much each day and hour may be costing. Our shame is well hidden, even from ourselves.

Pastor and Mrs. McCormick have retired to their bedroom, which is the only private space they have in the entire house. How hard it must be for Mrs. McCormick to have her house full of strangers, who are used to such crowding while she is not. We stay out of the kitchen in the mornings while she is getting ready to go to work. We look around carefully before going to use the bathrooms. The women polish the furniture, scrub the kitchen and weed the flowerbeds while

Mrs. McCormick is gone. We cook dinner while she plays the piano or reads the newspaper after work. Only part of this is an effort to make up for being in her way. We enjoy these tasks for themselves; it is a pleasure to do real things in a real house.

This afternoon we hear loud voices from the bedroom.

"I want them out," Mrs. McCormick shouts. "I want them gone, now. I can't stand them. Damned foreigners. I hate them." She slams the bedroom door, runs down the path bordered with marigolds that my mother is weeding, gets into her light blue convertible and slams the door. When Pastor McCormick sheepishly follows her out on the porch, she leans out and shouts at him.

"This is *my* house, mine."

She drives away. He gets into his car and follows. An hour later he calls to tell Mrs. Čigāns that he and Mrs. McCormick will be gone for a couple of days. Heaven.

Although it is only afternoon, the women and girls start working in the kitchen. We set bread to rise so that in the morning we will have the heavy sweet-sour Latvian bread instead of Wheaties soggy with milk. We talk about how much money is left in the cookie jar. Even before the new knowledge of the cost of our stay, we have always made sure nothing is wasted.

We are peeling potatoes, forming tiny meatballs, browning chicken, shelling peas. The table in the dining room is extended to its limits. There will be twenty-one people for supper, the meal will take all evening and conclude with the adults telling stories of strange shapes flitting by cemeteries at twilight, clever peasants recognizing the devil by the tail tucked discreetly in the back of the boot and terrified children with their arms stuck forever to floors in castles haunted by ghosts. There will be no stories about war or the camps.

The afternoon passes quickly. It is pleasant in the shady kitchen, women are laughing and humming; it would be nice if we could all still be together like this when school starts in September. I worry about school constantly. The other children will despise me for having long braids and funny clothes, they will torture me for not knowing English.

Verfluchte Ausländer, damned foreigners, the German children shouted on the rare occasions when my sister and I were allowed past the barbed-wire gates of the camps. The boys would throw stones or snowballs with rocks in them. We would stay away from the road leading to the village, we would walk warily in the woods instead, looking for wild mushrooms or anemones. We kept our eyes open for the bands of German boys who could suddenly rise out of the earth with slingshots and sticks.

I wish that I could run back to a kitchen like this from the taunts of American children that I fully expect. Mrs. Čigāns might be able to tell me what to do. I do not look for much help from my mother.

When the potatoes are almost done, Mrs. Čigāns notices we are out of napkins. We are afraid to use the linen napkins in Mrs. McCormick's cupboard, just in case one gets stained beyond the help of scrubbing and bleaching in the sun. Someone says that napkins aren't really necessary, we have eaten without them for years. But Mrs. Čigāns knows better. We had napkins in Latvia, no one ever ate without them, and furthermore paper napkins are American, they are modern and this is a special occasion.

Tālivaldis, Mrs. Čigāns friend/nephew/lover?, offers to go to Hooks Drugstore. It is probably the only place open in the city on a Sunday afternoon. He is a stocky young man in his twenties who doesn't say much, but his smile is nice, and he blushes easily. He is only a few years older than Mrs. Čigāns's daughter Jautrīte. Mrs. Čigāns does not explain her relationship with him, though he shares the space on the screened backporch with both mother and daughter.

Mrs. Čigāns prints "NAPKINS" on a piece of paper, finds two coins in the money jar, wets her handkerchief with saliva and wipes a smudge off his cheek before sending him out.

Mrs. McCormick's table is set. The dishes gleam on the white cloth, the chicken smells glorious. The men make jokes about which lady will be their dinner partner. Mrs. Čigāns tells the children to sit at one end of the table but mercifully does not include me in this category. She points to a woman, then a man, then a woman again.

"We must put one thorn between the roses. Now which man will be the next thorn?"

Everyone laughs.

Tālivaldis returns breathless and hands the paper bag to Professor Briedis. He tears open the blue package and starts handing out the solid thick pads of cotton that look more like bandages than napkins.

Mrs. Čigāns stops him. "Idiot," she says and grabs the box out of his hands. "Dumbbell." She seems to think better of it instantly.

"Forgive me, Professor, but I really must take this now." Professor Briedis holds on, pointing to the word *napkins* clearly visible on the box. Tālivaldis joins him, waving his slip of paper with the same word.

"Dumbbells both," Mrs. Čigāns cries. "Excuse me, Professor, for calling you that, but excuse me." She grabs the box out of his hand, shoves Tālivaldis out of the way and disappears into the kitchen. My mother has collected the rest of the pads and follows her.

There is an embarrassed silence. The women look down, the men are speechless, the children have not understood. Pale, snobbish, sixteen-year old Eģils, whom Beate and I call the Professor's Nursing Infant behind his back, leers at us triumphantly.

The kitchen door swings open and Mrs. Čigāns appears carrying a pitcher of milk in one hand and in the other a pile of the good thick white linen napkins, those everyone has been afraid to use.

When the silence continues, she says, "We'll wash and iron these, we ironed them for her last time anyway. But if there is a little spot we can't get out we'll just have to say excuse me."

She laughs. She ruffles Tālivaldis's hair. "Come sit by me, my little thorn." She turns to Beate and me. We are looking down embarrassed because we know our mother is.

"Come now, girls," laughs Mrs. Čigāns. "Practice it. Excuse me. Say it again, excuse me."

Everyone laughs. I would give anything if Mrs. Čigāns were my mother.

Mrs. Čigāns takes me to the Indianapolis Public Library, an imposing gray building that spans an entire block. Our steps echo over the marble floors, through the cavernous rooms and long galleries.

She conducts the negotiations with the elderly blue-haired librarian who looks at me suspiciously. Finally the librarian sighs elaborately and starts typing. She pecks out a few letters, sighs again, types some more and hands me a yellow card.

"Thank you," I imagine saying to her. These are the first two words of English I learned in the camps from Mrs. Saulītis. Mrs. Čigāns has listened to me on the bus and told me they are the right words. The *th* is hard to pronounce, there is no such sound in Latvian, but Mrs.

Čigāns assures me that I am pronouncing it almost right. Nevertheless I cannot bring myself to say anything now.

"With this you can take home any three books you want, any time you want. You just have to bring them back in two weeks, and then you can take three others. Don't let *her* tell you any differently," Mrs. Čigāns whispers.

Alcoves, balconies, dim rooms, all full of books. One ceiling-high bookcase after another, rows and rows of them. I have never seen so many books in one place; I have held very few books that are not flimsily bound, printed on cheap yellow paper that crumbles easily. I will read these one by one, I will try to read them all, I will learn everything I need to know. If I read three every week, how long will it take to get through them all? I cannot wait to begin. But first I have to learn English. Is that possible?

Mrs. Čigāns confers with the librarian once again. "Whoosh, whoosh," she says and waves her arms. The librarian stares at her. Mrs. Čigāns cups her hands around her mouth and blows.

"Oh," says the librarian and clicks away over the white marble floor. She returns with several books. *Gone With the Wind* is on top of the pile.

Mrs. Čigāns translates. I feel a smile of pure joy breaking out on my face, so that the librarian remembers why she became a librarian in the first place and smiles too. She stamps the books and hands them directly to me. My mouth is dry and my hands tremble, I can't wait to get home.

Gone With the Wind has been translated into Latvian and published in the camps in four separate small paperback volumes. My mother owns only the first volume, which I have read three times already. Will Scarlett O'Hara get Ashley Wilkes to fall in love with her and marry her? Will she fall in love with Rhett Butler instead? Will she have to leave Tara? What will happen to her during the war? Will she survive? Will she ever be able to return to her home? I burn to know.

As soon as I get back to the Pastor's house I find the English/Latvian dictionary that my parents, nonsmokers both, have gotten by saving and trading their cigarette allocations. At the head of the stairs going up to the attic is a door that opens onto a tiny balcony that no one ever uses. The railing is wobbly, the space is so small that it is suit-

A WOMAN IN AMBER

able only for one person. It is a perfect place—light, silent and shady most of the day. Nobody ever sits there.

I have had a few English lessons in the camps. "This is a pen, this is a pencil," the children would recite from memory. One summer we were sent for a week to a derelict house by a canal, an attempt by the camp administrators to recreate the summer country holidays they remembered. We learned to sing "My Bonnie Lies Over the Ocean" and "Oh, My Darling Clementine," the girl who had to wear herring boxes for sandals. Once we sang "*Man cepurei trīs stūri*," and the British woman officer laughed and joined in: "My hat it has three corners, Three corners has my hat." But I know there is a lot more to learn.

I begin by comparing words in the Latvian translation with words on the first page of English. I search the dictionary for those I do not know. Some of them appear with puzzling variations and approximations, others are not listed at all. But most are. Line by line, painstakingly, I work through sentences, then paragraphs of the material already so familiar in Latvian. I am interested in Scarlett losing her temper so I find that passage. When a word or sentence refuses to yield, I go to another, worried that I will always understand just parts. But I continue.

Hours later the book falls open in the middle. "I'm never going to be hungry again," Scarlett promises herself. This is not a part I have read before in Latvian. I look up each word, and then, keeping my fingers in different parts of the dictionary, I stare at the whole sentence. A miraculous intense knowledge, like light, fills me. I understand this, I understand it. "I'm never going to be hungry again." I realize I will be able to figure out the unknown parts of the book, I will teach myself English. I am elated. The sun setting over the maple tree in the backyard seems to confirm it.

I spend every hour I can on the balcony. I worry about the other two books that the librarian has given me, studies of air currents and weather patterns, but Mrs. Čigāns assures me that the librarian will not care whether I have read them or not. I experience absolute despair but also great elation in my solitude. Only Mrs. Čigāns asks me occasionally how I am doing.

"See," she says, "you'll speak English by the time school comes. You're smart like me. I learned in less than a year, but of course I could

149

practice it every day, there were so many young American men in and out of the camp office every day." This prospect terrifies me, since school is only a few weeks away.

But Mrs. Čigāns is quick to reassure me. "You've already learned how to look up the words you don't know and figure out how they fit. That's the hardest part. You've stepped over the dog, now all you have to do is step over the tail."

• 14 •

Real Life and Movies

The summer is over. Miracle of miracles, I can read English. Though I still have to look up many words, the sentences almost always yield their meaning when I do. I am pleased when one of the adults asks me to translate something on a job application, a box of cereal, a newspaper.

My family has moved from Pastor McCormick's house. On 24th and Park Avenue, on the near north side of the city, three four-unit apartment houses built in the 1920s are now filled with Latvians. Several families share each apartment. My family lives in the front part of a once-gracious but now rundown unit. We occupy the sun porch, a windowless living room with a fake marble fireplace and a dining room behind glass doors. Beds, boxes, a table holding a hot plate and a refrigerator take up most of the space. A family with three small children from the Kentucky hills lives in the other half, the two bedrooms and kitchen. The bathroom is either occupied or filthy. The other family does not clean, but waits instead until Beate or I do and then moves in for endless baths, leaving behind scum, pubic hair, dirty diapers. My mother says my father should speak to them, but he does not.

Other families share with other Latvians. The rooms are small for so many people; sound carries easily down the front stairwells and inner hallways. We are all used to the lack of privacy, but no one really wants to be so very quiet anymore. Isn't this America? Alcohol, almost impossible to obtain in the camps, now makes its appearance. Young men, who haven't had anything to drink since the war, stay up late arguing about politics and singing war songs. No one yet has a car. In a year or so three of these young men will be killed in collisions. Later this will seem an innocent and safe time.

Some of the older men rediscover alcohol as well. Mr. and Mrs. Melderis live in the apartment below us. They are a tiny, perfectly formed, perfectly matched couple, like miniatures, not quite midgets. Beate and I are fascinated by them. How did they meet and marry? How did he, so small himself, find an even smaller wife?

My mother reminds us that it is impolite to talk about people's physical characteristics. Size does not matter, she says. She points to tall, blond, beautiful Mrs. Liepa, who towers over her short husband. She is the great beauty who married the son of a millionaire for his money in Latvia. Now they are stuck together, poor like everyone else.

Each Friday night, after work at the Vonnegut Metal Works, owned by the family of a young man who will soon write about the war in Germany and the bombing of Dresden, Mr. Melderis and Mr. Liepa meet on the front steps. They are dressed in dark suits and ties, their shoes are shined, their hair slicked down. They saunter away, in the direction of Central Avenue. They usually return well past midnight, a little disheveled, singing or talking loudly. They flatter each other: "Good night, Inspector Melderis," and "Good night, Industrialist Liepa," they say at parting.

While they are gone, Mrs. Melderis stays in her rooms, cooking and cleaning. If she comes to sit on the front steps, she carries her knitting or mending. She cries a little when one of the other women stops to talk.

Mrs. Liepa, on the other hand, leaves Park Avenue an hour or so after her husband is gone. She wears a lot of makeup and even a false beauty spot on her cheek. Her hair is tightly curled, clouds of "Evening in Paris" perfume waft around her. She tells anyone who will listen that she thinks she will walk over to Central Avenue and take a bus to a movie. She saunters off. On the next corner she gets into Mr. Krūmiņš's car. Mr. Krūmiņš, whose father came to America in 1905, has a house and a car. He is as close to an American millionaire as anyone has seen.

At midnight, Mr. Melderis bids a fond goodbye to his companion and enters his own place. He shouts at Mrs. Melderis that his dinner is cold, that he is tired of looking at her long face after a pleasant evening, that she trapped him into marrying her, that she is from the wrong side of the tracks. He tells her he would never have married her if he had known that they would end up here. There is only silence from the Liepas' rooms. Mrs. Liepa has returned a little earlier and is running water for her leisurely nightly bath. She will lie in the soapsuds, humming to herself, till two in the morning.

One night Mr. Melderis goes further. The sounds of thuds, screams and slaps come from below. Mrs. Melderis is silent at first, but then begs for mercy.

"You must go down there," says my mother.

"No," my father replies, "it's between them, it's between a husband and his wife. They finally have their own room, let them do what they want."

"He's doing what *he* wants, not what *they* want. She doesn't want him to beat her. Go down before he kills her."

"No, we can't interfere."

"Well, then go to Professor Briedis's and use their telephone. Call the police."

"Are you dreaming? We can't get involved with the police. They will find out how many of us are in each apartment and arrest everybody. We'll all end up in prison."

Mrs. Cohen, the owner of the buildings, has cautioned us about revealing the crowding to anyone. She is doing us a favor by allowing us to double and triple up like this. Otherwise we would all still be living in Pastor McCormick's house and paying him back for the rest of our lives instead of the ten years it will probably take.

"You're the minister, you should go down there," my mother says. She gets up and starts putting on her shoes.

"What a life," she continues. "The house is full of men; I would think a man would go help her." As she starts down the stairs, the door across the hallway opens and Professor Briedis brushes past her.

"You must stop that," he commands, "stop that right now."

My mother and Professor Briedis escort Mrs. Melderis up the stairs.

She stumbles into our room, crying. Her nose is bleeding, there is a large red mark on one side of her face where her husband has punched her. She has a deep cut in the palm of her right hand. My mother calms her down and starts bandaging.

"Animal," she murmurs, "soldier, savage, barbarian." She does not include "Russian" or "godless Communist" in this litany, as many other Latvians do. All the words are of equal weight.

"You would think that after everything we've lived through during the war, we would have peace. I've never seen a *Latvian* man do this, not even when we had so much to put up with in the camps. I never thought I would."

She examines Mrs. Melderis's hand and sighs. Her hand is badly cut where she tried to take the knife away from her husband. "You'll need stitches. We'll have to go to a doctor tomorrow. We'll get a certificate from him about what that man has done to you. Agate, get the dictionary and look up the following words and copy them down on a piece of paper: brutal, husband, drunk, beaten, knife, affidavit, divorce."

I do as I am told, worrying all the while about my mother going to the doctor and maybe the police, but she seems quite sure of what to do.

But Mrs. Melderis does not get a divorce, no one ever does. Mr. Melderis appears with a dozen red roses the following day. On Friday he does not accompany Mr. Liepa on his outing. He and Mrs. Melderis, wearing a new dress and a sling around her neck for her injured hand, leave for the movies instead. Mrs. Melderis tells my mother the next day that the beating had nothing to do with her husband. Being crowded in with so many Latvians who watch and remark on every move is the real trouble. Shortly thereafter they leave for Cleveland, where Mr. Melderis has heard of a job in a factory that pays more. They will not make the mistake of living so close to Latvians again.

By now I can translate just about anything with the help of the dictionary, but understanding when others speak is more difficult. I can catch a few words or an occasional sentence on the radio. I then have to translate the words one by one into Latvian since I cannot yet understand them directly. Speaking English is even further away. I am afraid of making mistakes at school and of being punished for being stupid. The other children will certainly beat me on the way home.

School starts on a sunny September morning. My mother works in the kitchen of LaRue's Supper Club in the morning, and she also works there most nights.

"You're old enough to go alone," she says.

Since Beate is going to Shortridge High School, we will be separated. Beate will have to go on the bus; she will have to have eleven cents or a token for each ride. She is worried that she may miss her stop and never find her way back home. I will have to walk the two-block gauntlet to Public School 45.

Mrs. Čigāns cannot accompany me either. She has a job frying hamburgers at Hooks Drugstore, where she is also learning to make sodas and sundaes. The manager has told her she is too old for this job, but since she catches on fast, he has promised her that he will eventually teach her how to be a cashier. Then she can wear a nice dress, stand behind a counter and take in money.

I am scared but relieved my mother cannot come along to school. She is also learning English from books and newspapers, but is no closer than I am to speaking it. I blush when I imagine my mother trying to make herself understood. Besides, what would my mother wear? Her one good Sunday dress of dark blue wool with the white lace collar, rows of tiny buttons and long sleeves is shiny and stretched out in the back. She wears black shoes that lace up. No one has clothes like that. I am ashamed of my mother, and even more ashamed of myself for my disloyalty.

Mrs. Cohen, the landlady, has offered to take me. I am waiting on the steps when she arrives later than she has promised. Mrs. Cohen is dressed the same as when she shows apartments to new Latvian families. The hem of her dress is ripped, several threads dangle over her sturdy bare legs, food stains spread over her copious bosom. The dress is cut differently from my mother's, but it too is dark blue and has tiny buttons. Mrs. Cohen's stringy hair is greasy and uncombed, her face is flushed. She is wearing a man's scuffed bedroom slippers with no backs, which flap as she walks. Her purse is bulging with keys, cigarettes, envelopes of rent receipts. One of its straps is broken and pinned with two safety pins. She is eating a donut, and the powdered sugar makes more spots on her dress.

She takes out another donut, breaks it in half and offers it to me.

When I decline, Mrs. Cohen shakes her head sadly. She has done her best.

Groups and pairs of children are walking to school. They greet each other, hold hands, laugh with pleasure. There does not seem to be anyone walking alone. I hope they are not noticing me with Mrs. Cohen, but it is impossible that they would not. I believe I hear them laugh and whisper. They are probably making plans to ambush me later. When they do, I must not, *must not* cry or it will be worse.

Mrs. Cohen takes me to the principal's office. Miss Abbot, a tall elegant gray-haired lady, looks me over, points to Mrs. Cohen and asks, "Is this your mother?" She repeats the question slowly. Mrs. Cohen shakes her head and then launches into a long explanation that I cannot understand.

I shake my head vigorously too. Miss Abbot nods her approval. She points to a piece of paper and asks me to fill in my name and address. Mrs. Cohen translates the questions into Yiddish for me. There are many spaces on the form, but Miss Abbot dismisses most with a regal wave of her hand. She takes me by the elbow and firmly guides me towards the stairs. Mrs. Cohen shuffles away, then turns and waves at me encouragingly.

The corridors are as wide as rooms; sunlight pours through the immense high windows in the stairwells at both ends of the building. The wood floors are polished, and there are dozens of gilt-framed pictures of men in old-fashioned frock coats and uniforms of wars gone by. Glass cases lining one side of the corridor are full of books, stuffed birds, globes and charts. It is a beautiful school. I would like to be alone here, it should be easier to learn here than in the bare rooms in the camps. Maybe if I get all fives, I can help some of the other children and a few will accept me.

I glance at my freshly pressed gray wool skirt and gray wool blouse, which already feel too hot. On each pocket of the blouse are red strawberries embroidered by Ōmīte in the camp. My braids are tied with small red ribbons, my black laced shoes are polished. The other girls are carrying purses and wearing seersucker and madras cotton blouses or printed cotton dresses and penny loafers. I am not hopeful about my future. I *must not, must not* cry.

Miss Abbot guides me into a room where other children are already in their seats and points to an empty desk in the front. She confers briefly with Miss Buechler, the seventh-grade homeroom teacher, then addresses the other children. War, camps, Latvia, Russia, Germany, America—I catch a few words. The eyes of the other children bore through me; I feel like a freak. I wish that Miss Abbot would stop. Presently she does. She gently pushes me down into the seat and walks out.

Miss Buechler leans over me and asks a question, which I do not understand. She repeats. "Yes or no?" she offers. I drop my eyes in confusion. I do not know what will happen if I give the wrong answer or no answer at all. "Yes or no?" Miss Buechler waits.

When I do not answer, Miss Buechler reaches over and reassuringly pats my shoulder. This unexpected kindness brings tears to my eyes. I will them to disappear, but they do not. "There, there," she soothes. My tears spill out, I am powerless to stop them. Will Miss Buechler now make me stand in the corner for crying, send me out of the room until I have gained control of myself, tell me my mother must come to discuss my behavior?

"Oh, you poor thing," Miss Buechler says. She offers me a box of Kleenex, and when she sees me hesitate, she demonstrates by pulling out a few tissues and pressing them into my hand. She walks back to her desk, takes out a large yellow box of chocolates and passes them around the room. Everyone takes one, so do I. Miss Buechler sets an extra piece in front of me. If only Miss Buechler had not done that— I am too different already. Oh, if only I could go back to the moment before I cried. The eyes of the other children rake my back.

Miss Buechler gives directions, everyone takes out books. They turn quickly to the page she wants. She opens a book, hands it to me, points to a passage. I wish I had my dictionary, but I would not dream of bringing it or of asking if I may. I believe anything like that would be considered cheating and strictly punished.

In a few minutes the children open their desks. They all have brought pens, paper, pencils, notebooks, crayons and other supplies. Miss Buechler looks at me and sighs.

There is so much to learn that it seems hopeless. When must I stand and sit? Where is the bathroom and when may I use it? What time can I go home for lunch and what time must I be back? What are all the supplies that I need, where am I to get them, how am I to pay for them? What will happen if I return without the things on the list that Miss Buechler gives me? What if someone expects me to speak again? What if I cry?

The morning passes slowly. The teachers smile at me, the other children ignore me. When the bell finally rings and I understand that we can all go home for lunch, I get up quickly. I walk out of the building tensing myself for the ambush. I must try to protect my eyes and my face when the children start to push, hit and kick me as soon as we are out of sight of the teachers.

I walk the two blocks ready for blows, but nothing happens. The other children are behind me, whispering and laughing together, but they do not jump me. They watch as I go into the dilapidated building, relieved to shut the door behind me.

I hope they do not think that I will live here forever, I hope even more that they do not assume Mrs. Cohen is my mother. Most of all I hope that I can learn to speak English. Maybe that will make some difference, maybe I will be able to make a friend. It seems unlikely, but that is all there is to hope for.

And I do learn English in the months that follow. Math is the most useful for understanding what is being said. Miss Pinkerton, the math teacher, writes problems and equations on the board, and I listen intently to her explanations. The problems are easy, they are like those I had to solve two years ago in the camps, so I can concentrate fully on the words.

The air-raid drills for nuclear war are also familiar. Every week we practice leaving our desks quickly, crossing our arms over our heads, lying still on the classroom floor. The shades are drawn over the vast windows. In a few minutes, Miss Buechler rings a hand bell. "All clear," she says.

At other times, we are told to lie face down in the hallways, and the doors to the classrooms are shut. We have to lie still for five minutes, while the teachers whisper to each other as they mark time. The girls wrinkle their noses at having to get down on the floor. Later yet we are herded down to the basement, told to crouch and to cover our heads with our arms. Many wiggle and complain under their breaths that this is uncomfortable and boring.

At times like this I feel vastly superior to the American children. They seem to have no idea that they could be bombed any time. How grateful they would be then for a safe place to hide. I want to tell the teachers that the basement is really the best spot but that no one could ever crouch like that through a whole air raid. It would be so much better to have cots down there, so that we could lie quietly while the planes passed. The others seem childish for complaining and wiggling. In my imagination I repeatedly furnish the basement with comfortable chairs, warm blankets, working radios and batteries, vast stores of food. This is my favorite fantasy during recess while I stand alone, feeling exposed and awkward, and watch others play.

Thanksgiving is approaching, another unfamiliar holiday. Like Halloween, this holiday seems to be celebrated a lot at school. Cardboard pilgrims, turkeys and pumpkins decorate the walls. The skies are overcast, it is chilly and damp, the two-block walk to school is faster. I still walk by myself. A few times—I can count them on my fingers—the boys on the Safety Patrol have said "Hi" to me, but mostly no one speaks to me. I hurry home, do my homework, listen to the radio and read. Two nights a week I wash dishes at LaRue's Supper Club.

I am watching the clock, counting the minutes till the last period of the morning is over. At home I have *Little Women* waiting for me. I love the sisters confiding in their mother, getting to know Laurie, putting on plays, sitting in their cozy parlor. I can't wait to get home to read while I eat lunch, with the book propped up behind my soup bowl. Miss Buechler is talking about the pilgrims coming to a rocky shore to spend a winter of hardship in the new land.

And then it happens.

I suddenly understand everything Miss Buechler is saying— everything! I am not understanding just separate words, I do not have to translate sentences back into Latvian. I understand exactly what Miss Buechler is saying at the very moment she says it.

It's miraculous! My heart races with excitement, pure joy washes over me. I want to tell someone, everyone, what has happened. I understand English!

I look around the room. I cannot believe that others are not aware of the miracle, but they seem not to be. I wish I could tell them so they could be happy with me. But the gloomy skies seem brighter. Thanksgiving doesn't seem to be such an odd holiday.

I run home, skipping and humming to myself. I hope that someone will be around on Park Avenue I can tell, but there isn't. Everyone is at work. I get my book, prop it up and start heating the soup.

"I can understand English, I can understand English," I chant.

As if to celebrate my accomplishment, a letter from Ōmīte arrives that afternoon. She has passed all the tests and examinations and has been cleared to come to the United States to join my Uncle Jaša's family. She will come to Indianapolis later, as soon as there is money enough to pay for bus fare.

That day is by no means the end of learning English, but it encourages me to continue. It is well after New Year's when I finally have the courage to actually try to speak it.

Miss Buechler is in front of the room, asking questions about a story we have just read. I cautiously raise my hand. At first she looks past me, then she notices me and beams.

"He rode to warn them the British were coming," I say. My voice trembles. I can feel myself blushing and red blotches appearing on my neck, but there, I have said it.

"Why yes, that's right, that's very good," Miss Buechler smiles. "You said it," she adds. The other children behind me burst into applause.

"She talked," someone says, "she said something."

"Good for you," says John Stafne, the boy sitting next to me. I am embarrassed and totally gratified. I have learned English, I have done it. And I have done it by myself.

This event does not magically change my life in school, but slowly the children start speaking to me. A few of the girls walk home with me occasionally, most of the others say "Hi." I am still not invited to play after school or to go to any of the birthday parties that are passionately discussed during recess, but I do not always walk the long blocks home alone. During the next gym class I am not the very last one chosen for the volleyball team.

"You are making friends," Mrs. Čigāns says. "I saw you walking with two young American ladies."

"I guess so," I say, but I know no one is my friend. Friends meet each other's mothers, visit each other's houses, talk on the phone. My family does not have a telephone, and I do not want anyone to enter our rooms on Park Avenue. I could not bear someone seeing the crowded rooms or asking to look in our closet to try on my clothes. I have neither a dresser nor a makeup kit, items I believe to be essential, to practice painting eyebrows and cheeks. That is what other girls do after school.

Book reports are another way to learn. Some of the books, like

Little Women, are suggested by the teachers, but most Beate and I find in the library ourselves. Beate cleans houses most nights after school, and some nights I wash dishes at LaRue's, but on Friday evenings we are both free. If we have enough money we go to the main library downtown. Sometimes we go to a movie, though usually the only theater we can afford is on Ohio Street, and costs a quarter. The theater is next to burlesque houses and bars, so we have to be careful. It is filled with boys in army uniforms from Fort Benjamin Harrison and with seedy old men who touch our backs and legs. We have to move innumerable times to find a place where we can watch in peace. Usually we walk the twelve blocks to the branch library on 30th and Meridian. We spend the entire evening there, choosing books and reading in the comfortable leather chairs in front of the fireplace until an adult comes in and we give up our seats.

We read everything teachers have told us is important. Miss Buechler tells me to read *I Remember Mama*, which makes me gloomy instead of pleasing me as she has obviously intended. The story of another girl isolated at school because she is from a foreign country is at first comforting, then unbelievable. I cannot imagine my mother winning over the other children by inviting them in to a lovely sparkling kitchen, laughing, cooking them a meal, getting them to value her. To Miss Buechler's astonishment, I announce I have read *Anna Karenina* for one of my book reports.

"Did you understand it?" she asks.

"Yes, of course. I loved it." My mother read it too when she was twelve. I announce that I am going to read *War and Peace* for the next book report, but at this Miss Buechler draws the line.

"That's too old for you. Besides, you should not keep thinking about war. You should develop some normal interests."

I do not tell her that I have also read, with only partial understanding but passionate interest, *Farewell to Arms* and *For Whom the Bell Tolls*; that would make me even less normal. By accident I find a book that seems written for me, *A Tree Grows in Brooklyn*. It is about a girl living in poverty, who also has to walk alone on deserted dangerous streets, whose parents are seldom around. I have never read a story about someone in a situation that seems so real, someone like myself, in a city in America, rather than centuries ago or continents away. I tell Miss Buechler that it is the very best book I have ever read.

"*A Tree Grows in Brooklyn*? Really? That's a little too daring, isn't it? Did you understand it?" asks Miss Buechler, just as I have expected.

"Yes, yes, I understood it," I say. There are a few parts that I would like to ask Miss Buechler about, but that would only prove the book unsuitable for a book report. I wonder about one part especially. Francie and her brother look in a box that their sexy aunt has given them to play with but forbidden them to open, find something that looks like flesh-colored balloons, blow them up and hang them out the window. Why is everyone so very angry and embarrassed, I wonder. It will be years before I will understand the significance of these little balloons.

Movies are the best source of information about America. For several months I have the most perfect job of my life. Mr. and Mrs. Kalniņš are newlyweds who have moved into the front part of the apartment once occupied by Mr. and Mrs. Melderis. Mrs. Kalniņš's mother lives with the young couple, sharing the living room and sun porch with them. Mrs. Tumsītis is a sensitive old woman who speaks fondly of her daughter and her new son-in-law. She regrets she is so much in the way of the young people, who really should have some time to themselves. She takes a slow walk around the block each evening or lingers in the hallway.

One evening Mr. Klalniņš comes to talk to my father. If I will take Mrs. Tumsītis to the movies each Sunday afternoon, he will be glad to pay for my bus fare and ticket. He looks a little embarrassed talking to the minister, man to man, rather than negotiating with my mother or with me.

So every Sunday Mrs. Tumsītis and I set off to the movies. I get to choose which movie to see. I pore over the Sunday newspaper, looking at the movie advertisements and the eight tiny photos of movie stars that are printed each week. When everyone on Park Street is finished with the paper, I cut these out, save them, discuss them with Mrs. Tumsītis on the bus. Debbie Reynolds, Jane Powell, Mitzi Gaynor are Mrs. Tumsītis's favorites, she likes musicals "with nice girls in them." I adore Stewart Granger, James Mason, Robert Taylor, Montgomery Clift, Cary Grant. Only later, when Jimmy Dean appears on the screen, do I fall in love with someone close to my own age.

We enjoy ourselves hugely. On the bus we review the movie we saw the previous week and speculate whether the one we are going to see will be better. If I have read anything about the movie star, I report that. On the way home, I translate conversations and explain parts that Mrs. Tumsītis has missed. We speculate as to what will happen to the characters in later years. We laugh about the funny parts again.

When we get back to Park Avenue, Mrs. Kalniņš, freshly washed and dressed, opens the door right away and invites me in for a cup of tea or a slice of cake. Other times she takes a long time in coming to the door, and when she does, she is wearing a bathrobe and her face is flushed. Mr. Kalniņš is lying in bed, entangled in the covers.

But one evening Mrs. Tumsītis and I have an unpleasant encounter on the bus. Two American women wearing hats and white gloves, carrying plastic purses, sit down in front of us. They glance over their shoulders a few times and move closer to each other. When Mrs. Tumsītis and I continue talking, one of the women turns around and says angrily, "You have to speak English, this is America. For your information, we speak English here."

I start to apologize that Mrs. Tumsītis does not speak any English, but the woman interrupts me. "That's no excuse. She should learn. She should be grateful that she is in America. If she can't speak English, she shouldn't speak at all. She should go right back where she came from."

"We have enough foreigners in this country already, we don't need any more," agrees her friend.

"You people who don't speak English, most of you are Communists or you'd learn. Thank God for Senator McCarthy, he'll flush you out. He'll put you on his list."

"You should be ashamed of yourself," they mouth slowly to Mrs. Tumsītis, who sits dignified and silent on the edge of her seat. She may not understand the words, but the feelings are unmistakable. Mrs. Tumsītis and I ride the rest of the way in silence.

"Good riddance," "overrun by foreigners," "Communists," "leeches sucking us dry" echo behind us as we get off the bus.

Mr. Bumbieris, a former cellist in the Latvian Symphony, is also a movie fan. He goes whenever he has a chance after his job at Vonnegut Metal Works. Mr. Bumbieris has fallen in love with Marilyn Monroe. He talks about her constantly, praising her hair, her legs, but mostly her breasts. He smiles slyly and moistens his lips, cups his hands under his own breasts, shivers.

"Isn't she something? *Zaftig*, I say. And what about those breasts?"

When *Niagara* is released, Mr. Bumbieris is entranced by Marilyn Monroe nude under a sheet, with nothing between her and exposure but a bit of cotton material, so he goes to see the movie seven times. He talks of nothing but waterfalls, unfaithful wives, cotton sheets, her co-star Joseph Cotten, and of course, her breasts. When Professor Briedis, irritated by this obsession, asks him why he wastes so much time and money in going to see the same movie, Mr. Bumbieris replies, "I was waiting for the sheet to slip." He is only joking, but this story makes the rounds of Park Avenue, and an innocence is ascribed to him that he does not possess.

Mr. Bumbieris is learning English too. During the common meals and parties that take place in the crowded rooms, he motions to Beate or me.

"Come here, girls," he says, looking around carefully for Mrs. Čigāns, who pokes him in the ribs and tells him to behave himself whenever he gets too far out of line. He pulls out a small paperback, dog-eared from frequent reading. On the cover a woman with an off-the-shoulder blouse, legs spread apart, beckons invitingly. He has several other books, all showing women with big breasts that make him shiver and perspire and mop his brow.

The book falls open in a favorite place.

"Now," Mr. Bumbieris says, "Agate, teach me English. I want to hear you say it. Say it out loud. What does it mean, I wonder? It says here *coont* and *foock*." He exaggerates the vowels, half whistling as he pants.

"Come now, Beate, you're the one who's such a great actress in the plays at the Latvian Center. Reading aloud will be good for sharpening your dramatic skills. Enunciate clearly now. Read the part where it says *coont* and *foock*." We try to get away from him by going to sit next to someone more respectable.

"Stay away from him," Beate advises. "He's terrible."

"Say them together. Say, I want to *foock your coont*." He has me wedged in a corner of the sofa. "Say it, I want to hear how you pronounce it."

Mrs. Čigāns, dishcloth in hand, advances towards him.

"You're a dirty old man," she says. "Leave that girl alone. I know all about you."

"I wasn't doing anything. What was I doing? She is going to school, she has many educational advantages that the government has seen fit to deny me, she is getting a free education, they are teaching her English. All I want is for her to help me learn English too."

"Don't talk back to me." Mrs. Čigāns waves her dishrag. "Get away from that girl. Get!" When Mr. Bumbieris does not move, she throws the dishrag at him, hitting him smartly on his bald head.

"Mrs. Čigāns should learn more self-control. I thought she was from a better family," my mother says reprovingly later.

But this highly irregular action only silences Mr. Bumbieris until the next time. "What is this? What does this word *prick* mean?" Mr. Bumbieris whispers. "They're not defining it correctly in the dictionary. Come, girls, let me hear you say it."

All the Latvian families have signed a pledge that they will contribute a sum to the Latvian Society for the next twenty years, and they have bought a house on 25th Street and Central Avenue. It is a dilapidated three-bedroom bungalow, which is gradually being painted and repaired. Poetry readings, plays, lectures, discussions, even concerts and folk-dancing practice take place in this small space in the evenings and on weekends. Beate, who loves social occasions and teases me about my solitary ways and constant reading, goes to the center every chance she gets after school and work. She does her homework late at night, sitting on the floor in the hallway so that her light will not disturb anyone else's sleep.

I am not supposed to go to the movies alone, but they are my passion. Mrs. Tumsītis no longer wants to go with me after the encounter with the two women on the bus, and Beate, when she is not working, is more interested in rehearsing plays at the center and shrugging off the compliments of the half-dozen young Latvian men who try to get her exclusive attention during breaks.

I go to the movies by myself one autumn evening. I know I have to be very careful. Ohio Street with its burlesque houses is out of the question. The cinema on 16th Street shows black-and-white films about crime and punishment, like *Unchained* and *I Am a Fugitive From a Chain-gang*. At the Esquire Theater more disturbing things happen. Montgomery Clift knocks on Olivia De Havilland's door and is not admitted at the end of *The Heiress*, Farley Granger plans his wife's murder in *Strangers on a Train*, and Montgomery Clift watches Shelley Winters drown in *A Place in the Sun*. But the movies downtown are in Technicolor, they show women wearing beautiful dresses and falling in love, and they always have happy endings. So I go to Loew's Theater on Pennsylvania Avenue. Getting home from there will be safe since the bus stops a block away, on a well-lit corner. Then I only have to stay aware of who is sitting behind me on the bus and run quickly if I am followed. Lights are extinguished early on 24th Street between Central Avenue and Park Avenue. A small grocery store and a shoe repair shop are open only until five o'clock. But I do not want to think now about the danger going home. I am looking forward to seeing Mitzi Gaynor dance, sing and be courted.

At Loew's, I carefully choose a seat in the center a few rows from the back. No one is sitting behind me, and if someone should sit next to me and start touching me the way the old men do on Ohio Street, I can quickly move out the other side. The theater is almost empty, which is not unusual for a week night. Towards the front of the theater is a married middle-aged couple. I wish that I could sit next to them and so be under their protection, but they would not like it if, of all the empty seats, I chose a seat by them. Before the curtain opens a few more people come in, mostly men, mostly alone. I record where each of them sits, so that I can move if I have to. There are no young men in pairs or groups, who would try to block the aisle the way the young soldiers from Fort Benjamin Harrison do on Ohio Street.

Red satin shines and sequins glitter as Mitzi Gaynor dances across the screen. Her legs, in fishnet stockings, move gracefully, she fans herself with an ostrich feather. Two men adore her—whom will she choose?

Warm fingers touch my shoulder, they linger there. I feel moist breath on the back of my neck, and fingers touch my arm. Not taking my eyes off the screen, I move a couple of rows closer to the middle-aged couple. I am aware almost immediately of the insistence of the man as he follows to the row behind me.

I sit still, willing him not to touch me, but he does. His hand slides over my shoulder towards my breast. I get up and move again. I see white flaccid flesh swing against the dark material of his pants. I can smell him behind me, my neck and shoulders so sensitive they register his movements before I see them.

I move twice, but he pursues me. In the shadows of the theater he seems huge, dangerous, insistent, totally selfish. He has every right to do what he is doing; I shouldn't be here alone. In desperation, I move to the row with the married couple, but almost immediately his breath is on the back of my neck again. He puts his hand on my shoulder. It is pale and lumpy; the tips of the fingers are curled slightly backward. His repulsiveness nauseates me, but I keep my eyes resolutely on the screen, terrified of what he will do next.

I feel him tensed to attack, but something interrupts him. There is a commotion behind me, someone motions him to leave, there is a brief scuffle and he is gone. I do not turn around to look because if he is still there he will think I am encouraging him to return. I try to concentrate on Mitzi Gaynor's costume, which is like a corset that Mrs. Čigāns still has from Latvia, except that hers is black and meant to be worn under her dress, whereas this one is all red glitter and worn in full view of women and men both.

But I cannot keep my mind on the movie, which now seems false and cloying. I do not even care whether there is a happy ending; I wish I were at the Esquire instead. No matter how sweetly provocative Mitzi Gaynor and other nice-girl heroines are on the screen, no one ever pursues them in dark movie theaters, no one circles the block ominously in cars as they walk home, no one hides by the back stairs to ambush them, no one drags them across rough cement floors. I wish all such nice girls were pushed out of cars on dark streets in Indianapolis, shoved into a basement in Lobethal. I wish I could see a movie that told the truth.

Suddenly there is a tap on my shoulder, and I jump in terror. A man in uniform. I am so petrified that it takes me a moment to realize it is a policeman, not a soldier. He stands in the aisle, beckoning to me. I must be guilty of whatever he says I have done, I should not be here alone. I will probably be arrested and taken to jail. I blush, my heart pounds, I control my tears, but I feel warm urine run down my legs. I am overwhelmed by this yet greater shame.

The policeman motions again. The urine stings the backs of my legs, my slip clings to me. I am wearing a full circle-cut cotton skirt, my first, which I have made in home economics class. It has a pattern of yellow and brown leaves against a flecked background. It is too much to hope that the policemen in the jail won't notice that I have soiled myself. My face and neck are flushed bright red. I tremble as I walk up the aisle with the policeman. The men in the back rows turn and look.

The policeman takes me into a tiny room, the manager's office, and asks my name, age, address, the names of my parents. I know I can hide nothing. I am most sorry for the trouble I have caused my parents. I hope against hope that the police will not go to Park Avenue and arrest everyone for housing violations, as Mrs. Cohen has warned they will.

"Why are you at the movies alone?" he asks. "Where are your parents?"

"My mother is working at LaRue's. I don't know where my father is right now, I think he is at a meeting, but later . . ."

"Is he going to pick you up when the movie is over?"

"No." They will probably find him at the Latvian Center and lead him out handcuffed. He will be angry with me. Being here alone is just one of my crimes.

There is an abrupt knock, and the door is pushed open. Outside is my pursuer, the menace in the dark.

"This is the man who was bothering you," the policeman holding him says firmly. "You have to identify him."

I hesitate. I have a definite recollection of the man's fingers and of his moist sickening breath on the back of my neck. But this man is smaller, older and much more human than I remember. His skin is an unhealthy white, a few limp brown hairs are scraped over the bald spot on his head, he is perspiring. He is dressed in a shabby navy blue suit and a soiled white shirt; he carries a raincoat. He looks very frightened.

The policeman feels I am hesitating too long.

"He was bothering the girl at the concession stand before, so she had the usher call us. We were in the back of the theater, watching him follow you whenever you moved. Is this the man?"

I look at the man's hands, the pale recurving fingers, the slightly dirty fingernails.

"Yes, I think so."

"Well, is he or isn't he?"

"Yes."

"Are you sure?"

"Yes.

"Good, then we can take him down and book him. We'll get him out of the country for this, if we're lucky."

"Out of the country?" asks the second policeman.

"Yeah, he's another one of these filthy foreigners, they're all over the place these days. A frog. He's from the carnival, only got a visitor's permit. Send him back where he came from. Good riddance."

The man begins protesting. "No, no, I didn't do anything, she winked at me. No, no."

When the two policemen ignore him, he starts begging and crying. "Please, please," he repeats, wiping his face on a handkerchief, then on his sleeve. He is still pleading as the policeman takes him away.

"Come on," the officer says, "we don't need any foreign scum in this country."

"Now, we'll need a statement of what the suspect did. When did you first notice him? Did you see him before you sat down close to him?"

The interrogation continues. I expect to be questioned and not believed about winking at the man, but the policeman does not seem interested. Mostly he wants to know my movements and the position of the man's hands and body.

"Were his pants open? Was his penis exposed?"

When I look puzzled, the officer points to his own lap. I know exactly what he is getting at, I remember the Russian soldiers in the basement. My face and neck are so flushed they throb.

"Yes."

Finally the policeman hands me a telephone number.

"Call if you have any questions before the court date."

"Court?" The worst has come true.

"Yes, you'll make an excellent witness. We'll lock him up for good. Your mother will want to come with you."

"Does my mother have to come?" I have a fantasy of somehow going to the court alone, of my mother and father never finding out.

"Yes, your mother will have to come. It won't take long. All you have to do is to tell exactly what you have told me. Think you can remember it?"

"But what about the girl in the concession stand? Couldn't she go and testify instead? Didn't he bother her before?" It is a measure of my terror of my mother's reaction that I dare question the police.

"Oh, she told him right away where to get off. He didn't have a chance with her."

There is no escape. I will have to tell my mother, who will cry about the disgrace. Sometimes she sobs convulsively, her arms hugged around herself, but mostly she does not say a word. The pain I have caused her is my worst offense.

"Look," says the policeman. "I know it's scary. I have daughters myself. But your mom will take care of you, she'll be with you, there's nothing to it."

This policeman does not know my mother.

But at least he does not take me to prison. He asks me if I would like to stay and see the rest of the movie; he is letting me go. When I shake my head, he nods approvingly. Then he puts me in the back of the squad car, wet skirt and all, and drives me to the bus stop.

"Let me give you some advice," he says before he lets me out. "You're a very pretty girl. That's why you have to be real careful. You're the one who has to watch out."

I wait. I do not understand what being pretty has to do with it, though I am very pleased the policeman thinks so.

"I've got daughters of my own. I'll tell you the same as I tell them: Don't go to the movies alone, don't ride the bus alone. Stay home. You're just asking for trouble if you're outside after dark. You encourage these guys, you lead them on, and really, the poor saps can't help what they do. I don't want to have to question you again."

I know there are men lurking in movie theaters, in the backs of buses, in cars that pull over to the sidewalk. "Come here, gorgeous," they say, although darkness covers my face and body. "Come for a ride, baby, come with me." I never walk on the east side of Central Avenue by 11th Street where the bars are, I always cross the street and walk against traffic. After working at LaRue's, I run as fast as I can when I get off the bus after midnight. I know men are dangerous, I move when someone bothers me. But that is not good enough. I am the one at fault.

No one is at home when I let myself in. I try to read, but the words make no sense. The enormity of what I have done, the trouble that I have caused my parents is too painful. I would do anything to help my mother get through this.

When she comes home, I tell her. It takes a long time because she sobs, goes to the bathroom and runs some cold water, rinses her face, says she cannot bear to hear any more, but then repeats the same questions.

"How could you go to the movies alone? How could you get us mixed up with the police? How could you do this to us?"

I try to explain, but mostly I wait. My mother is punishing me by letting me watch the pain I have caused. "How could you do this to us?" she asks again and again.

Finally she stops. She takes off her shoes and gets into bed. She picks up a book. "All right, I'll have to go with you. I'll have to take off work and lose a day's pay. I don't know how we'll pay the rent. Don't tell your father. Now I don't want to talk about it again, I want to read."

My parents are asleep when Beate comes home. I tiptoe past their bed to join her in the bathroom.

"She's very mad. I did something terrible," I whisper. I tell the whole story quickly. Beate does not act puzzled or surprised by any detail.

"What did *he* say?" she motions towards where our parents are sleeping.

"She hasn't told him yet. She didn't say anything when he came home."

"She probably won't then, so don't worry about that. Did this guy have his pants open? Was his thing sticking up? Like this?" She wiggles her finger. "Did he touch you with that filthy thing?" We have both seen the man with his pants undone who sometimes lurks by the darkened grocery store we have to pass on the way home from the bus.

"No."

"Well, that's good then. I'm glad he didn't hurt you with that. You must have been scared."

"Yes, I was. I thought they would put me in prison."

Beate laughs.

"He's the criminal. He's the one who's locked up right now. I hope they chop off his hairy carrot. Are you still scared?"

"Yes. And I'm sorry for what I did to her."

"She'll get over it." But we both know our mother will not forget it.

Beate puts her arms around me and gives me a quick hug. "You can come sleep in my bed. I'll take care of you. Remember, you're the littlest."

We try to arrange ourselves comfortably, but Beate's bed is too narrow. I cannot fall asleep, my heart pounds, I think I will never sleep again.

"Let's push our beds together. We'll move them back tomorrow," Beate suggests. We are not allowed to block the passage from the porch where our parents sleep, but it will probably be all right for one night. We get under the covers.

"That filthy pervert, he's abnormal," Beate says. The words make me feel a little less guilty.

"They said they would deport him. He's from a foreign country, just like us. It will be my fault if they send him to the camps."

"Well, let them. He should have thought of that. He's the one who stuck his slimy thing out. Don't be scared. It will be all right."

Beate leans over and tucks me in. So comforted, I finally fall asleep.

When I go to court a few weeks later, my mother does not speak to me on the way. I know she will not speak to me for several days afterwards; I hope that it will not be longer. I have to tell my story twice in a private room, and then again in the courtroom, directly in front of the judge. I expect to be questioned about what I was doing at the movies alone, or why I have gotten the man into such serious trouble. I am also afraid that he will be released and that he will do something terrible to me then.

He is there in his shabby navy blue suit, but today he does not speak English or is pretending not to. I have to point him out to the judge. The man gives me a pathetic pleading look before I do.

"Thank you for bringing her," the judge says.

My mother smiles at him. The small Frenchman mops his brow. I can feel his eyes on me as I leave the courtroom. No one says what his sentence is.

"What will happen to him? Will they send him back to Europe?" I see him being led handcuffed into a concentration camp.

My mother pauses, to indicate the favor she is granting by speaking to me at all.

"I expect so. They won't want to pay for keeping him in prison here." I feel the gates shut on the man, who is now wearing a striped uniform. I have sent him there.

That is the only thing my mother ever says about the trial. She never refers to it again, and as far as I know she never tells my father. After about a week she starts speaking to me again, but there is always a slight unnamed difference in her tone.

◆ ◆ ◆

During my freshman year, I have Miss Guthridge as an English teacher. Miss Guthridge is unlike all the other teachers in Shortridge High School. With the exception of strict Mrs. Vitz, the Latin teacher, all the other women are single, "old maids," as they are called. To us they seem to have no lives beyond teaching. The few men who teach biology, math and chemistry are all married except Mr. Milligan. Miss Guthridge, as she freely tells everyone, is divorced. She makes our class read "The Love Song of J. Alfred Prufrock," she says *Silas Marner* is boring, she herself can't see much point in *Julius Caesar* and we don't have to finish it if we don't want to. She gives us full details of Tennessee Williams's suicide attempts and F. Scott Fitzgerald's drinking bouts. She wears tight skirts with slits in the back, sits on the desk, crosses her lovely legs and announces that she does not like teaching English, she never thought she would have to do it, but there it is, one never knows how things will turn out. She advises our class of fourteen-year-olds not to marry.

Some mornings Miss Guthridge arrives in a car driven by a man. The girls speculate breathlessly where she must have spent the night. Miss Guthridge tells Miss Peterson, the guidance counselor, that vocational aptitude tests are meaningless. Her own said that she should never teach, and here she is doing it. She tells me not to pay any attention to Miss Peterson, who says I should take the commercial course rather than the college preparatory one. "You'll go to the university," Miss Guthridge breezily assures me. She says Miss Peterson is a fool for saying I am failing to adjust because I have admitted to her I can still remember the war.

Miss Guthridge announces to our class that writing themes is silly because no one ever buys a book of themes to read. She asks us to write about the first thing we see coming towards us when we shut our eyes. I write a story about a furious rider announcing exile and war. "Complete this story," Miss Guthridge says after she reads us the first paragraph of a story in *The Atlantic Monthly*, about a homeless woman in a city park. I write about a woman who has lost everyone dear to her in the war and to whom possessions are meaningless.

I adore Miss Guthridge. I discover that I can partially close my eyes and write anything if I imagine Miss Guthridge will read it.

"You can be a writer," Miss Guthridge says. "You have a lot of valuable experience, you have a lot to say. I expect to see some of your things one day. I'll go into a bookstore in New York or Paris, I'll pick up a magazine and I'll see a story of yours."

In spite of the thrill of those words, my heart contracts. When will Miss Guthridge leave?

At the end of the school year, Miss Guthridge gives me a copy of *The Diary of Anne Frank* and tells me that I must write my own story: "You have just as much to tell."

I read and reread the book until I know passages by heart. I study Anne Frank's photograph on the cover, I see her face at night before I fall asleep, I wonder what other books Anne would have written if she had survived the war.

At the public library downtown I return obsessively to the photographs of concentration camps. I wish I had the courage to rip out the pages and steal them, so that I could really study them. There must be something everyone else has missed. I pore over the hopeless, resigned faces, the emaciated bodies, the stick-like limbs. I believe that if I try hard enough I will be the one to find Anne Frank, unnoticed by everyone else, standing quiet and dignified among the survivors.

Finally I resign myself to the truth: Anne Frank is dead, she will never write anything else.

I study the mountain of eyeglasses taken from the dead. The volumes fall open to the right pages as soon as I pick them up. This is where the real story of the war is, these are the people who really suffered. How dare I even think of writing about my own minor inconveniences, my privileged experience?

Miss Guthridge does not return to Shortridge the following autumn. Rumor has it that she has been fired, but I prefer to think that she has quit and gone off to New York or Paris, that she is leading a much more exciting life.

I am not surprised that Miss Guthridge is gone. No one has ever stayed. I try once more to write a story, but cannot find the first sentence. I am relieved when I get sick once again, just as I have before at times of unbearable tension. That autumn I am diagnosed as having TB, which allows me to stay in bed, silent and alone.

Whenever I return to Indianapolis, I drive to Park and 24th Street. The sidewalks are littered with trash, the elm trees are gone. The grocery store is still standing, but it is a pawnshop now. Like all the other small businesses in the neighborhood, it has bars on the windows. Half a dozen family homes have been torn down and a huge liquor store erected in their place, also with barred windows. The three houses where the Latvians lived are even more dilapidated. The soil is packed hard where the patch of lawn used to be, some windows are broken and covered with cardboard and plastic. I doubt that the people living in the apartments now have the kind of supportive community we briefly had.

Public School 45 is closed, the windows boarded up, the walls defaced with graffiti. The movie theater on Central Avenue is closed, but the seedy bars are still there. I make sure that my car doors are locked. There are a lot of men drinking on the corners, who eye me suspiciously as I drive by. I expect that the three houses where we Latvians lived will soon be torn down too; they hardly look habitable now.

Only Mr. Bumbieris stayed on in the apartments for years rather than moving to another part of the city. No longer thinking of Marilyn Monroe, he shot himself when he was eighty.

Always ahead of the rest of us, Mrs. Čigāns moved to California. She had been the first to buy a toaster. She sent Tālivaldis to the store for a large loaf of Wonder Bread and knocked on doors, issuing invitations. Everyone stood in her crowded kitchen, watching the toaster work in the middle of the table, taking turns pushing down the bread. Butter, bologna, grape jelly and peanut butter were tried and commented on. Mrs. Čigāns sent Tālivaldis back to the store for more bread.

"Get two loaves this time," she told him, "so we have plenty for everyone. And you, Agate, come with me. Let's see if between the two of us we can figure out the directions for Mrs. Briedis's pressure cooker, so she doesn't have to wash carrots off her ceiling again. Aren't you glad that you learned English?"

"Yes." I am glad I did. Learning English was thrilling, the most wonderful part of learning America.

·15·

Leaving Home

I cannot wait to leave home. I want to escape the tiny house on Park Avenue, five blocks from the Latvian Center, where we have barricaded ourselves. The seedy, hopeless neighborhood is quickly growing even more dangerous. Half a block away, a woman is raped and stabbed to death behind an abandoned church. Another is strangled in a house facing the dilapidated apartment buildings on Park Avenue, where a few Latvians still live. But most move away as soon as they are able. The close, supportive Latvian community is withering away.

I lie awake in bed, listening to the loud music, shouts and occasional women's screams that come from the house next door after the bars close. Men line up in the yard, smoking and passing around flasks and bottles while they wait their turn inside. Sometimes they misread the house numbers, and they pound on our door, demanding to be let in. If my father is at home, he hastily buttons on an American minister's collar before he turns on the light. A glimpse convinces the men then that they have come to the wrong place.

At other times, Ōmīte and my mother go. They cover their hair and foreheads with scarves, they keep their eyes downcast, they try to appear old and unattractive, just as they did in the basement in Lobethal. During the day the heavy dark brown curtains stay drawn over the French doors of the dining room, making it hot in summer and perpetually dark in winter. My mother checks frequently whether these doors are locked, and she tells Beate and me to push the dining-room table against them at night. Men are outside drinking, they are looking at the house; they may be planning right now how to force their way in.

The owner of the house next door wears a white cowboy hat and a long shiny leather coat, like a German officer's. My mother holds him in contempt, and the number of his customers distresses her.

"More drunken men for the Nazi Cowboy," she calls out as fists pound on the door. "Don't let them see you, Agate. And Beate, both of you girls get into the closet if someone starts to break in."

She waits until we are in the back bedroom. Then she shouts through the locked front door, "Go away! This is the wrong house."

"Not at home." Ōmīte speaks the only words of English she has learned, which serve her for answering the phone as well.

Only if the men continue pounding or start kicking the door does my mother turn on the porch light and point to the other house. Ōmīte shakes her head vigorously so that the men can see her too denying them through the small glass panes of the flimsy door that opens directly into the living room.

"I could talk to them about more meaningful ways to spend their lives, but I'm not learning English," Ōmīte says as the steps recede. "I've had to learn too many languages—Russian in Siberia, French in Moscow, German in Latvia. I'm not starting to learn another at eighty to direct customers for the Nazi Cowboy, to make *him* rich."

"Those poor creatures," my mother sighs. She never refers to the women next door as prostitutes.

"Martin Luther said . . . ," my father begins.

But she does not listen. "Such wasted lives, such terrible humiliations. They must wish for death every single day."

The women are never outside, and the long low porch remains empty when it is light. Perhaps they sleep all day after their long hard hours, perhaps they are locked in. The Cowboy's black Cadillac is gone during the day too. He lives elsewhere, probably surrounded by luxury, but he often reappears unexpectedly. The Cadillac slides up the street noiselessly, the Cowboy gets out, slams the door, hustles yet another woman into the house.

Occasionally a weary, middle-aged bleached blonde, her skin dry and white, glares as she is being pushed along, but most of the women are black. Some are heavy and soft, with eyes as sad as my mother's. Others are slender jaunty girls, like the ones who get off the bus with me at Shortridge High School. Or they are just a few years older, like the black women who are doomed to spend their lives working as maids in the mansions on North Meridian Street.

The men who tramp through our yard, grinding broken liquor bottles and cigarette butts into the patch of lawn, urinating against the back porch, are white. Talk of integration of the city swimming pools is causing many whites, afraid of even such proximity to black flesh, to join Westlake and other "private swimming clubs" during the day, but at night the Cowboy's business flourishes.

My mother is still working as a dishwasher at LaRue's. She spends the rest of the time in her tiny space behind our kitchen. Exposed pipes run along the walls, the linoleum is worn and dented where a washer and dryer once stood. Two boards are laid over the unused double sink, and these serve as her dressing table and desk. There is just enough room for a narrow single bed. As soon as she gets home from work, she goes there and closes the door. She studies for the one class she manages to take each semester at Indiana University Extension, or she brings translations of Russian novels home from the library and reads them to improve her English. The only time she gets animated is when she finds a mistake in translation.

"Who gave this naive man the significant job of translating Dostoevsky?" she asks. "He doesn't understand the first thing about Russian. Dostoevsky was writing about purity, not chastity or virginity. He valued Maria's purity. She had been humiliated and used, but Dostoevsky knew she was pure. He was a great writer because he saw beneath the surface."

On his way to yet another meeting, my father nods absentmindedly. Both he and my mother value and take seriously their responsibilities as naturalized citizens of the United States, but otherwise they have entirely different attitudes towards their new country. My father spends most of his time with Latvians. He works ceaselessly for the Latvian congregation he has founded, for the Indianapolis Latvian community and for the Latvian Lutheran church in exile. He prays every night that Latvia will someday be free and that Latvians there can survive Russian oppression and torture.

Although still doing manual labor, my mother puts her faith in

America. Her English is increasingly sophisticated, and she keeps up with current novels, films, music and literary criticism. She defends American culture against those uninformed Latvians who assume that drugstore paperbacks represent the best that's been thought and said in the United States. She tempers my father's longing to return to Latvia by reminders of women having to do backbreaking work there, without the benefit of running water, central heating and electric appliances.

My father's salary from the Latvian congregation is smaller than my mother's dishwashing pay. People are just getting started in a strange land, they need practical and spiritual help, and he is happy to give it. He worked for nothing except satisfaction in the camps, and at least now they pay him something, but even he worries that we will never pay off all our debts.

Ōmīte falls down the basement steps and breaks her hip. She has no insurance. We try to take care of her at home, but finally she has to be hospitalized. I am sick with TB for an entire year, also without insurance. I stay in bed, mostly at home, with weekly visits from a doctor and a nurse who gives me shots. I can call myself lucky because streptomycin, the miracle drug, is newly available. Unlike my mother's beloved sister Velta in Latvia, I will recover. All of my mother's efforts to save her sister, all her long hard trips from Riga when she carried the heavy oxygen tanks on the train, proved in vain then.

I have innumerable X-rays, over half of which the kind Jewish radiologist on 34th Street takes without sending a bill, but I have to be hospitalized repeatedly for bleeding and for bronchoscopies. I daydream that I am going to pay my parents back for all the hardship I am causing them. I want to pile gold and silver coins and dollar bills into my mother's lap so that she will never have to go to LaRue's again. I wish I could give my mother silky slips and smart suits. I long to pull out a chair and tell her that she can rest as long as she likes.

In the late afternoons, too feverish to sleep, I imagine every detail of the house that I will buy for my mother someday. It is a graceful, well-proportioned brick house, covered with ivy, encircled by lawns, flowers and trees. It is in Latvia, which has been freed from occupying Russian soldiers. With my eyes shut, I furnish the house with comfortable chairs, good lights, new books, musical instruments. My mother's face is radiant; she smiles and puts her arm protectively around my shoulders as the two of us stroll up the long winding drive.

We sit in the library together, we read through endless evenings, we talk softly to each other. The windows are open, and at night scented stock perfumes the air.

Except when worrying about catching up at school or when gasping for breath during bouts of coughing or spitting up blood, I do not mind being sick. It is restful. I do not have to walk down the long hallways of Shortridge High School, I do not have to feel disapproving eyes scalding my back, I do not have to hear sniggering whispers that I am strange and different. I am relieved to put aside the story that Miss Guthridge expected me to write, but which I know I will never finish. I have nothing at all to say.

The smell of disinfectant and fatty food from LaRue's is finally out of my hair and skin, so that when my mother comes in I am momentarily repulsed breathing a whiff of it, mingled with cold air. I turn my head aside if she comes close to my bed. I play cards and Chinese checkers with Ōmīte, but mostly I read, doze, dream. School and work have dropped away, leaving me safe in bed.

Only Beth interferes. For reasons I cannot begin to fathom, my classmate begins telephoning me.

"How are you? Are you any better? What are you reading? Do you have any errands you'd like me to run for you?"

"No," I say.

I do not know Beth well, and why would Beth want to have anything to do with me anyway? We only sat next to each other in Latin class, and once we did a chemistry experiment together quickly and efficiently when Beth's regular lab partner was absent.

"Are you ready for some company?" Beth persists. "I'll come and see you next week, or the week after, whenever you say. You must be getting bored, aren't you? Tell me when I should come."

"No, please, don't bother. It's too much trouble, and I'm still too sick to see anyone."

One late afternoon, as I wake from a nap, Ieva, a Latvian friend, who loyally stops to visit me almost every day, gently opens the door.

"Someone to see you. A young American lady is getting out of her shiny little red car in front. She's coming up the walk, carrying flowers."

"Oh no," I wail. I see the room with the coldly judging eyes of a stranger. Beate's and my beds are jammed so close together I have to crawl over my sister at night, the embroidered cloth over the cardboard boxes does not transform them into a bureau, the piece of mirror propped against the wall is cracked—all details commonplace to Ieva and me. Even more, my own sheets are crumpled and damp from my regular afternoon fever, the wastepaper basket is overflowing with bloodied Kleenex, the pillowcase is bloodstained as well. I am ashamed of the house and of my illness, but much worse is my fear of what I will say to Beth. What will we talk about? We have nothing at all in common.

"Please," I beg, "don't let her in. Tell her I'm too sick to see anyone."

"It would be nice for you to see another friend."

There is a knock on the front door.

"No," I whisper in terrified appeal, "she isn't my friend. Don't let her in."

I turn my back and close my eyes. "Please, go away," I pray.

When Ieva returns, she is carrying a vase filled with spring flowers—yellow trumpet daffodils, creamy tulips, a dark blue hyacinth.

"She left these for you. She was very disappointed not to see you."

"Did you let her into the house? Did she look around?"

"No, I went out on the porch to talk to her. But really, what does that matter? She must have gone to a lot of trouble, getting all dressed up, wearing a hat, carrying white gloves, bringing such lovely flowers. How nice to have a friend who wants so much to make you happy. She must really like you."

But I do not believe Beth likes me. No one who is not Latvian does, no one could, why should Beth? Maybe Beth has only come to look, to disapprove, to report back to the others.

I turn my face towards the wall. I feel sorry for Beth, a tall, serious, red-haired girl, carrying a bouquet carefully in her freckled hand, her thin face registering disappointment and embarrassment at being denied admission. Beth is too intelligent not to realize that she has been snubbed. She will never call again, I think. And she never does.

So many secrets to keep. Debates on irresolvable topics are held in the Latvian Center on Central Avenue. Would Latvia still be an independent country if Latvians had united with the Lithuanians and Estonians and then fought simultaneously against both the Germans and the Russians in 1944? What steps should be taken now to guarantee independence for Latvia in the future? Who had the hardest time during the war, men or women?

One muggy Indiana summer evening, I sit in the back row, next to my mother. The small airless room is packed with young men, many of whom fought in the war. Some were prisoners of war. They speak of exhaustion, wounds, death. They cite numbers and percentages of casualties, they give names of comrades who lost eyesight and limbs. Their voices rise high in anger and pain.

The women are silent.

Finally, Miss Regīna, an intelligent, decisive woman who was an actress in Latvia, says, "A man at least had a gun in his hand. What did we have?" She motions to the women and girls in the back row. "We had nothing."

She is quickly shouted down. Can she produce the number of women killed and wounded? No, bombs don't count. And anyway, everyone knows that more men are killed in wars than women. Where are her statistics? Where is her proof? How can she even think such a thing? She is overdramatizing.

Miss Regīna starts to answer, shakes her head defiantly, then bends her head to study her rings.

In the awkward pause, my mother says loudly, "Other things happened to women, terrible things, more destructive in their own way."

"What can be more terrible than being wounded and killed?" someone interrupts her.

"Terrible things," my mother repeats. It sounds lame, even to me. "Rape" is an unsayable word in mixed company; people have been shocked that it has actually been printed in a recent controversial novel. I hope my mother does not say it out loud, I hope she does not *tell* anything. It sounds as if she is making light of the suffering of the men, which is very real. Is she trying to take something away from them? Why has she spoken at all? I am embarrassed for her, I must defend the men against her.

But even as I wish my mother had stayed silent, I feel an overwhelming desire to speak myself, to shout at everyone, to make them see what happened to women and girls. My chest is tight with tension, my head filled with images to bursting.

I do not say anything, but only in part because I would be shouted down too. I am ashamed of the basement; everyone would despise me if they knew what the soldiers did. They would ostracize my mother too. I will never tell.

"Men had a harder time," is voted the winning proposition. The women and girls raise their hands to indicate agreement. Miss Regina continues polishing her rings as if she has not heard the question, but when it is repeated, she shrugs and raises her hand too, making it clear it does not matter to her one way or the other.

My mother sits stubbornly looking down at her clenched hands. I vote with the winning side. I glance at my mother's flushed face and wish she were different. Longing washes over me to see her smiling directly into Sniegs's brooding eyes, accepting a flower from Pastor Braun's outstretched hand, laughing with my father about a funny story he has just told. As much as I would then resent my mother's inattention to me, I prefer her previous compliance to men to this bitter resistance.

But the men's victory pleases no one. The men stand about looking awkward and defiant, while the women file out silently. The chief spokesman for the men pushes papers around irritably and kicks at a chair. The tightness stays in my jaw and chest as my mother and I walk home without referring to what has happened.

I am familiar with that tightness, I feel it every day. Only when I was sick did it abate. Now I am paralyzed by my desire to make others see and my absolute need to conceal.

In the spring of my senior year, I am a finalist for a scholarship given by a group of Jewish businessmen. I stand alone in an immense empty space while a dozen middle-aged men behind a long white table littered with napkins, ashtrays and half-empty cocktail glasses examine me. I am adept at summarizing my past in one sentence.

"I was born in Latvia, went to Germany during the war and came to the United States when I was twelve."

"How did the Germans treat you? What was it like to be in Germany during the war?"

"It wasn't so bad."

They look surprised and begin to question me in earnest.

"Why did you go to a Nazi country in the first place?"

"Were your parents Nazis?"

"Were they Communists?"

"Why didn't you come directly to the United States?"

"Why don't you go back to Latvia now that the Nazis are no longer there?"

I feel assailed by their questions. Will they ask me what every other Latvian thinks about the Nazis? If I speak about the majority of Latvians, how will I explain the exceptions—Mr. Ziemelis and his false dueling scar or Mrs. Saulitis's Nazi husband? They too are Latvian, so I too am responsible for what they did.

"Who was worse, the Russians or the Germans?"

"Do you prefer the Nazis to the Communists?"

I must not, *must not* cry.

"I don't like any of them, Nazis or Communists," I blurt out. "I don't like Germans or Russians. Both have occupied and brutalized Latvia."

When that does not satisfy them, I stand silent, successfully controlling my tears while pretending to study the intricate pattern of the Oriental carpet. It is all too complicated to explain. And I am ashamed of my last answer. How can I say I dislike the Russians? My mother still mourns leaving "dear Mother Russia," she recites Pushkin, she rereads *The Brothers Karamazov* constantly because she says it contains all the great human truths. Like the Greek Orthodox Russians, she prefers Easter to Christmas, she says Lutheranism is German, lacks ritual, deadens the soul.

"Christ is risen," she says, as she hands out small presents to everyone, just as she once did as a girl in Russia. She cries when she speaks about the Russian people having to eat grass during the siege of Leningrad.

And what about the Germans? I believe these men would understand about the Nazi guards at Lehrte, but how would I explain my love for Pastor Braun whistling "Nearer, My God, to Thee"? For Hilda offering herself to the Mongolian soldiers in place of the twelve-year-old girl? For Frau Braun quoting the inscription on the statue of the stone Christ welcoming the homeless and the maimed to Lobethal and then taking me by the hand so I would be given carrots?

Why do others insist on making such comparisons? Why must everyone who lived through the war *compete*? I do not recognize that I myself still compete too. I believe that I am finished with the war because I no longer study obsessively the photographs of concentration-camp survivors. But I have them memorized, and I feel responsible for them in a way that I could not begin to put into words.

So I shake my head again and remain silent.

The odd thing is, I win the Isadore Feibleman Scholarship, so that my silence must have seemed unbearable only to me. Perhaps I gave away more than I knew, probably they understood better than I gave them credit for. Certainly they were unusually enlightened men since in 1956 they offered a generous scholarship to anyone solely on the basis of academic achievement, "regardless of race, creed, ethnic background or sex."

I feel a bit like an impostor, and I hope that they do not discover that I really do not deserve their generosity, but for the moment I am elated. I will go to Indiana University, just like my sister. Beate has a work-study scholarship and is already completing her second year at Bloomington. I am also very excited: I believe that finally this time, by going to yet another new place, I will leave behind the gray fog that I expected to lift when I arrived in America. I will escape the guilt that suffocates me the moment I see the thin strip of light under my mother's closed door. In Russia she did not even have to lace her own boots because the servants did that for her; here she sighs as she puts on shoes to go wash dishes at LaRue's. In the summers she works additional hours at Stokeley's cannery, and her hands are blistered and burned.

"Come in," she says in answer to my second knock. "What is it? Be quick. I have to get ready to go to work in a few minutes." She keeps her eyes on the page.

"I won another scholarship, a large one this time. So now I have four altogether. I have more than enough to go to the university in September."

"Oh, precious, did you win?" she flings aside her book and holds out her arms.

I start towards her, but stop halfway. It is impossible. When have we last touched, when did she last call me precious? Too long ago.

"So you won the big one?" she asks.

"Yes," I say as formally as I can.

"I *knew* you would. You're my daughter."

She folds her arms in her lap. The distance is reestablished between us.

"I am glad you are pleased," I say.

"I am. It's exactly what I wanted for you. Just imagine, only a few months from now you'll be at the university with intelligent people, who love books and ideas and music and art, who talk about something besides making money and accumulating possessions. You'll have a wonderful, exciting life, going to lectures and concerts, listening to famous professors. How wonderful it will be for you, the fragrance of new books, and sitting up late at night by yourself, studying. Talking with others about ideas. How fortunate for you. That's why I didn't want to go to Brazil."

"I know," I say stiffly. Whenever my mother and father worry about money or the dangerous neighborhood, they probably remember that life might be different for him if we had all gone to Brazil.

"I always wanted to go to the university too," she is saying. "I would certainly have gone, if only the war hadn't come, if only I had not been driven away from dear Mother Russia, if only my father had not died."

I imagine myself outside, daydreaming under the peach tree that blooms luxuriously in defiance of the trampled soil in the backyard.

"If only my Uncle Žanis had not disappeared during the Revolution, he would have helped me. He believed in education for women too. He and my father were both such enlightened men, so different from most people here. But then the second war came, and we lost everything again, and we lost our beloved Latvia too. Oh, how different life could have been."

I long to escape. I feel helpless whenever she recites her losses. Should I apologize for winning the scholarship? I try to harden myself, push the guilt away. Why does she have to ruin everything? But in the midst of my anger, I wish again that I could give her a gift that would make up for everything. I would even give up my scholarship to her.

"Life is just one terrible repetition after another," she is saying. "We go through one war in Russia, just to go through another in Germany. We see women raped in Lobethal, we think we can escape by coming to America, but now we run from the bus stop every night, afraid of the same thing. We hide from drunken Russian soldiers there, we bar the door against drunken Americans here. We hope they don't break into this house instead of brutalizing the women the Nazi Cowboy keeps in his prison next door. It's the same nightmare. I can't wait for my life to end."

"Oh no, don't say that, it's not true."

"I know you don't want to hear that, but that's how it is. But *you* finally have a chance. You can have a different life, a larger, freer, better life. You must escape, even if it is too late for the rest of us. You can live like people were meant to live. You must not let anything stop you."

"But everyone has a chance," I say, wishing it were true, irritated with my mother for reminding me that it isn't.

"Well, I'm sure they teach you a lot of nonsense like that in school, fairy tales about every child growing up to be president, and equality of opportunity, and rising to the top by hard work, and America as a melting pot, where we are to lose our nationalities by being boiled alive, like missionaries by cannibals. None of that applies to most of us. But I don't want to start talking about politics, it doesn't matter what I believe about that. *You* can have a real life. You can graduate from the university. Maybe you can even teach in those beautiful ivy-covered limestone buildings someday."

"Yes, I know, I have to get all A's to keep my scholarships," I say, deliberately misunderstanding her.

"You'll get all A's, I always did. No, what I mean is that you must not let anything interfere with your education. Not anything or anybody. Remember Skalbe's poem about no one being able to take away the riches of the heart? Don't let any man stand in the way of your getting an education."

I burn to be gone before my mother starts in on the dangers of marriage, how it sends women on endless rounds of carrying wood, drawing water, scouring pots, flattering husbands. She rereads *Anna Karenina*, hums sad romantic songs and talks about the dashing Russian officers in white wool uniforms, yet she expects me to give up all dreams of romance. How can she be so inconsistent? I *will* have love and passion, I will not settle for a drab life, I will do better than she has.

"Don't you marry," she sometimes whispers while the two of us assemble platters of tiny elegant open-faced sandwiches for church-board members and other guests who crowd into the house for my father's birthday and name-day celebrations. "See how you have to spend your whole life in the kitchen if you do? Wouldn't you rather be in the living room talking about philosophy, and pretending that the platters of food are appearing magically, prepared by female angels happy to serve mortal men?"

I open the door to leave the room.

"One more thing."

"Yes?"

She says exactly what I know she will.

"Don't you marry."

·16·

My First American

I see him while I am waiting to register for classes during my junior year. In lines I always count people ahead of me and imagine the worst. I will not be admitted, I will not get enough credits to satisfy the scholarship committee, I will finally be unmasked as an impostor not deserving my scholarships, I will have to leave school in disgrace. Upperclassmen are ushered past, the line doesn't move for a long time, then finally it inches forward, stops again.

He strides past all the freshmen and speaks to the official checking identifications. He is tall and dark, his brown eyes intense above his high cheekbones. Only the too-narrow lips, pursed in a determined, almost spiteful way, keep his face from being handsome. There is something military about the way he holds his shoulders straight and stiff, as if an invisible rod were driven through them. In contrast, his manner is ingratiating, even wheedling. His long dark hair curls over his frayed shirt collar, he wears jeans and cowboy boots instead of neatly pressed slacks and polished loafers like the other students.

I stare at him, and he briefly catches my look before I drop my eyes. I scarcely notice that he would be considered handsome, even desirable. Something about him is so totally familiar that I can barely stop myself from greeting him in recognition. I have never seen him before in my life, and yet I am certain that I have known him or someone like him somewhere before. I cannot place where, and this familiarity is both vaguely unpleasant and compelling.

He has no proof that he is an upperclassman, but he is trying to convince the official to let him through the turnstile ahead of everybody else anyway.

"You and I know this is a lousy system, don't we, buddy?" he says. "We've both been around."

. Pointedly turning his back on those in line, he stage-whispers so that some words—special case, for everybody's good, a grown-up, not a damn college kid—are clearly audible. The guard shakes his head at first, then gradually softens. A long conspiratorial conversation ensues, punctuated by jokes and laughter. Finally the guard steps aside and motions him through the turnstile. A few people waiting in line mutter in disgust, others sigh. A little embarrassed, the official starts whistling to show he isn't listening.

An hour and a half later, when I finally have all my classes and am leaving the gym, he steps into my path.

"Hi," he says, "my name is Joe. Glad to meet you. You look like the only one with half a brain around here."

He extends his hand towards me.

I hesitate. The grudging admiration that I felt when he managed to get ahead of everyone else in line returns.

"Dumb shits." He motions towards my classmates. "Bunch of fucking sheep."

I draw in my breath sharply, as much at the language as at the sentiments.

"Oh," he continues, "don't do that, you don't need to defend them. I know you're a nice girl, I can tell by your cashmere sweater and those knockout pearls, you don't have to prove it to me. I bet you're in one of the best sororities, aren't you?" He gives me no time to answer. "All right," he adds, "I won't say 'fuck' out loud, if you don't want me to."

I drop my eyes in confusion. I feel the faint flush on my neck getting darker, rising above the soft collar of my sweater, which is dark blue lamb's wool topped with imitation pearls.

"I'll even say 'geez', if you want me to. As in, 'Geez, you're pretty.'"

He takes my elbow, and I let him because he is so certain of what to do next. Besides, he has mistaken me for someone entirely different—an average girl, a real American. We are two outsiders, mistaking each other for insiders.

As we walk past the guard who admitted him earlier, Joe says, "You've got to learn how to work the system, kid, you'll never make it otherwise. I can see already you need someone to take care of you." He makes a show of lowering his voice but whispers loud enough for the guard to hear, "Dumb bastard, I could have talked him into anything."

He has lived everywhere, in the sophisticated East and the wide-open spaces of the West. He does not think much of the Midwest, which he calls a backward, dumb but snobbish place. He does not think much of the students or professors either. He's only at the university to learn enough so that he can keep his own accounts when he sets off to Alaska or California to make his fortune. He himself grew up in slums, in one-horse towns, in abandoned oil fields. He had to work hard for every penny he ever had, driving cabs, parking cars for nightclubs, betting on horses. He had a foolproof method for winning, he says, until the crooked officials in New York kicked him off the track.

He has been everywhere, seen everything, he's been around, he knows what life is like. Women are always chasing him, he says, but he doesn't think much of them, they have no principles and no loyalty, just like his goddamn ex-wife. From this general condemnation he kindly exempts me and tells me I should be pleased by his singular devotion. He does not think much of foreigners either—they come over here to take away the best jobs from Americans and then, to add insult to injury, they refuse to learn English. But at least I am different from those funny guys in pinstriped suits, whose accents he can mimic to good comic effect. At least I look and try to act like an American. I could probably fool anyone, since I fooled him. All I need is a little polish.

He sets about enlightening me.

"Why do you stand in line? Why do you study all the time? Why do you think you have to tell your scholarship committees if you get a B? Tell them you got all A's. Send them someone else's transcript, just blacken out the name."

When I object, he laughs at my naïveté. "Jesus fucking Christ, studying isn't the only way to get an A. Ever read *The Scarlet Letter*? Don't know much American lit, do you? Remember how Hester Prynne got her A? Ha, ha. Only a jerk goes by the rules all the time. I had hoped you were smarter than that."

He is crazy about me, he says; he would do anything to please me. He points out each gesture and every act he performs only for my sake and at great inconvenience to himself. Nobody else will ever love me as he does. He can tell my mother certainly does not give a damn about me, so why can't I appreciate him? That's really one of my problems. I've got lots of problems, that's for sure. Still, he is absolutely, madly in love with me. It's lucky he knows more than enough for the two of us. If it were up to me, I wouldn't know enough to come in out of the rain, I would be up shit creek without a paddle.

When Joe is with me, he never takes his eyes off me. He watches my lips when I speak, he remembers everything I say, it breaks his heart when I have opinions different from his. He calls himself my servant and my slave. He cannot endure being away from me. He cannot restrain himself from touching my hair, my body, my face, no matter how public the place. He never closes his door against me, he cannot stand it when I shut him out. It destroys him, I am so cruel. I have vast, absolute power over him. He can't help it if he gets angry with me—sometimes I really make him furious.

Dazzled by the intensity of Joe's attention, afraid of his anger, oblivious to his belittling, I sit as if mesmerized, when I should try to escape while there is still time. If I sense some of his faults, I give no sign while he circles around me, praising, entreating, bullying. I shrink when he talks about marrying me as a matter of course, but I believe I have no real choice in the matter. Perhaps Joe will grow tired, lose interest, go away. All I can do is wait.

Deep down I know that I do not deserve any better. My dreams become repetitious, insistent, terrifying, but I pay no attention to them. The drunken soldiers kick over the half-filled bowl of milk for which I have had to beg. Who do I think I am? I should have known I am not worth feeding. The soldiers force an amber pin from my hand while I frantically try to remember the right words to recite in a foreign language. Angry soldiers seize my father and prod him with their guns while he walks alone, terrified but trying to appear brave. I wake with tears streaking my cheeks and determined not to hurt Joe any more by my remoteness and coldness. It would be terrible if Joe were as powerless as my father was, it would all be my fault. It never occurs to me that Joe's situation is in no way parallel to my father's. It is beyond me to consider that I may be the one who has been seized.

Resolutely I try to concentrate on Joe's good points. He is, I believe, a real American. He has a lot of experience. If there is another war, he will get me on the last ship, the last train, the last plane to safety. As long as he is with me, I will not have to stand meekly in line. He will take care of me. He is pulling me forward, towards life, not death, as my mother had.

Meanwhile, I can at least try to be nice to him and not hurt him or make him angry. I know how to be very quiet. Perhaps he will still go away. All I can do is wait. I compose my face into a smile.

·17·

This Jagged Break

On a cold rainy morning the day after Thanksgiving, I do not want to get out of bed because I dread having my mother finally meet Joe. He had arrived unexpectedly last night, after she had already left for work, insisting on the introduction I have repeatedly postponed. He'd slept on the living-room couch.

Beate tiptoes in and hands me a cup of tea. "It's Joe," she whispers urgently. "He's really upset. He says he's going to wake Mama and have it out with her."

"He what?"

"Have it out with her, give her a piece of his mind, tell her you're going to marry him, I don't know what all else. He sounds pretty upset. I got him to promise he wouldn't do anything until he talked to you."

I find Joe fully dressed, pacing back and forth, flicking ashes carelessly in the direction of the already overfilled ashtray.

"I'm going to have a little talk with her," he announces as soon as he sees me. "Who the fuck does she think she is? If she thinks she can scare me, she's got another think coming."

"Shhh, Joe, be quiet. She's tired. She worked late last night."

"I don't care what she did. I'll tell her about us, if you won't. She can't pull that superior foreign aristocrat shit on me."

"What are you talking about? You haven't even met her yet."

"Met her? Thanks but no thanks. I don't want to meet her, the fucking Dragon Lady, she isn't even human. I'm going to put her in her place."

But he makes no move to get past me. "Look, do you have any beer?" he asks instead.

"Beer? No."

"Jesus H. Christ, no beer? No turkey for Thanksgiving, and now no beer. And that bitch driving me to drink."

"Please, Joe, don't call my mother that. Just tell me what happened."

"All right," he sighs. "It was weird. She's batty, if you must know. I was minding my own business, sleeping, when I heard something. I sat up, wondering what the hell! It was four o'clock in the goddamn morning. I could see the clock, the room was full of moonlight. And there she was, like a ghost or fury or something. She was wearing a long white gown, her hair hanging down, like a crazy woman. Scared the piss out of me. She was standing by that door, just like you, staring at me."

"Are you sure? Maybe you were dreaming."

"Sure? Is the Pope a Catholic? Of course I'm sure."

"Well, did she speak to you? What did she say?"

"'Hiya,' I said, 'pleased to meet you.' I put out my hand, real polite-like. But of course she wouldn't say anything. She didn't even move, she just stood there, staring at me."

"She must have . . ."

"There you go again, defending her. That's really one of your problems. Wait until I finish. She just kept staring at me. 'Hiya,' I said again, trying to be pleasant. You know, you must be so and so, but she just smirked. 'Well, pleased to meet you,' I repeated. I started getting up, but I couldn't; all my clothes were over on the chair. Holy Mary, Jesus and Joseph, she sure knows how to humiliate a guy, she knew good and well I didn't have a goddamn thing on. Bitch."

"Joe."

"Anyway, she didn't even have the decency to turn her back. Just stood there, while I had to sit here bare-ass naked, as she damn well knew. It must have been an hour."

"Didn't she say anything at all?"

"Oh yeah, finally she did. After she'd been there forever and a day, she came towards me, loomed over me, didn't even try to be polite. You'd think she'd have some manners, but not her. You'd think she'd apologize or something."

"What did she say?"

"She said, 'Get out. I won't let you have my daughter!' Just like that. And then she said it again, as if I couldn't hear her the first time. 'Get out! I won't let you have my daughter, she's *my* daughter!' And she just glared at me. I've never been so insulted in my life."

"Oh, Joe, I'm sorry . . ." I am blushing with embarrassment for my mother, but another emotion stirs somewhere, jubilation perhaps, too faint to reveal to Joe, too faint for me to note it properly myself. My mother does not want to hand me over to Joe. Maybe my mother loves me, after all. My mother will protect me, she will save me from Joe without my having to hurt him.

"So I'm going to tell her off," Joe says, but he remains sitting. "Well, it's either that or I have to leave. I can't stay here as if nothing had happened, after all the shit she's put me through."

"Yes, yes, you better leave, that would be best, really."

"Well, what can you expect from a bunch of fucking foreigners, huh?" Joe laughs, and I laugh weakly with him. "I better get my stuff together."

Relieved, I start helping him. I hand him his cowboy boots and start folding the crumpled sheets.

"Yep, I can't wait to blow this dump. Go get your coat."

"But . . ."

"Look, you're going to have to grow up one of these days, you're nothing but a spoiled brat. You've never had to deal with anything tough, that's really one of your problems. If you'd been through some of the shit I have, you'd at least have some sense. You can't have it both ways. It's either me or her."

"I'm not ready to go, I'm not even dressed."

"Well, get your ass in gear, go get dressed. I need a drink."

"No."

"Hey, I'm not going to stick around forever. You can either come with the man who loves you or stay with that bitch in there. Don't imagine anyone else would ever put up with all your shit either. And there are plenty of women who'd give their left tit to be with me, unlike you."

"I can't just leave her like that."

"Hell, I knew it! I *knew* you'd pull something like this on me. After all I've done for you. What the hell has she ever done for you? Don't imagine she gives a flying fuck about you, she doesn't."

"She does," I say, though I am far from certain. "You just don't understand why she . . ."

"Yeah, yeah, don't start that song and dance about all she's been through, I'm sick of hearing it. Everybody had a lousy childhood, I sure did. Jesus, all my parents did was fight. My old lady didn't give a shit about me, all she did was whine about how hard it was for her if my old man so much as had a beer. Frankly, I'd give anything to have had a childhood like yours. Compared with most people, you were pretty damn lucky. But you never appreciate a goddamn thing. Now, once and for all, are you coming with me or not?"

It takes all my strength to say it.

"No."

He stares at me in disbelief, so I add, "I'm sorry, Joe."

"So you should be, after the way you've been leading me on. I bust my balls trying to please you . . ."

No matter how afraid of his anger I am, I must, I will endure it.

But suddenly Joe's shoulders slump, his eyes mist over, he seems ready to cry.

"That's the fucking story of my whole fucking life. Nobody ever treats me right, no matter how hard I try. I thought at least you'd act different, I really did. My mother couldn't wait until I was old enough to go to school, 'Gimme a break,' she'd say and put me out on the sidewalk to play, no matter how cold it was. And that bitch Elaine, she only married me so I'd have to support her for the rest of my life. She went running back to her mother every time I'd so much as raise my voice, it was pretty damn humiliating. But honestly, I really tried with you. I really did. I don't know what I've done to deserve your treating me like dirt too."

I have seen a photograph of Joe at six, a serious little boy, standing stiffly, holding tight onto the railing in front of a rundown house. I have imagined him bravely making himself walk down the steps and face the hoarse shouts and attacks of the bigger boys.

Joe wipes his eyes, looks at me, squares his shoulders. The gesture pierces me to the heart. He must be as hurt and frightened as my father was when the Russian soldiers were coming into Lobethal. I must not hurt him further.

"You know I can't live without you, and you're the one who got me into this state. I don't know how I'll manage," Joe whispers, "I'm crazy about you."

I hold out a moment longer.

"I guess I'll be alone for the rest of my life," Joe says bravely and makes a slight movement towards the door. He needs my love and protection so much. Who do I think I am to withhold it so selfishly?

I reach out to comfort him, but he shrugs away from me.

"Don't," he whispers fiercely. "You sure know how to hurt a guy. You're making me cry."

I cannot bear to see him cry. I am completely overcome with pity. "Don't, Joe, please don't. I'll . . . I'll go . . ."

"Good," Joe says, "I knew you'd come to your senses. Go find that coat. Let's get out of this dump."

Three months later Joe and I are walking towards the house on Park Avenue again. I stop, unwilling to go further, but he half coaxes me, half pulls me along.

"Come on, let's get this over with. I haven't got all day," he says.

"I can't."

"Crybaby."

"I don't want to."

But I know I must. I cannot hide being married to Joe from my parents forever. Just let them be all right, I repeat to myself. Please let this not be too hard for them, please let them get through this somehow. Yet another blow for my mother and father, and I the one to strike it.

"What's the matter with you?" Joe jerks on my arm. He is angry, he is getting pretty damn sick of my passivity. I must do what he says.

"Nothing. I'm coming."

He is on the porch already, pounding on the door.

Ōmite peers through the pane, shakes her head and steps back. Joe jerks me forward and knocks again.

"Think they'll offer us a drink? Shit, I could use one, having to stand out here until they get good and ready. What's the matter with them anyway, don't they know it's colder than a witch's tit out here? Why do they have to act like such jerks?"

"Ōmīte didn't recognize you," I say and step forward to tap lightly on the door myself.

"I bet. I bet she was just *pretending* not to recognize me. She knew me all right. They've already made up their minds not to like me, just because I'm an American. And that fucking mother of yours, God knows what she'll say. I bet she'll throw a goddamn fit, no matter what I do."

"Oh . . ."

"Come on, admit it, they won't like me, no matter how hard I try. I try and try to please everyone, but nobody likes me, I can tell."

Suddenly he looks pathetically young and scared. He needs all my loyalty.

"There, there." I stroke the small of his back. It is my responsibility to keep him from being hurt. "They'll like you, of course they will," I reassure him. "Anyway, they probably will. After a while." But I know they won't.

"Prejudice," he says. "I've suffered from it all my life. But quite frankly I didn't think I'd have to put up with it in my own family, from my wife's goddamn parents, of all people."

"I'm sorry." I continue stroking his back.

He kicks the door with his black cowboy boot.

"Never mind," he says harshly. "You've never had it rough. My parents never gave me a penny after I turned sixteen. I've had to get every fucking thing myself ever since. But you, with all your scholarships handed to you on a silver platter, you imagine telling your old lady you're married is such a big deal. A real woman would be pleased, but not you. Boo hoo."

I see that he is angry again, and I accept it as my fault. If Joe's being an American were the issue, I too could be energized by indignation. But I cannot hope to explain my mother's absolute contempt for Joe without hurting him further. I remain silent, stroking his back, vowing to protect him.

Joe and I are sitting side by side on the living-room couch, waiting for my mother to come home from LaRue's. My father is in his study with the door ajar. He hasn't cried since I was seven, but he cried when I told him I was married to Joe.

"How could you do this to us?" he calls out. "What will people say?"

I have no answers.

My father gets many calls every evening from people needing help finding jobs, settling disputes, wanting to get married, and tonight is no different. While he talks on the phone his voice sounds normal, even cheerful, and I feel the weight on my chest shift just a tiny bit. He is all right; at least I haven't hurt him so much that he cannot speak. After each conversation, he calls out more unanswerable questions.

"What the hell is he saying?" Joe whispers. "I can't stand that mumbo jumbo. Why the hell doesn't he speak English? Doesn't he see that I'm here?"

"He wants to know how I could do this terrible thing to them."

"Terrible thing? What terrible thing?" Joe whispers more loudly. "There isn't anything terrible. We're in love, we're married, that's all. It's not terrible, it's pretty damn romantic. A normal person would be happy."

He starts to stand up. "I'm going to tell him he's acting like a real jerk."

"Please," I whisper, "please, don't say anything. Let's talk about it later."

"And another thing," Joe continues, settling back, "he's not upset at all. All he cares about is what other people will say. He doesn't care about us, he doesn't care about you. I'm the only one who gives a flying fuck about you. You know that, don't you?"

I nod. For the few seconds while I contemplate Joe's version, the weight of my guilt lifts.

"Well, why don't you act like it then? I can't stand seeing you put on that long face. Come on, act cheerful at least."

I compose my features and smile at Joe.

"When's your old lady coming home?" he asks.

"My mother," I correct him automatically.

"La-di-da, your mother then. When is she going to show up? Or are we going to have to wait here forever? Isn't he going to offer us a drink or something to celebrate? It's the least goddamn thing he could do."

"Please, Joe," I whisper, "don't upset him more. Just wait till my mother comes home, we'll go after that."

"All right," Joe agrees reluctantly, "but any halfway civilized person . . ."

I am listening to the slow scraping of my mother's key in the door, the reluctant lifting of the latch, the exhausted sigh of the hinges when it finally opens.

My mother's eyes flick sideways to register but not acknowledge Joe. She faces me.

"What have you done?" she asks.

"I . . ."

"You must have done something. What is it?"

Joe steps in front of me.

"We're married," he says triumphantly. "I married her."

Ready for congratulations or a concession of defeat, he extends his hand.

My mother stands still, inspecting him as contemptuously as she does the strangers who beat on the door at night.

"She is married to me," Joe enunciates loudly in slow motion. "So there."

She scans my face for confirmation. I nod.

She lets fall the groceries she holds, glass shatters as the bag hits the floor. Then she screams. It is a long, piercing, pain-filled cry, which seems to go on forever. It is engraved on my heart.

"Holy Mary, mother fucking . . . ," Joe starts to say.

My mother swings her heavy black purse at Joe's eyes. Her aim is forceful and accurate and her purse has metal embossed corners, but he is too quick. He raises his arm and jumps aside, so that the powerful blow grazes his elbow instead.

"Holy mother . . . ," Joe repeats, outrage mingled with fear.

She cries out a second time and lunges at him. Her face is filled with fury, her hands are on his arm, she is ready to sink her teeth into him, to gash his flesh even through the heavy protective layer of cloth.

But she is pulled away. My father and Ōmīte, brought to the living room by her screams, encircle her. She struggles silently for a few seconds, then subsides. The brief powerful flash of triumph that I felt as my mother attacked Joe, strange and unacknowledged, subsides as well. I see my mother's defeat, and my own.

"Let me go," she says in a dead authoritative voice, and they do. Cradling his arm against his body, Joe steps back. He rubs his elbow vigorously.

"Holy mother," he says again. Then he too pulls himself together. He cups his hand around his mouth and turns to me.

"Crazy foreign bitch," he says, as if no one but me could understand him. "She almost broke my fucking arm."

He takes a threatening half-step towards her.

Shame over my mother's outburst floods me, but my guilt is much stronger. I have stood still instead of fighting on her side as I did in the basement in Lobethal. Then my mother's fury was roused on behalf of a stranger, directed at the Russian soldier holding the old woman's teeth. Now she has tried to save me and failed. I do not acknowledge the possibility that her rage might spring from love.

"Agate, how could you do this terrible thing against me?" she asks in Latvian. She gives me no opening to express loyalty to her.

I cannot justify myself. I keep my eyes on the pattern of my mother's shabby cotton dress. The purple irises are faded to a dull gray on her shoulders and breasts, but still dark and rich in the folds of the skirt. I study the flowers, try to memorize them. I feel Joe move towards the door behind me.

She draws a deep breath and rises high above her mother and husband, who are supporting her by the arms.

"He isn't any good," she says about Joe, "he's not a real American. He's the worst America has to offer. Hostile, manipulative, crude. He's not nearly intelligent enough for you. And you're from a much better family. He'll never understand our history. He's too limited to value you." Her lips curl in brief contempt at Joe, then she turns to me.

"You won't be happy with him."

"I know."

"And what kind of wedding did you have? What kind of wedding could you have?" A fierce tenderness crosses her face. "I would have helped you bathe and dress, I would have made you a white dress, silk or linen. I would have bought you a new slip, of satin, trimmed with lace, or embroidered with roses. Your sister and grandmother and I would have gone with you."

Her voice catches. Tears start to my eyes. No matter what, I think, I must not, *must not* cry. If I do, it will be harder for my mother, even harder for myself.

"What kind of wedding did you have?" she repeats.

I do not answer. I met Joe downstairs in my dormitory a half hour before we were due at the courthouse. I was wearing my good black wool dress, scratchy against my collarbone, the skirt cut so straight I could hardly walk. I had to lean on Joe's arm.

"Have I got a treat for you!" Joe said. He led me to the black Cadillac that he had thought important to rent for the afternoon and opened the door. "Pretty romantic, isn't it? Something to tell the kids."

"I would have made it a beautiful day for you, even if you were marrying him," she says, "so that at least you'd have one lovely memory. We would have all been together."

She studies my face. "Who was with you?"

I shake my head. I want to say, "Nobody," but that isn't really true. Joe had called an old army buddy. He and his wife drove from Fort Wayne and arrived at the courthouse a few minutes before the forty-five second ceremony. I had not met them earlier and had not been able to think of anything to say to them at the Van Orman Hotel, where Joe had bought a round of drinks for everyone in the bar. Several people shook my hand and congratulated me; one or two strangers kissed me on the cheek.

"You should not have married him. Now you won't finish your education. If you graduated from the university that would have made up for at least a few things I've been through."

I have denied my mother the one gift that would have meant something.

"You will suffer daily, living with him," she says harshly.

It is part prophecy, part curse.

"I know," I say. "Please forgive me." The words seem to tear my throat. But at least we are speaking in Latvian so that this exchange does not hurt Joe.

If it would do any good, I would kneel in front of my mother and beg until I was forgiven and embraced. I would tell her about the plans I have made to continue school, to work full time, to face anyone's, even Joe's opposition. I will get my education, no matter what.

But it is pointless. Like a bone long weakened by imperfectly healed injuries, something finally breaks violently clear through. This jagged fracture will not heal.

My mother's black purse, the clasp open, dangles awkwardly from her hand. She makes no move to pick up its contents mingled with glass from a broken jar: keys, change, notebook and pens—meaningless possessions.

"Please forgive me," I say again as Joe yanks on my arm.

"Come on, let's get out of here. I've had about all I can take."

A flicker of contempt crosses her face again, but it is followed by a look of such resigned defeat that I, unable to stand it, say, "Yes, let's go."

"You better go," my mother says. "You've chosen between me and him, you've abandoned the Latvians for the Americans, go on, go with him."

When I hesitate, she adds, "You've made yourself a hard and narrow bed. You better go sleep in it now."

"Come on, let's hit the road," Joe says. He grasps me firmly by the elbow and steers me towards the door.

My mother draws her arms around herself and begins rocking back and forth silently. She lifts her eyes past me, towards the horizon, or where the horizon would be if only she could see it.

I put one foot in front of the other and follow in the path made by Joe's cowboy boots. I am leaving my mother, I am a guilty exile from the community of Latvians, I have abandoned Latvia itself.

When I am almost to the car, Ōmīte, using the affectionate diminutive, calls to me. "Agatiņa, wait a minute, precious. Come back here."

I stop. If I wait, this too will soon be over.

"Take this, precious," Ōmīte says. She holds out a bundle towards me.

I let her put it in my hands.

"Those are the new sheets that Jaša and Zenta sent me for my birthday, so that at least you'll have something new and nice. I haven't used them yet."

"I couldn't accept those," I say automatically.

"Take them, precious, you need them more than me. And I put in two of the new towels, they're still very good. And the blue bowl, we can get along without it."

"Thank you," I say.

Ōmīte reaches in her apron pocket and takes out her small red coin purse. "Take this too," she says.

"I won't. That's all your money." I know that there are probably five or so dollar bills in there as well as some loose change, money sent to Ōmīte occasionally by her sons. It is Ōmīte's fund for presents and small treats.

"Go on," Ōmīte urges, "you'll need it. It's a hard way for you to start out, alone in a strange land, precious."

I accept the coin purse, which is warm from her hand. I am shivering. My legs are blue and mottled from the cold. I have forgotten to put on stockings, and some loose threads from the hem of my coarse wool skirt dangle unpleasantly against my bare calves.

"Thank you, Ōmīte," I say.

Ōmīte dabs at her eyes, which are surrounded by hundreds of fine lines. She uses a white cambric handkerchief embroidered with violets.

"Thank you," I repeat. I myself believe I will never cry again.

"I wish you a lucky journey," Ōmīte says. She makes a motion to button my coat, but I am already starting down the path.

By the car I glance back at the house. Ōmīte is still standing on the steps, following me with her eyes. My father's dark shape is outlined in the doorway, but my mother is not there. She is probably in her room, reading or pretending to read, I think as I get into the car with Joe.

Inside, my mother turns my high school graduation photo face down on the board over the double sink. Then she thinks of something else. She searches for a pair of tweezers, pulls the picture from the frame and systematically tears it in a dozen small pieces. She pushes the empty frame behind the library books piled on the double sink.

She takes off her shoes, gets into bed and picks up her book, but she does not look at it. Her eyes are on the dark horizon, far away from the house.

"Jesus fucking Christ," Joe says, "I need a drink. A double." He pulls into a parking space in front of the Stardust Lounge. "Coming?"

I meekly follow him.

"Well," says Joe, "I've never been so insulted in my life. What the hell is the matter with them anyway? All we did was get married, for chrissake. What if you'd done something really terrible?"

"I did."

"Oh, there you go, talking crazy again. What's a little thing like getting married? A normal woman would be grateful to me. If they hadn't acted so shitty about it, we'd have asked them to the wedding. Quite frankly, it's their own goddamn fault. And anyway, I'm crazy about you, you're crazy about me, we're crazy about each other, so what the hell does it matter?"

I want to believe him; it would be so much easier if he were right. Perhaps he can help me salvage something positive.

"Maybe if Beate marries Uldis," I begin. Beate has recently gotten her B.A. in political science from Indiana University, and she is seeing Uldis, a Latvian, a man my parents like.

"There, see how shitty your old lady is? I bet your parents will spend big bucks on her wedding, but they won't give you a dime. Injustice—I've suffered from it all my life."

"They don't have any money. I just meant my mother will have something . . ."

"All right, all right, I'm willing to overlook it this time. Come on, we're crazy about each other, aren't we?" He grasps my knee and squeezes it. "Answer me for once, why don't you?"

His hold on my knee tightens.

"Yes," I say.

"Then act as if you meant it. The least you can do is try to act cheerful."

I smile, and he lets go of my knee.

"Actually," Joe says, "it was very funny. Your old man pretending he was so upset, then going to the phone and yammering away in Latvian, your old lady heaving that purse at me, shit flying all over the room. It's a good thing I'm so damn quick on my feet. What a bunch," he laughs, "overdramatizing everything."

"My mother was heartbroken. My father too. I won't be able to go back there again."

"Don't start that song and dance again. You're just like them, you like to make a big tragedy out of nothing. Can't you ever see that something is funny, can't you at least laugh once in a while?"

I show him a fixed smile. I would like to believe that Joe is right, that what happened is a little thing, that it is in fact funny.

Joe studies me. "That's really one of your problems—you don't have a sense of humor. Now take me, I've been through so much shit today, including what you've put me through, but I can still laugh. My arm is practically broken, I don't know if I'll ever be able to use it again, but I have a sense of humor about it. Come on, laugh, why don't you? It was funny."

He takes a gulp from his second drink. "There we were, doing every goddamn thing just for them, going out of our way to see them and tell them that we're married, but did they appreciate it? No way. They couldn't wait to have their big tragic scene. I was just waiting for them to start going on about your childhood in war-torn Europe. That's about the only thing they didn't say. Boo hoo."

The bartender, tired of polishing glasses at the empty bar, comes and stands in front of Joe.

"What's that I hear? You folks get married?"

"Yeah, that's right, a couple of days ago. Finally went to tell her goddamn parents. Foreigners, not Americans like you and me, buddy. You can't imagine; I've never seen anything like it."

"Please, Joe." I tug on his sleeve. I do not want a total stranger to laugh about my mother.

But Joe ignores me. As he tells it, it does sound almost like a stage farce. Not exactly funny, I think, but predictable and almost bearable. Maybe he is right.

"Well," says the bartender, "it's funny, all right. Makes me think of that other play, though."

"Which one?"

"Can't think of the name of it, it's from the olden time. My wife dragged me to it."

"What's it about?"

"Oh, it's got these two kids in it who are crazy about each other, but their parents don't want them to get married. Lots of sword fighting and stuff."

"Yeah." Joe is suddenly serious. "Listen to what this man is saying, Agate, it's pretty damn profound. Romeo and Juliet, he thinks we're Romeo and Juliet."

He turns back to the bartender again. "That's pretty damn good, buddy, that's exactly right. Her goddamn mother just about killed me. Here, let me buy you a drink now."

He does and takes another himself. I wait till he is almost ready for the next one.

"Joe, I want to go home. I've got a test tomorrow."

"Jesus, you and your studying."

But Joe does not argue or order another; the bartender has put him in a good mood.

He opens the door for me, settles me into the car.

"From now on, it's just you and me, kiddo. Just like the man says. You saw how they treated you, like dirt. They don't love you. But don't you worry, I'll take care of you."

"Thank you." I smile at him. He is all I have.

Joe is whistling to himself when he gets in on the other side.

"Yep, you better thank me for all the shit I put up with, just for you. Geez, I'm nuts about you."

He reaches over and locks my door. He holds me, rearranges my hair, nibbles my ear. "Isn't this nice? I can tell you're glad we're finally married."

I hear his words but am too exhausted by guilt and remorse to answer. And I have nothing to say. I feel like a plant torn from the soil.

Joe starts driving. "Nothing can separate us now. And hey, how about that bartender? Wasn't that good? Like fucking Romeo and Juliet."

Part IV

◆◆◆

·18·

"Blow, Wind, Blow My Boat . . ."

Twenty-one years later, I am weeding my mother's flowerbed, work that is beginning to be too hard for her. The creeping charley, dandelions and crabgrass do not yield easily, the ground is dry and caked, but the chore is satisfying nevertheless. Sometimes I daydream about working as a gardener rather than as a professor, but I like much of my academic work, teaching twentieth-century literature and women's studies at the University of Wisconsin-Whitewater.

I straighten, push aside my hair, look at the sun. It must be after four, almost time to quit, to go into my parents' comfortable apartment in a safe neighborhood, where they moved after Ōmīte died, and perhaps close my eyes for a few minutes while Latvian folk songs in praise of nature and hard work drift over me. Then I can shower and dress, and accompany my father to a lecture, concert or another of the seemingly endless activities at the new Latvian Community Center on the prosperous far north side of Indianapolis. Or maybe, since Joe is not with me this time, I could visit friends I usually do not get a chance to see. Joe does not like my meeting with other Latvians. He believes we talk in our own language just to exclude him and that they try to arrange romantic assignations for me with former lovers. He suspects them of laughing at him too.

I look at the progress I have made in my mother's flowerbed, wipe my hands on my shirt and try halfheartedly to clean the soil from under my nails. I like gardening without gloves, feeling the warm moist earth in my hands. I even like the slightly acrid smell of my own sweat mingled with dust and the gritty feel of soil on the inside of wrist and elbow, before washing and then starting work on something else.

I examine my hands critically. It is striking how similar they are becoming to my mother's. The skin is flat and collapsed and marred by small scars and age spots. But my palms are smooth and hard. My hands are capable and strong, a gardener's hands, not a professor's. They do not hint at my inner conflicts, hesitations, weaknesses.

I feel a sense of accomplishment as I regard my mother's rose-colored cosmos, purple asters and burgundy chrysanthemums. No longer choked by weeds, they look more vivid, but I myself could do with a rest. I imagine cool water sliding through my hair and down my shoulders. No, I tell myself, I must not quit before I have finished. I can be done in less than an hour if I just keep working.

This habit of work, which is by now natural to me, has stood me in good stead. I finished course after course, won scholarships, graduated with highest honors, went on to receive a Phi Beta Kappa key, a fellowship and my M.A. from Indiana University as well. While teaching mostly full time, I completed my Ph.D. in twentieth-century English and American literature at the University of Wisconsin in Madison.

Finishing every step gave me a sense of accomplishment and control, which I did not expect to find in my marriage. I forbade myself to think about the romantic dreams I had as a young girl, but concentrated on other sources of satisfaction. I was able to provide a secure and comfortable home for my son, Boris, who is now ready to go off to college. I liked teaching, and I was respected by my colleagues.

Where did I get the energy to keep going? My sister, who had married Uldis and moved to Texas, was separated from me. Although she had been very supportive immediately after I married, we saw each other seldom, and spoke on the phone irregularly. My father came to see me a few weeks after I married Joe. He forgave me and reestablished regular contact, but my mother did not. Without my father's and sister's love, my life would have been bleak indeed.

Fortunately, like Ōmīte before me, I was always blessed with women friends, who gave me a lot of affection and comfort. As I moved increasingly into American society, I made friends with several wonderful American women. There was also the heady excitement of discovering feminism, reading women writers for the first time, working on women's issues in the profession, connecting with colleagues who shared my interests. Developing courses and a program in women's studies at the University of Wisconsin-Whitewater gave my academic activities focus and meaning. My passion went into my son, my work, my students, my friends and colleagues, my garden and women's issues, and I received a lot of positive energy in return.

Pride kept me from admitting unhappiness in my marriage even to close friends. In fact I made every effort to pretend the opposite, just as I struggled to hide my sleeplessness, anxiety, depressions and suicidal thoughts.

Although I was unable to talk about my wartime experiences, stories of others helped me immensely. Sometimes I think it was primarily the stories that saved me from suicide, because they gave me a harmless way to *try* to exorcise the past. In retrospect, I taught a disproportionately high number of novels about war and its aftermath to my undergraduates, which I justified on various theoretical and critical grounds.

More than any other book, my students hated *The Painted Bird*. They called it "too depressing," "ugly," "completely gross." They blamed the six-year-old boy, who during the war is separated from his parents and denied all adult protection, for being abused and brutalized. They offered irrational suggestions as to how he could have remained safe: he should have practiced "better communication," "developed greater self-esteem," "given up co-dependency," "taken charge of his life." They shouted angrily that the boy should have tried harder—he should have gone to a different village, avoided all human beings, burrowed into the ground and stayed there.

Patiently I led my students through the text, helping them search for evidence for their assertions, until the unfairness of blaming the boy became obvious even to the most hostile. They turned their anger from character to writer then. They accused Kosinski of lying, exaggerating, complaining. They suspected him of making millions from the war. The war was such a long time ago, why keep talking about it, they asked. They were angry with me for assigning the book.

It mattered terribly to me that they understand the boy's experience. I did not say that I myself had been in Europe during the war, but my voice trembled and tears rose to my eyes each time I read aloud the final passage in which the boy, mute because of the horrors he has undergone, finally feels an overwhelming desire to speak and words rise to his lips "heavy with meaning."

I became fascinated with Jerzy Kosinski himself. How did he learn to transform his experiences into fiction? I read every one of his novels as soon as it appeared, I regretted bitterly that I had not seen him on a late-night talk show, I kept copies of all his interviews, just to study his face. On my way home from classes I constructed elaborate fantasies about him. I would meet him on a plane, we would talk. I would offer him perfect sympathy, he would understand me the way no one else had. If not exactly his muse, perhaps I could be his subject. He would write a book about a girl and her mother, which he would dedicate to me.

But would he? Kosinski's protagonists attracted and repelled me. I often simplistically equated their attitudes and his. Their sadistic sexual athletics, their casual use of women, their amorality, above all their obsession with revenge chilled me. If I angered Kosinski, he might eliminate me, the way that Tarden cleverly exposed Veronika to radiation without her knowledge. I wished he would.

My fantasies always ended with Kosinski saying, "It wasn't so bad what happened to you. There is just no comparison. I was separated from my mother and father for six years, I lost my entire family in the Holocaust, I was irrevocably changed by war. You better be quiet."

Imprisoned in his own pain, Joe could not bear to hear of anyone else's. "Yeah, you better," he would chime in.

But now, working in my mother's flower garden, I am considering her life and achievements instead of my own. My mother, at seventy, has earned her Ph.D. in comparative literature from Indiana University.

"How would you like it if I called the *Indianapolis Star* and told them? You've achieved so much, in the face of such overwhelming odds. I'm sure they would want to do a story about you."

"No," she says, though I can see she is pleased. "I don't want it in the paper. They would make a big fuss over me being seventy, that's what they would oooh and aaah about. They would not understand what a bitter struggle my whole life has been. Or they would write how 'cute' I am. That would be worse."

"But you could tell the interviewer what is important to you—how you had to leave Russia when you were a girl, and then Latvia too, about living through two wars. About your father and Uncle Žanis believing in education for women, about how hard you had to work in America. But that you graduated as a Phi Beta Kappa nevertheless, and now you even have your Ph.D. in such a difficult field. Those are all amazing achievements."

"They would not want to hear about hardship. They wouldn't understand it. They would say, what was she doing getting a doctorate, a minister's wife at that? Why didn't she help her husband more instead? Why didn't she do more work for the congregation?"

"But you could talk about how you had to wash dishes at LaRue's, about having to work in the cannery, your hands scalded and stinging. And how you learned English by reading Dostoevsky and talking to David . . ."

Her face lights up. "You remember David too?"

"Yes, the busboy. The one who was so crazy about music. He was always telling you about jazz, and you helped him with his German."

"Now *he* is someone who really did well. He got his Ph.D., ten or so years ago. He's on the faculty at the Indiana School of Music, I've seen his name in the catalog. Last spring, the Indianapolis Symphony performed one of his compositions. Isn't that a triumph? Because he was black they didn't even see him when they looked at him. They thought the blacks were just like us immigrants, happy to be working in the kitchens of America, grateful to be allowed to serve the rich, too stupid to do anything else."

"That's wonderful about David. You could write to him, he would be delighted to hear from you."

"No, I'm sure he wants to forget LaRue's too. It was humiliating to work there. He had to hear every day about Negroes and natural rhythm, and they laughed that a black man talked about music theory and wanted to be a professor. Well, each of us had to put up with different things to earn our food. But I wouldn't give anyone from

LaRue's the satisfaction of patting themselves on the back now about giving us those terrible jobs and insultingly low pay."

But we reminisce anyway about LaRue's, Park Avenue, Indiana University. Suddenly she asks me a real question.

"Do you think Beate is all right?"

"Why?" I too have a vague sense that something is wrong because Beate never mentions her husband, Uldis, when we talk. But then I seldom mention Joe.

"I'm worried about her. Beate has so many teaching and committee responsibilities at Texas A&M, she can't find time to get to her Ph.D. dissertation."

I feel a stab of envy in spite of myself. My mother is worried about Beate, but she has never once asked me how I have managed. She has never acknowledged any of my three degrees with the slightest approval, let alone congratulations.

"It's rough, working and writing a dissertation at the same time," I agree. "I hope she can get to it, I hope everything is all right between her and Uldis."

"Yes. I hope that too. I wonder what he does all day long while she's at the university. He's had more than enough time to finish his own dissertation by now."

To my surprise, my mother and I are having something like a real conversation. Maybe it is the first of more to come.

Otherwise my mother has been distant and formal with me, as she usually is. Although I have come to share her opinion of Joe, it has not brought us any closer. The break between us is more final than that; it goes back to the sandy path where I struggled with her, further back even than that, to her own early displacements and losses, to her always looking towards the horizon, away from the house.

Nevertheless, I think, this has been a good visit, much better than last winter. Then her eyes had filled with disappointment when she greeted me. Her expression did not change after she opened the gold embossed box and held up the cream-colored silk blouse, which I had bought because it reminded me of the clothes she used to wear in Latvia. Fervently wishing for some change in our relationship, I had offered it hopefully.

She had glanced indifferently at the heavy silk folded in tissue paper and closed the lid.

"Thank you," she said.

She left the box, as if forgotten, on the floor of the living room for the rest of the visit.

On the plane I started to cry in front of Joe, instead of waiting to be alone. Surprised, Joe said, "Come on, kid, cut that out. Quit dwelling on the past, that's really one of your biggest problems. Admit it, you really loved it over there in war-torn Europe. 'Soldier, soldier, chocolate bar'—I bet you got off on saying it."

When his formula did not make me respond, he said, "Jesus fucking Christ, you really *don't* have a fucking sense of humor. I don't know who else would put up with you. Come on, what you need is a good stiff drink."

We got off the plane during the stopover, but when we tried to return, there was a long line at the security check and hundreds of Christmas travelers ahead of us. Joe took me firmly by the elbow and steered me forward.

"My wife just got out of an institution," he stage-whispered for everyone to hear. We got back on the plane in time, retrieved our coats and possessions, settled down into the sad half-light of the late winter afternoon. We did not say anything to each other.

I was angry with him and ashamed of myself for allowing him to maneuver me like that, but at the same time I still felt cared for. I repeated my own shopworn formula that if another war came, Joe would always get Boris and me onto the last boat or last plane leaving for safety. Joe would never leave me, as everyone else always had. So how could I leave him?

I put the incident aside, just as I had hundreds of others. I learned not to notice. If, for strangers, he turned into jokes the few stories I had mistakenly told him early in our marriage, I turned aside and looked away. When at parties he called on everyone to pay attention, then squatted, crossed his arms and kicked out his legs vigorously in imitation of the Russian soldiers doing *kazačok*, I walked into another room before I could hear him explaining that I had loved sexing up the Russians. I avoided every reference to the past. When Joe got into bed groaning with exhaustion and smelling of scotch, I kept my eyes firmly shut and pretended to be asleep.

◆ ◆ ◆

I believe that nothing will ever change, yet change is in the making all around me. Within me too, but so faintly I have not noticed yet. All I know is that the words between my mother and me seem more significant. Do I sense that this is the last visit unclouded by her illness? She will die a year later. Is that why events seem to carry clues and hints and why I feel such urgency to talk to her now, more than twenty years after marrying Joe? Or is the gray film, which has smudged everything since I was seven, finally too much even for me? Am I at last tired of meekly waiting for my life to end?

This Sunday afternoon in late summer, I accompany my parents to Mr. Bērziņš's ninetieth birthday celebration. Several women in the Latvian community have reached this ripe old age, but hardly any of the men. Like most milestones, this is celebrated publicly, with representatives of all the Latvian organizations arriving with roses, speeches, cognac, wine. Friends come throughout the evening to eat, talk, sing. It is unusual for me to participate or to feel I belong if I do. Since the break with my mother I have lived outside of Latvian communities and I miss speaking in Latvian, my mother tongue. My marriage has exiled me in all the ways I predicted and more.

The Bērziņšes' spacious house is in a wealthy suburb of Indianapolis. It is filled with fine furniture, delicate china and Latvian woodcarvings, ceramics, embroidery. No one would think that thirty years earlier its inhabitants had been refugees.

Mr. Bērziņš, a cadaverous old man, almost totally blind, receives the congratulations with a great deal of pleasure and approbation. Raising a glass of wine in a liver-spotted but remarkably firm hand, he offers a toast to his own long and event-filled life. He speaks about fighting in World War I, of seeing the Czar wave from a carriage in Russia, of hearing Hitler address a jubilant crowd in Berlin. Like other Latvians, like the earth of Latvia itself, he has survived both Russian and German oppression, and he is proud of it. Neither Hitler nor Stalin has been able to triumph over him, he says.

When Mr. Bērziņš takes my hand and thanks me for having traveled so far just to help him celebrate his birthday, I start to explain that that was not my purpose in coming to Indianapolis, but I stop because I can see that his version gives him such pleasure. He whispers that he has privileged information that Anastasia was not executed along with the rest of the Czar's family, and that I should tell this to my mother because she grew up in Russia. He says he knows someone who saw Anastasia alive more than ten years after the Revolution, that she was hidden during the Stalin purges, and that someday her real story will be known, as will other stories of the terrible days in the past.

More people are waiting to talk to him, so I get up and look around for another seat. Jānis Kalniņš beckons to me, but I know better than to sit next to him. Although we always joke that we have much in common because we share the same birthdate, I do not have the patience to listen to him. A professor of economics, Jānis is well respected in the Latvian community for his professional achievements, his stable marriage, his large beautiful house that he built with his own hands. Like so many of us, he cannot stop working.

He compulsively collects books about World War II, and he talks more frequently than other Latvians about the 1939 secret codicils to the Molotov-von Ribbentrop pact. This collusion between Hitler and Stalin, between Nazis and Communists, gave Latvia to the Russians in 1940. He hopes to prove someday that the Russian claims to Latvia are false, that Latvians did not welcome the Russians with open arms and that Latvia did not voluntarily join the Soviet Union. Latvia was brutally occupied instead, no matter what propaganda the Soviet Union wants the rest of the world to believe. Jānis cannot stop talking about all this. He has memorized every reference to Latvia in his war books, and if given an opening, he can recite these for hours, complete with page numbers, implying a significance in each that usually escapes the listener.

Now he smiles at me expansively, cups his hands around his mouth and whispers something that I cannot catch. He takes a long contented drink from his glass. He looks perfectly happy, his past and future far away on this festive afternoon. When Jānis was six, and sitting in his father's lap during an air raid, his father was killed. Jānis himself escaped without a scratch. He has told his gentle wife, Lidija, that he cannot understand the point of his being alive, but his remarks do not seem ominous. No one knows that he is planning to kill himself next year, shortly after his forty-third birthday. Because he feels he has to offer some explanation, he will carefully place a note on the dashboard that he has not found life worth living since his beloved dog Pērlīte ("Little Pearl") died. His suicide will shock the Latvian community and diminish the news that I have finally left Joe. Jānis will not live to see the truth emerge about the secret pact and the forcible occupation of the Baltic countries when it is finally, fifty years later, reported as fact in American newspapers.

Not inclined to listen to Jānis's recitation of footnotes and page numbers, I wander into the kitchen in search of Mirdza, to ask her about her dead cousin Anna. Anna died three years ago, killed by her husband, Ivars, who shot himself afterwards. I often think about Anna's daughters. How is the sixteen-year-old who married an old man a few weeks after her parents' funeral? The twelve-year-old to whom Ivars bowed as he raised the pistol to his own temple?

But lately I have begun to feel intensely curious about Anna herself. What happened to her during the war? Did she ever say? Could that be where the explanation lies as to why she gave her already suicidal husband twin pistols as a Christmas present? Did she say, it doesn't matter if you kill me, as I do when I meekly get into the car and let Joe drive, no matter how much he has had to drink? Why couldn't she bring herself to leave?

Mirdza is busy supervising the setting out of desserts and slicing a beautifully decorated mocha and almond torte. On the table in front of her are apple cakes, chocolate tortes, raspberry turnovers and the traditional *kliņģeris*, a saffron cake made with raisins and almonds and shaped like a huge pretzel, which every guest attending has to taste. She is gesturing and smiling, her cheeks flushed with pleasure that there is so much to offer. She waves, but she is too busy to talk, so I wander back into the living room in search of someone else.

The room is filled with the fragrance of roses and wine and rich coffee, it is warm, I have already talked to half a dozen people whom I have not seen for years and I am completely overcome by nostalgia. This emotion usually does not attack me until I am on my way home from Indianapolis. If I am in the car by myself, I let myself cry because my parents seem frailer each time I see them, because I have to leave behind people with whom I feel so at ease yet in whose community I do not belong, because I have no opportunity to speak Latvian or to participate in familiar traditions, because I myself am doing nothing to bring about an independent Latvia and because I feel harshly judged by those who do. But mostly I cry because my mother avoids talking to me whenever possible and because the longed-for reconciliation with her seems unlikely.

If Joe is with me, I turn away and look silently out the window until

I manage to control myself. I wish absurdly to return to Indianapolis to live, to go about as my father does from one Latvian event to another, to spend my weekends teaching Latvian to children, helping to organize the upcoming Song Festival, setting tables and washing dishes at the community center. But then I would intensely miss my American friends, with whom I share my daily life and all my adult professional and political interests. I know I will never fully belong anywhere. I remind myself then that I don't even like washing dishes, and I make myself smile at Joe. So that by the time I arrive home I have put this nostalgia behind me.

But there is no reason not to give in to it now, so I go out to sit on the porch swing next to Laimonis. We were friends when I was in high school.

"Come," Laimonis grins at me, "tell me what the life of a woman professor is like. Is it worse than being a woman doctor? I've heard that professors are even more sexist than doctors, but such behavior would be unbelievable, a caricature really. It sounds impossible to me."

Laimonis himself is a doctor. Much of his practice consists of Latvians who prefer going to him rather than to another doctor with whom they would have to speak in English, even if they speak it fluently.

"And how is that American husband of yours? I bet he would be jealous if he knew we were talking to each other," he says, joking.

I laugh. Laimonis would be surprised at how close he has come to the truth. Joe still reproaches me for a wood carving Laimonis gave me when we parted to go off to different universities. It was of a slender, windblown girl playing the *kokle*, a Latvian zither, which he said was of me. Not wanting to hurt Joe, I compliantly packed it up and returned it the year after I married. It was part of my systematic giving up of photographs, letters, poems, opinions, memories, friends— everything that Joe demanded in the name of love.

"How is your mother?" I ask.

"She's fine. Nagging me to get married again."

"Oh yes? And how many times will that be if you do?"

"Number three."

"And are you going to?"

"I don't know. Who would have me? And anyway, it doesn't seem worth the bother. I'm beginning to think I have no talent for marriage. It takes someone with much firmer character."

Laimonis laughs self-deprecatingly, and I just barely stop myself from comforting him. He is a handsome, solid, even imposing man, but I recognize in him the restless, dramatic boy I knew in high school.

"Anyway, how *is* your mother?" I ask now.

Beautiful, dark-eyed, competent, charming Mrs. Kļava! No wonder Laimonis was obsessed by her. I loved to listen to her talk about the clothes she had worn to the National Opera House in Latvia, the French perfume she had brought back from her trips to Paris, the artists who had kissed her hand. She had questioned me about what I wanted to do—and wear—once I graduated from the university.

"Well, her eyesight is going," Laimonis says. "She's practically blind. All she can see is shadows."

"Oh, I *am* sorry."

"Well, she always had trouble with her eyes, remember?"

"Yes. But I haven't seen her for more than twenty years."

Back then Mrs. Kļava's glossy good looks were only slightly marred by her poor eyesight, which caused her to squint because she refused to be seen wearing glasses. She said she had ruined her eyes by crying too much when her husband died.

Mr. Kļava, a prominent lawyer in Latvia, spent the workweek in Riga and idyllic weekends on their large wooded estate in the country. When the Russians occupied Latvia in 1940, they arrested him and took him into the woods. There they bludgeoned him with clubs and guns and left him for dead. He regained consciousness and crawled back to the house to be taken care of by his young wife. He lived for four days, groaning in agony. Laimonis was five, but he could remember his mother's constant crying and his own ineffectual efforts to comfort her.

In America Mrs. Kļava lived with a man to whom she was not married. The Latvian community equated extramarital sex with criminal behavior, officially anyway, and regarded her as a scandalous woman who had forfeited her right to good society. But they did not judge her lover harshly. After all, so the reasoning went, he could not marry because he had a wife in Latvia from whom he had been separated by the war.

"I miss seeing your mother. She was always so gracious to me."

"Well, she certainly took a great deal of interest in your future. She remembered every detail of your plans and courses. She cried when she heard you'd gotten married before you graduated. You were lost to the Latvians, she said. I only wish she'd paid as much attention to me. Or so says little Oedipus."

This time Laimonis's self-deprecating laugh does not cover the pain, and something else, hostility perhaps.

I lean back into my own corner of the porch swing and hold on to myself. I do not want to be drawn into complicity with Laimonis again. When we were in high school, I used to admire him because he was so talented. He wrote poetry, painted, sculpted, played waltz music on the piano at parties and accompanied the singing of "God Bless Latvia," the national anthem, at the Latvian Center. Gradually I was drawn into sharing Laimonis's fantasies. Sometimes he toyed with ideas for humiliating his mother's lover. But mostly he plotted about going secretly to Latvia and taking revenge on everyone responsible for killing his father. Sometimes he believed his mother did not love him, and I, recognizing a similarity I did not put into words, tried futilely to comfort him. During intermissions of concerts and plays, we would whisper together in Latvian. Studying around the dining-room table on Park Avenue, we would look up simultaneously.

"Hunting knives," Laimonis would say and I would nod, knowing just what he was talking about.

I helped him by offering suggestions when he was stuck for ways to conceal a weapon or evade the customs officials on his imaginary missions of revenge against his father's killers.

"Tell Mrs. Kļava I think about her," I say to distance myself from Laimonis's appeal. "Please give her my regards."

I do not know that five years from now, Mrs. Kļava—frail, suffering from delusions and violent outbursts, and totally blind—will die under suspicious circumstances. Her body will be covered with bruises, as if she had been beaten to death. As Laimonis's father was bludgeoned to death, so will his mother be, one killed during a war, the other in the endless aftermath. Laimonis and his third wife will be briefly suspected.

"All right," Laimonis says, "I'll tell her you're moving onward and upward, unlike me. . . . *Ad astera per aspera*, and *gaudeamus igitur* . . . ," Laimonis mumbles in Latin.

I am glad that my mother's coming out interrupts Laimonis, so that I am saved from further pressure for reassurance.

"Have a drink." Laimonis waves his empty glass affably at my mother, who never drinks. "I'll get it for you," he says, and jumps up to yield his seat to her.

My mother and I swing back and forth silently.

I do not know Laimonis's future, but I have begun thinking about the element of repetition, even duplication, so common in the lives of people who have survived the war. Facing the past will soon change my own future. But repetition is what I am acutely aware of now. Roman Polanski, a survivor of the Holocaust, experienced more carnage when Sharon Tate, his pregnant wife, was brutally murdered by the Manson gang. Recently I read that Polanski's mother was also pregnant when she died in a concentration camp. I cannot put this parallel out of my mind. It lies unassimilated on the edge of my understanding; there is something I must learn from it.

Jerzy Kosinski not only knows how to escape, he is an escape artist. During the war he narrowly escaped death dozens of times. On his way to visit Polanski, he fortuitously escaped again. He was delayed in New York by lost luggage, and so was not murdered along with Sharon Tate and the others. Another repetition. (His suicide, his final action in a life spent trying to exorcise the trauma of war, is far in the future. In 1991, a dozen years from now, a huge fire will rage on the east side of Madison, bringing traffic to a standstill. Alone in my car, unable to move, I will howl then with grief as I listen to the same brief measured announcement of his death again and again and again.)

I had recently learned a few details of my father's childhood. He was seven when World War I started. His earliest memory is of a furious uniformed rider tearing down the village street in Latvia and shouting, "War! War!" He hid under the cellar steps, afraid they would kill him before he could get into the tiny basement where his brothers and sisters were hiding. His mother had died when he was two; his stepmother was already sick. He does not know where his father was, perhaps out searching for food.

My father does not remember the fighting, but he remembers terror, hunger and cold. There was no bread; they ate *stagarus*, tiny fish with many sharp bones, potato peels and leaves. The room was cold, the windows froze shut. All the children huddled under an old coat made of animal skins, which was full of lice. His stepmother died. His father had to beg for food for his starving children, and he hurt his back dragging home a sack of carrots. As soon as he recovered enough to walk, he set off again, for the last time. He died far from home, probably of smallpox. My father does not know where his father is buried.

At the age of seven my father became a homeless orphan. He had been sent to a distant farm to watch cattle in exchange for a sack of potatoes. News of the death of his stepmother and then of his father reached him there. He had nowhere to go. The wife of the farmer wanted to adopt him, but with winter coming on there was not enough food for an additional child. The farmer gave him a pair of shoes and sent him out alone on the road.

My father was a boy in Latvia when he heard a rider cry war. He lost his parents and home, he was separated from his siblings. My mother was a girl in Russia when another man riding furiously announced displacement and loss.

He must have had immense courage because so much was required of him at such an early age. I do not know what wounds were inflicted on him, a seven-year-old orphan, in the aftermath of war. I am afraid to imagine them. Yet he survived.

As a boy my father did hard manual labor: he dug ditches, hauled wood and cleared stones, carried heavy crates of dirt and vegetables for the owner of a greenhouse. He went without sleep and food to study, but he was denied all pleasure: he was even forbidden to attend his own grade-school graduation. He won one of the very few scholarships to the University of Latvia, graduated, went on to get an advanced degree in theology, served actively in several congregations. He fell in love with my mother, married, made a life for himself in independent Latvia.

When my mother was abstracted or sad, he was the one who romped with my sister and me. He recited funny verses and made jokes, which made my mother smile too. He tried to keep a straight face when Beate and I asked him to baptize our dolls, to sign their birth certificates so that we could demand clothing coupons for them from Ōmīte or to marry us to huge wobbly husbands we had made out of brown wrapping paper. He often sat with me when I was sick.

Even after living through yet another war, he kept alive his strong faith in God, his optimism and his compassion. He worked hard to help others.

I would like to talk to my mother about patterns and repetitions, but do not know where to begin. The painful silence between us, its awkwardness so familiar to me, lengthens, until I blurt out, "How were the students in the last Russian class you taught at Marian College?" American students and United States educational policies are safe and neutral subjects. We make small talk about them on the short visits that began three years after my marriage, but which I still find excruciating.

"Fine. And yours in English?" she asks.

"I've got some excellent students this time."

"Are they better prepared in grammar, do you think?" she questions.

"No . . . maybe . . . I doubt it. One of them wrote a paper about her uncle who was a prisoner of war in Vietnam. He and his cellmate were repeatedly tortured. The most terrible thing was that he was forced to watch while his captors cut out his friend's tongue with a straight razor."

She shudders and looks away.

But I am compelled to go on. "And now this uncle, after drifting and drugs and divorces, after doing everything to estrange himself from his family and from everyone who loved him, has killed himself. He cut his wrists, also with a razor."

"What an unsuitable topic for a paper. It is much too horrifying. Much too personal to bring into an academic setting, to discuss anywhere really. American students are so indulged, they are so extraordinarily coddled. Hence they have too little self-discipline, too little sense of the appropriate. I can't imagine handing in such a paper to a professor."

"But it was an excellent paper. I believe she needed to write about it. The element of repetition . . . the same weapon . . . the way that wartime horrors affect even those in the next generation who never went to war . . . I've begun to think about that myself."

"Amazing you should say so. What assignment did you give that allowed her to go off on a tangent like that?"

"It wasn't a tangent really. It was in a class on the contemporary American novel and the students had read *Slaughterhouse Five* and *The Painted Bird* and they started discussing the aftereffects of war, so that—"

"Ah yes, and what other novels are you having them read?"

The conversation skims over sufaces, accumulated reading lists, polite interchanges. A few lines from an Irish folk song, overdramatic yet persistent, reminding me of Vietnam, run monotonously through my head.

You haven't an arm, you haven't a leg,
You'll have to be put in a bowl to beg,
Johnny, I hardly knew you . . .

I try to silence the lines and pay attention to my mother, though I am disappointed once more that I cannot talk with her about things that seem so immediate to me. I would like to tell her that I have been worrying that my own unhappiness has affected Boris, that I deeply regret now that I obeyed Joe and did not teach him Latvian when he was little. But at least my mother and I are speaking to each other.

"Are you enjoying the party?" my father asks. He has come out unobserved for a breath of air.

"Yes," I say. As a matter of fact I am. My expectation that my mother and I would finally reestablish a real connection, and in this one visit, is surely not reasonable. Besides, we have talked much more than usual.

"It's a very nice celebration," I say, and my parents nod.

"Mr. Bērziņš is a wonderful old man," I continue.

"That old man is a bastard," my mother says.

I lean towards her to see if I have heard right. My mother has to be really provoked to use a word like that, and I am even more surprised that my father, who always gives the kindest interpretation of other people's behavior, does not contradict her.

"But Mr. Bērziņš seems so gentle and appreciative. He was so touched by all the presents and honors." I do not want my nostalgic mellow mood ruined, but I can see that it is going to be.

"That's just for public show," my mother says.

"He *is* cruel," my father admits. "He's punished his wife for more than thirty years for something that happened because of the war."

Mr. and Mrs. Bērziņš have moved to Indianapolis from Boston, and I have never met them before. Mrs. Bērziņš, a thin shy woman dressed in black, is at least twenty years younger than her husband. She had quietly taken the roses presented to him, placed them in water, efficiently distributed the crystal vases on sideboards and tables. She unobtrusively guided his hand to the food in front of him. She looked gravely attentive but was always too busy with some task to join the general conversation.

"What does he do to her?" I ask, disbelieving.

"He berates her every hour. He curses her, he pushes her out of his way, he threatens her. He holds her responsible for their seventeen-year-old daughter being left behind in Latvia," my mother says.

During their last summer in Latvia, my mother tells me, Zaiga had been working in a knitting factory, enjoying living in town and being free from school and the hard work on the farm. She was devastated when her parents wanted to leave Latvia, because she had fallen in love. She wanted to see the boy she loved, just one more time. They had walked through the town park together, and he had put his hand on her elbow at every curb and held it there protectively. Even though she did not need his help, his solicitude had thrilled her. By herself she could jump over fences and ditches better than her brothers. He had seemed on the verge of saying something. She had to see him once more to learn what that was, even though it meant going inland, away from the sea.

When her mother objected, Zaiga insisted she tell her father she had gone for her pay as well as sweaters and socks that the manager had promised for the cold winter in Germany. Mrs. Bērziņš, who remembered herself as a young woman, did not strictly forbid her to go.

Zaiga did not return. Her parents and brothers waited till the sound of guns was no longer intermittent but continuous before they started for the seashore. They asked everyone who overtook them, they looked behind them for her, but she never rejoined them.

"You should not have let her go," Mr. Bērziņš had accused his wife. "You are a greedy woman, you sold your daughter to the Communists for a pair of socks and a handful of coins."

Sunk in her own grief and guilt, Mrs. Bērziņš did not reply. When she rallied enough to tell him Zaiga's real reason for going, Mr. Bērziņš laughed bitterly. "Love? You let her go for love? There is no such thing. You let your daughter go so some young hooligan can root under her skirts. She'll be rotting in the ground because of you."

But Zaiga had not died. The boy she loved had gone off at the last moment to join the partisans in the woods and had disappeared forever, but she survived. Almost thirty years after she had last seen them, Zaiga came to visit her parents in 1972. No one could imagine then that the Soviet Union would crumble only twenty years later. Married to a Russian government official and trained as a physician herself, she had been allowed to visit the United States on money her mother had sent her. Her sons spoke Russian better than Latvian, her husband was a member of the Communist Party.

Mrs. Bērziņš had hoped that she and Zaiga would talk as they used to, she had even daydreamed that someday Zaiga might come to the United States to live. But her daughter had no interest in doing so. Because of her husband's nationality and party membership, she did not share with most Latvians the terrible grinding poverty, the lack of adequate food, aspirin, bandages, coffee, clothing, housing. Her sons would have opportunities for education denied to most Latvians. Moreover, she was living in her own country.

A florid, solid woman, Zaiga bore little resemblance to the lithe, romantic girl her parents had lost. She was reserved with her mother. She waited while her father praised life in the United States and cited the advantages of capitalism. When he finished, she enumerated the goals of communism and criticized America for selfishness, consumerism and sexual license. She scolded her parents for giving way to superstition when they attended the Latvian Lutheran services. Her own future was in the Soviet Union, with other workers. Besides, unlike her parents, she was not in exile; she was living close to the family farm, she walked every day on the familiar roads through pinewoods and birches.

Ignoring his wife's sharp disappointment, Mr. Bērziņš blamed her again for letting the Communists brainwash her, for robbing him of his daughter and letting them turn her into a commissar shouting Soviet slogans.

"But why did Mrs. Bērziņš put up with it?" I cry. "Why didn't she tell him it wasn't her fault?"

"Oh, she probably did, but by then he was used to blaming and she to being blamed. And besides, it isn't so bad. When you compare what happened to others . . ."

"But it *is* terrible," I cry, surprisingly not willing to accept the familiar formula. I can recognize now that the lines around Mr. Bērziņš's mouth are set in a bitter grimace, while just a few minutes ago they seemed the marks of a serene old age. I can see Mrs. Bērziņš's defeated hesitancy as she fingers her amber necklace. In the very midst of comfort and celebration, each carries scars of exile and war so many years later. But to see them one has to know how to look.

"It's war that damages people," my mother says. "Who knows what we all put up with because of the past? How many unhappy marriages and other misery?"

Her eyes questioning, my mother looks directly at me.

But this time I withdraw. "Oh no," I say, "the war was such a long time ago."

"Was it?" she says flatly and stands up to go.

"But people are stronger because of what they have survived, aren't they?" I insist. "Anyway, they should be, everyone says so. Once you've survived the war, you should be tougher rather than more vulnerable, nothing else should matter, you should be able to handle anything."

It doesn't come out quite as convincingly as I want it to, it sounds arbitrary and even brutal. It isn't even true, but I continue. "You should forget about the past, you shouldn't continue feeling sorry for yourself, others had it . . ."

But my mother either does not hear or does not want to agree. In any case, I stop because the words I have heard and also unthinkingly repeated hundreds of times finally sound thin and false even to myself.

Other people are beginning to drift out onto the porch from the warm festive rooms, and my parents and I get up to go. Mrs. Bērziņš comes out and warmly thanks us again. Nothing in her dignified, slightly deferential manner reveals her husband's twisted grief and cruelty, her meek acceptance or her mourning for her lost daughter.

Indoors Laimonis is starting to play a folk song with a lot of odd Liberace-like flourishes, but voices are joining in and carrying the tune in spite of the accompaniment. Mirdza looks up and waves at me. Like everyone else in the room, she seems happy. Maybe if Joe lets me come by myself another time, I can ask her about her murdered cousin Anna's daughters. It does not seem the right moment now.

> "Pūt vējiņi, dzen laiviņu,
> Aizdzen mani Kurzemē.
> Kurzemniece man solīja
> Sav meitiņu malējiņ.
> Solīt sola, bet nedeva,
> Teic man lielu dzērājiņ.

Blow, wind, blow my boat,
Blow me back to Kurzeme.
A woman promised to give me
Her daughter who grinds the corn.
She promises, promises,
But then she refuses,
She calls me a drunkard . . ."

This song is almost the unofficial Latvian anthem. Its plaintive melody expresses perfectly the intense longing to return to Kurzeme, the western district of Latvia. It is sung at family celebrations like this one, but also at more formal occasions. At the national Song Festivals, which were held in independent Latvia and continue to be held in the United States, hardly an eye remains dry as thousands of voices join in singing it.

I pause on the steps to listen to the words. I identify with the longing; I too would like to return to a place where I belong. Usually I sympathize with the lover who has been denied the young woman he loves—ah, how painful and romantic his situation seems. But this has been an emotional afternoon; perhaps that is why I now hear it differently.

"What tavern did I drink empty,
What horse did I race to death?
I drink on my own money,
I ride my own horse,
I marry my own wife
Without her parents' permission."

I don't like the man in the song very much, I think suddenly. He is so boastful, so ready to justify himself. He is completely unaware of the pain endured by the mother and daughter who have been separated from each other. The suffering of women is as real as that of men. I have seen both this afternoon. What a foolish debate that was long ago in the old Latvian Center.

Who suffered more in the war, women or men?

All of them. And all children too.

What did the mother from Kurzeme say to the suitor as she tried to drive him away? Did she say, "Get out, I won't let you have my daughter!"? What did she do after she lost her daughter? What song did the daughter sing—alone, among strangers, in a strange land? Did mother and daughter remain apart forever? Were they ever reconciled? There must be such a song, I think. If not, someone should write it.

·19·

Second Escape

Two years later, I am sitting in bed alone. The lamp casts a circle of light on my smooth white cotton sheets and a much-worn rose-colored afghan made by Ōmīte. On the nightstand are piles of books and a handful of letters from Boris, who is away at college. The rest of the house is dark, all the shades drawn, all the doors firmly secured. I am surprised that everything seems so peaceful, when I myself am in such a turmoil of grief and guilt and remorse.

My mother has been dead for more than a year. We did not reach a reconciliation before her death, and except for one wild fit of weeping at a shopping center, I have not cried for her. Two elderly women, strangers to me, held my hand then and patted my shoulder, but I did not tell them what the matter was. I am aware of my mother's death all the time, but I have not been able to put into words my grief, love and hurt.

But tonight I have locked the doors against Joe. He had come home, as usual, after the bar and restaurant he owned closed. Although his heavy tread, the rattle of ice cubes for a final drink and his stumble on the stairs woke me, I lay still, pretending to be asleep, knowing the pattern. He would take a long time emptying his pockets of change, shedding his clothes, asking me where his pajamas were. He would sigh about how hard his day had been, recount the slights and insults he had suffered, then blame me for not sympathizing enough. Finally he would get into bed groaning and turn out the light.

"Another day of my life shot to shit," he would say. Then he would lean over me and ask, "Are you asleep? Come on, I know fucking well you're not. You're just pretending." I would keep my eyes resolutely shut while he studied my face.

Eventually he would turn away, either because he accepted my pretense or because he was not sure it was one. He would rearrange the pillows and pound them a couple of times.

"These fucking pillows," he would say. "You would think that with all the money I make, I could at least have a decent place to sleep. But all you care about is your goddamn family and your fucking students and having your nose in a book." He would shove the pillows around some more. Finally he would stretch out, his breathing would become more regular and he would drift off.

I might get up then and go into my study. More often I fell into uneasy sleep myself. I woke regularly at four each morning, terrified of something I did not put into words, my heart beating hard, my body covered with sweat. I was used to my bad dreams and the attacks of panic that followed them. All I had to do was wait until my breath no longer came in short gasps and my body quit trembling. When I was calm enough to get out of bed without disturbing Joe, I would tiptoe downstairs and work until it got light. During the day I forbade myself to think about the panic I felt at night.

But this time Joe did not go to sleep.

"Jesus fucking Christ," he muttered, his voice gradually rising. "I might as well stay out all night as come home to you. Might as well be drunk all the time, there's never any sex around here anyway. You're a cold bitch, just like your mother. She was always in her room with the goddamn door shut, locking your old man out. What she needed was a good—"

"Please, Joe, go to sleep."

"Christ, don't get your balls in an uproar. You never let me say a damn thing about her, that's really one of your problems. No wonder a man has to go out once in a while." He sighed elaborately, then started again.

"Aren't you listening to me? Say something to me, for chrissakes. Say you're sorry I got all those unsold steaks and expensive liquor sitting in the restaurant. Goddamn environmentalists, goddamn animal rights activists, I bet they'll ruin my business during the summer too. Can't you talk to me for once in your life? What the hell's the matter with you anyway? You're a crazy foreign bitch. Frankly, you've gotten even crazier since your mother died."

He was winding down; he would finish soon.

"I'm sleepy," I said.

"Sleepy? Why the hell are you sleepy now, when I am finally home? That's another one of your problems." In an aggrieved voice he enumerated my other problems before concluding, "You're just feeling sorry for yourself about that mother of yours dying. I'm getting pretty damn sick and tired of it. You don't mope around the university like that. Just because I'm not one of those high-flying phony academics and feminists you respect so much . . ."

I could hear the hurt in his voice. It was all so dreadfully familiar. We had made our way through scenes like this a hundred times in our twenty-two-year-old marriage. I would wait until I sensed that he was ready to quit. Then, filled with pity for his pain, I would reach over, comfort him, tuck him in.

I should do that now. I should put aside the harsh words that had been said, I should try to make the best of everything. He worked so hard to please me. I believed him when he said that he loved me, that no one else would put up with me. He would never leave me, as everyone else always had. He had even tried to stop drinking a couple of times for me, though of course it never lasted.

But if I touched him, nothing would ever change.

"There's plenty of women who would bust their balls to have me in bed," Joe was saying. "Don't think they don't beg me for it either— they do, all the time. Quite frankly, I could get a piece of ass anytime I want to, the bar is full of women just asking for it. But you, you don't give a flying fuck. Poisoned by feminism. And after all I've done for you and your family and your precious son."

Suddenly he yanked at the covers and lunged towards me. I grasped them and pulled them closer so that they would not give, as he fumbled ineffectually for me under the taut sheets. I drew my knees to my chest and clasped them tightly. I dared not make him angrier. If I was very quiet and if I only waited, he would stop. His fury would eventually be spent and he would leave me alone. *I must not, must not cry or speak.*

But he grabbed me harder than he ever had before. His fingers pressed into the soft flesh of my arms as he tried to force apart my hands. When that failed, he straddled me, digging his knee between my legs, trying to straighten my body, prying apart my limbs to get me to unclench and to pin me firmly under him. For an instant I thought I could passively outwait even this. After all, what did it really matter if he raped me? So many women had been raped, it was hardly worth remarking on. If I was very quiet and waited, it would soon be over. If I resisted, he would get even angrier.

He succeeded in pulling apart my clenched arms and started on my legs. I tried to keep them locked, as I had seen Hilda do before she subsided into compliance. Joe succeeded in wedging his knee between my thighs.

At this, anger finally surged in me. Rather than only recoiling, I began to struggle actively against him. I fought silently at first, as if that would make him believe I was not really resisting. I managed to wriggle free of him and then to push him aside. He was much stronger, but his movements were slowed by drink and mine fueled, finally, by fury.

I jumped out of bed and stood trembling. Only by holding onto the oak bureau did I control myself. I wanted to lunge at him, pick up my green ceramic Latvian vase and heave it at him, to smash it over his head, to beat him senseless. My rage shocked me.

My long hair wild about me, my voice rasping, I shouted at him, "Leave me alone. Don't you dare touch me again."

Suddenly I felt exhilarated. I had not known I could speak louder than he did; I had never tried to before. I always stopped talking when he interrupted me.

"You're fucking nuts, just like your old lady," Joe yelled.

I became aware of my own fists knotted hard and my tensed legs under my demure white Victorian nightgown, ready to spring. I was poised to attack; I felt wonderfully powerful.

It made me ecstatic to contradict him. "No, I'm not crazy. I'm not listening to you anymore. I want to live by myself."

He looked as if I had slapped him. His face crumpled, and a short, harsh, painful sob escaped him.

"How can you say that? How can you be so selfish? You used to be crazy about me, remember? We used to be like Romeo and Juliet, remember? No one else was in love as much as we were. You used to adore me. Why did you have to go and wreck it all?"

I stood at the end of the bed, looking down at him.

"Come to bed," he pleaded. "Everybody always treats me like shit. I thought you at least would be different. I work my butt off for you, while that restaurant is doing worse and worse. Christ, you should know, you do the books. The least you could do is to act cheerful and take care of me once in a while. Come on, we wouldn't fight like this if we weren't in love. Admit it."

But fighting had given me energy. I would not be drawn into complicity with him again. I would not surrender my autonomy.

I looked past him, out the window. The bare trees were silvered in the moonlight. It poured over the expanse of lawn, glistened on the few patches of remaining snow. It would be spring soon, but I had been too deadened to notice.

I heard his voice, insistent, wheedling, repetitious. "Come on, I know you love me."

"No," I brought out finally, "I don't."

At these words, immense relief flooded me as the burden of lies I had helped create lifted off my shoulders. Out of guilt, but also out of real feeling, I added, "Please forgive me, Joe. If we stay together, one of us will die—of depression, suicide, drink. I have to save myself. I am really sorry."

"So you should be, you ungrateful bitch. I'm not staying here tonight." He was pulling on his pants. "I'm going where someone appreciates me."

"Please don't drive now," I said automatically.

"I'll do exactly what I want," he said, his voice deadly calm. "Just remember, you won't get to keep the house. You'll be out on the street in no time without me." He picked up his keys.

After I heard his car roar away, I went downstairs to make sure that all the doors were locked. I felt very tired, as if I had just completed the first stage of a very long journey. As I turned out the lights, I caught a whiff of the intense fragrance of hyacinths. Delft blue, in a shallow white bowl, three sturdy flower stalks rose from the cluster of dark leaves at the base. I leaned over and breathed deeply. They were the only ones that I had forced into bloom this winter. I wished I had planted more.

But then I remembered that only a few thin patches of snow remained on the lawn. It would be spring soon, others would bloom in my flowerbeds, it would be all right.

I got into bed and closed my eyes. I expected to lie awake, tossing and turning, tormenting myself about my cruelty to Joe, blaming myself for everything, especially for failing to assuage his pain and heal him in all the years we had been together, but my eyes shut, and I slept almost immediately.

I dream that I am lying in a narrow white bed. It is very old, eighteenth century perhaps, made of rosewood, the graceful slim legs elegantly curved. White silk sheets caress my strong naked body. Intensely green and flourishing ivy and laurel and ferns are clustered on a low table at the head of the bed, but otherwise the room is empty. The early morning sun pouring through the stained-glass windows glistens on the parquet floors, then is lost in the dimness further on. The room is so vast that I cannot see the end.

I stretch my arms and legs, and I am surprised at how vigorous and competent I feel, not tired at all as I have expected. I let the silk sheets lie around me loosely, enjoying their luxurious softness, as I watch the light fall on the thriving plants.

Suddenly I become aware that I am not alone, someone else is in bed with me, though I feel neither crowded nor invaded. Ōmīte, weary and worn past the point of exhaustion, is lying next to me. She is even older than when I last saw her a dozen years ago, a month or two before she died. Her body is nothing but transparent skin, and even her bones have thinned. She is colorless except for the fresh bruises and old scars that cover her face and hands.

"I am going to die now," Ōmīte says. "I've lived here much too long. I want to be dead." She loosens her hair, then sinks back slowly and closes her eyes. She is weightless, she makes no dent in the pillow.

"Please don't die," I cry, "you must stay with me."

But Ōmīte does not seem to hear. Her breath is so light that she might be dead already.

"Please," I beg, "stay with me, I don't know what I'm going to do without you. I'm afraid to be alone."

Grief and loss and pain wash over me, maybe even more intense than I felt returning home the night after Ōmīte's funeral. I had been on the bus by myself, feeling calm and in control, telling myself that Ōmīte had lived a full life and had been in much pain the last year, that it was inevitable that she die. But suddenly I had remembered again Ōmīte's grave in the Latvian section of the Indianapolis cemetery. It was covered with flowers, it was true, but everyone had gone away and left Ōmīte there alone, abandoned her to the cold rainy November night. I had wanted to jump off the bus and rush to her so that she would not be afraid, but of course I had not. I'd cried all the way home, surprised at myself. I had not cried at the funeral or before it.

"Jesus," Joe had said, impressed with my swollen eyes in spite of himself. "You look fucking awful. Well, come on then, I'll take care of you. You really lose it when you get around your family. I don't get it, after all the shit they've put you through, you still let them walk all over you, that's one of your problems. Oh well, come on, I'll buy you a nice Chinese dinner," he had said kindly. "But we have to hurry, otherwise the Golden Dragon will be closed, and nobody else even serves drinks with dinner in this dump."

I had been shaken by the strength of my feelings then, but after that night I had been able to keep them to myself. Gradually they had lessened, gone underground, and yet here they were in my dream, all their intensity and depth distilled, bringing back memories and pain, the way one whiff of the fragrance of lilacs can bring back a dozen springs.

"Please," I continue begging, "I'm used to you, Ōmīte, I have no one else." I have to keep her alive.

"I'm too old," Ōmīte says, "I've lived with you too long. It's past time for me to die. You're young yet, precious. You haven't really started to live your life yet. You must begin."

Ōmīte closes her eyes, her breathing slows, then it stops altogether, in spite of my concentrating my entire will on keeping her alive.

Ōmīte lies light and still on the white smooth pillow. I stroke her lifeless cheek, and as I do the deep purple bruises seem to fade a little. Perhaps in time, if washed by tears, they will become indistinct and a few will disappear altogether.

Even in my grief and fear of the future, I know Ōmīte is right. It is time for her to die. Time to put aside the hopelessly scarred and old, to allow something new to be born.

I wake, surprised that I have slept the whole night through for the first time in years. The dream gives me the strength to consider the future.

To leave the house and the garden, that is the hardest. I walk around the spacious rooms, too many for just Joe and me, too many really even when Boris was still at home. When Joe and I moved here, we talked about having other children, it was only a matter of time. I said that I wanted to wait just until the next summer, when I would only be working rather than working and going to school. But when the summer came, I always found an additional job, took another course, studied for my prelims, worked on my thesis. Finishing each task gave me great satisfaction; it was the one part of my life that I felt I could control. It never seemed the right time to have another child. But now I think, of course, I knew by then that I could not trust my real self to Joe, it's as simple as that. It would have been a mistake to have another child with him.

Rivulets of water are snaking their way down the hillside, the first green shoots of snowdrops and scilla and crocus are breaking through the hard ground. I study my flowerbeds. Years of planting and dividing and cultivating have produced well-established perennials, some already waking from dormancy. The garden promises spectacular blossoms, something to look forward to, every flower blooming predictably and reassuringly in succession. Flame-colored tulips yielding to bleeding hearts and fragrant wild blue phlox, succeeded by sky blue delphinium punctuated by madonna lilies and daisies, followed by salmon daylilies and crimson roses, to be completed by cream-colored chrysanthemums and purple asters.

The swollen buds of lilac, birch and mock orange, which shield the house from the road, are ready to leaf out. I remember they were only as high as my little boy when I planted them. Boris must have been eight or nine years old then. A blond, long-limbed, serious little boy, he had worked hard helping me dig and rake. If only I could have been a happier mother to him, I think again. If only I had had more willpower, so that my unhappiness had not marred his childhood.

I walk by the flowerbeds, recalling what each plant looked like the previous summer, noting which need to be divided and transplanted this year. I remember the history of so many: the resurrection lilies I saved from a garden that was to be bulldozed to make way for a shopping mall; the dark red peonies I bought as a private celebration the day I passed my Ph.D. orals; the flourishing bleeding heart seven-year-old Boris brought home as a tiny plant one Mother's Day. I remember too my intense unhappiness that I took with me into the garden, which lessened as I worked: cultivating the soil on Friday nights when Joe stayed late in the bars, planting the climbing rose the day I got home from visiting my dying mother, who was even more distant and remote than usual, weeding all the flowerbeds systematically after my mother's funeral.

In the bare spots in the beds, dozens of different lilies will bloom later in the summer, white and rose and burgundy and even pale green. Lilies are the last to come up in the spring, as if their luxurious blooms and heavy fragrance explained their early caution. How can I leave them? How can I bear not to see them? All I have to do is call Joe and tell him I am sorry and say that we should try again to make a go of our marriage. He would never leave me, and he will say that I am crazy to leave him, that I will not survive for a day without him, that everyone will laugh at me for trying.

I count the bare spots in the flowerbeds, where tender plants have been killed by the harsh winter. Normally I would compile lists, study catalogs and make out orders for new plants to fill in, or I would buy annuals at the greenhouse down the road. I would work hard to cover the devastation with new growth. Snapdragons, nicotiana, evening-scented stock have a heady fragrance on summer nights. I have often come out here alone after dark to breathe it in.

I do not start the tasks to make the garden flourish again, but neither do I pack my things and leave. I am waiting for another dream, though I myself do not know that is what I am waiting for.

One night I go outside and scoop up a handful of soil. It is dark, rich and crumbly, the way garden soil can be that has been well tended and repeatedly enriched with mulch. I cannot bear to part from it, I think. I hold it tight and carry it inside, search on a high shelf in my study and find an empty *vācele*, a round wooden box, hand-carved, with Latvian designs. I empty the soil in it and put it on the shelf.

There is another round wooden box on the shelf, though the wood is darker and the design more intricate. It contains soil from Latvia, brought back by one of my colleagues from a tour to the Soviet Union five years ago.

"I'll be in Latvia for two days," Jim Leaver had said. "What would you like me to bring you from Riga?"

"Nothing," I started to say. I had been too young when I left Latvia to remember Riga. All I remembered was the Parsonage, a hundred kilometers away, and he would not be permitted to travel there. Besides, what I wanted was silly, too sentimental. I was afraid he would say, like another of my colleagues had recently, that people who kept talking about their war-torn childhoods in foreign countries made her want to throw up.

But then fear that I would miss an opportunity that would never come again made me say urgently, "What I would really like is a handful of Latvian soil." I waited for Jim to start laughing.

When he didn't, I looked down the long dinner table and really saw him for the first time. His eyes were kind, his expression attentive and calm. Next to him, Rose Mary, his wife and my good friend, smiled warmly. No one else was laughing either. They seemed interested, even encouraging.

In the car, Joe said, "Jesus, what a ridiculous thing to ask for. You've made yourself into a real joke this time. Dirt, for chrissakes, dirt. You should have asked for something real, some Russian caviar or vodka or even some amber jewelry. There's a chance you'd actually get those. But *dirt*. You might as well go piss up a rope."

"But he'll bring it, he said he would."

"Sure, dream on. Another one of your ridiculous foreigner fantasies. He's an American, kiddo. He'll go out in his backyard and scoop up some shit right before he comes over, just so you'll make a fuss over him. And then he'll grin and act like King Kong with a hard-on. Don't think he'll go digging around in Latvia while some piss-ant Russian policeman is watching. You don't know a goddamn thing about what people do."

But Jim brought the soil, just as he had promised. The ground had been frozen solid in Latvia, so that he had to borrow an ice pick from the tour guide, a young Latvian woman who understood immediately. He had brought earth from a flowerbed next to the National Opera House.

"It was an adventure," he said as he handed me the jar. "I wouldn't have missed it. And I knew it was important to you."

"Important? Oh yeah," Joe said, "ask her about her childhood in war-torn Europe. 'Soldier, soldier, chocolate bar.' Boo hoo."

Jim ignored him. "Now if I could never return to America, I wonder what I would want for someone to bring me?"

"Yeah, a McDonald's hamburger and a bottle of Jim Beam, huh?"

"No," he continued calmly. "I might ask for sand, though I doubt it. Maybe something from Arizona, some mesquite or sweet grass perhaps, it would be hard to decide."

"Well, the soil is exactly what I wanted. I love that it's from the National Opera House. One of my father's cousins was a landscape architect, and he helped design the flowerbeds. He was later deported to Siberia. Oh, thank you, this means the world to me."

I was afraid I would cry in front of everybody. I was amazed that everyone did not think me abnormal because I still thought about Latvia.

Cradling my mother's amber pendant and the container of Latvian soil, I get into bed. I study the amber until the waves of indecision and conflict about leaving Joe and the house recede. I slip it under my pillow and turn out the light, but then I reach for it again and hold it tight. And then I sleep.

Usually I dream in English, but this time everyone speaks Latvian. I know this is unusual, just as I know that I am dreaming. It is a lucid dream.

I am in the Latvian Lutheran Church in Indianapolis, waiting for the service to begin. Soon my father and other men in black robes, with heavy silver crosses on chains around their necks, will climb into the pulpit and speak to the silent congregation.

The church is very crowded. Everyone is wearing black, the men are in somber suits, the women in severely cut unadorned dresses. It is someone's funeral or Good Friday, with everyone mourning the death of Christ. The altar, without flowers, is draped with a black cloth. It is evening, a steady cold rain is falling outside and gusts of wind rattle the shutters. It is a very long time until Easter and the resurrection.

People in the choir file in silently. They lift their eyes to the darkened stained-glass windows and begin to sing. The song is controlled yet very passionate, but at first I cannot distinguish any of the singers or understand the words.

Gradually I become aware that one voice is more distinct and more powerful than the rest. It is a woman's voice, an alto, rich with experience. As this voice rises, it expresses, elaborates, deepens what the others have suffered. The song is haunting and very beautiful.

I scan the rows of singers again. "Where is the singer?" I ask the people around me.

"Look, she is right there, in the last row," replies my sister, who has been next to me all along.

I look, and yes, I too see the singer.

"Why that is Anna," I whisper, "Mirdza's cousin Anna, whom Ivars shot." But she also looks like another Latvian woman named Anna. Hopeful, intelligent and very beautiful, with clear blue eyes and a lovely voice, this younger Anna was one of my friends in high school. I have recently heard that after twenty-two years of marriage to an alcoholic, she herself is an acute alcoholic and very sick.

"Yes, that is Anna," Beate murmurs. The two Annas seem to have merged. I can no longer tell whether it is the one murdered by her husband, or the one destroying herself by drink.

"But she is well again. That is a miracle. The last time I saw her she looked terrible. Her skin and hair were dry and coarse, as if she had been starving, but her body looked bloated. At first I didn't even recognize her. Her eyes were so dead and empty, it was hard to talk to her. She didn't have anything to say."

"Yes, poor girl," says Beate, "that's what she looked like when she was married and her husband was drinking all the time. Of course, she hid everything from everyone, she had to. Her pride wouldn't let her tell anyone that she suffered. He had been fired from one job after another for drinking, but he always blamed her and humiliated her, even though she was the only one working."

"But I'm so happy to see her. I thought she was dead. Who would have thought that her husband was in such torment that he would kill her, then kill himself? Their life seemed so prosperous. Remember those glittering parties, the lanterns lining the drive, the string quartet playing Viennese waltzes? And the musicians and artists and actors who came? The beautiful sun room where we had champagne for breakfast?"

"Yes, where her husband shot her." Beate is bitter. "'Go ahead and kill me,' she must have said. How *could* she? It was her duty to live for her daughters. Control, willpower, endurance, pride—she should have had those."

"But she was so vulnerable. And she was only seven when the Russian soldiers . . . ," I begin, but realize I don't know whom I am speaking of. "But look, Beate! She is alive again. She has escaped! And now she is the one singing."

I cannot take my eyes from Anna's face. There are fine lines around her eyes and mouth, her hair is graying and there is a large scar on her throat. But her face is radiant. She has saved herself! Miraculously healed, she is in full possession of her powers. She has suffered, but now she has much to sing about. That is why her song is so haunting and powerful.

I rise and walk slowly towards her. We recognize each other and embrace. I am crying with happiness.

"I am so glad you are alive."

Anna touches my cheek. Her hand is very warm. "Yes, precious," she says, "I escaped. All of us have to escape the second time if we are to live our lives. Only we can save ourselves."

I wake joyful, believing that I too can escape. But during the day pity for Joe invades me once more. How selfish I am. He is my husband, and he has loved me and stood by me all the years that I have been estranged from my mother and from the Latvian community. He is in so much pain himself; otherwise he would not drink or get so angry. I have failed to heal him with my compliance; all my efforts have not been good enough. And now when he begs me to reconsider, his voice seems full of tears which he makes a brave effort to control. I waver.

Tormented by conflict, I am wakeful the next night until my hand brushes against my mother's amber pendant again and I fall asleep easily. Then I have the final dream I have to have.

I am back in the Parsonage in Latvia, walking barefoot past the daffodils under my bedroom window. I must be quite small because the fragrant blossoms are so close to my face. I scarcely notice that my feet are cold and wet. I feel completely safe and happy.

I round the corner and start towards the barn behind the kitchen gardens. Zilite, the white mare, is kept there, and if I want to ride, I must saddle her myself. But as I get closer to the barn door, I become apprehensive. Something dangerous is happening inside, which I will have to confront. It can't be anything very bad, I tell myself. I am in Latvia; nothing bad ever happens here.

I hear thuds and blows, and then someone is moaning in pain. I make myself open the door. A Mongolian soldier is viciously whipping a glossy pregnant mare in a small enclosure. His dark skin glistens, his slanted eyes above his high cheekbones are cruel, his thin lips are determined. The mare regards him with patient supplicating eyes, she tries to avoid the slashing blows that fall on her bloodied mouth, but she is not really struggling to break free.

"Don't," I yell at the soldier, "don't beat her, let her go."

The soldier strikes another blow with a whip that sings and stings.

"Let her go," I shout. I hurl myself at the soldier. I try to grasp his leg, but it is hard to hold on. The coarse cloth of his trousers, tucked into polished leather boots, is too thick.

The soldier kicks me to loosen my grasp. The black boot bruises my chest. The searing pain is too familiar.

"Let her go," I gasp.

The soldier threatens me in a foreign language, so that his precise meaning is lost but his hostility is coruscating. He is cursing me, he will beat me next if the mare breaks free, he is certain to kill me. His hand is buried in the mare's mane, he is asserting his right to do anything he pleases. He can be as cruel as he wants.

"You have to fight for yourself," I shout to the mare, "you must break free and run, you have to save yourself. No one else can do it for you."

And the mare, as if finally understanding, begins to strain, tosses her head wildly, pulls at the reins. I pummel the soldier's leg with my fists, hoping to distract him long enough to loosen his grip. The three of us struggle intently, silent except for our harsh breathing. My life depends on the outcome.

Suddenly the mare neighs, tosses her head, rears up and kicks her shining silver hooves at the soldier's head. He stumbles, and while righting himself, lets go of the reins. The mare thrashes about in the enclosure for a moment, then finds an opening and moves easily through it. She pushes aside the barn door, her hoofbeats resound on the hard ground outside. She is running, she is running, she is free.

I let go of the soldier's leg and run with the mare. We must reach safety. But the season has changed. It is no longer spring, but early November. The ground is frozen, thin ice covers the puddles between the furrows of the empty gray field. Ahead of me, the mare is running hard. I try to keep up with her, although it is difficult; the ground is rough, filled with stubble that cuts my ankles. But I keep running. The

Mongolian soldier is in pursuit, his rope ready to ensnare the mare once more, his whip raised to slash at my neck.

The mare has raced across the open field and is now making her way down a steep hillside to a half-frozen lake below. She too has a hard time keeping her footing, so I put out my hand to touch her smooth warm flank, to steady her, to soothe her, to feel the colt safely inside her. But the mare leaps forward again, rushing towards the dangerous deceptive ice of the lake.

"Don't," I cry a warning, "it isn't frozen yet."

At that moment everything changes: the fields, the light, the lake are no longer autumnal but malevolent, the sky ominously threatening. The soldier is closer, his boots crush the stubble, his whip splits the air. The mare struggles, writhes, strains.

And then, to my horror, the mare begins to change. Her black mane turns into short reddish hair, her muzzle retracts and flattens, and a freckled vulnerable face, Hilda's face, emerges. Hilda's thin pathetic arms rise from the powerful front legs, the silver hooves drop away and disappear. Hilda's legs, blue and mottled with cold, are braced against the steep earth, her stockings in disarray around her ankles. She is prepared to sacrifice herself again for someone else. Her face is a mask of patient endurance.

But the Mongolian fetus, clamped onto Hilda's emaciated frame, sucking nourishment from her, is pulling her towards the dark depths. She tries to speak, to call for help, but she is mute. Only I can hear her, only I can help her, there is no one else. I must scream, I have to, yet I too am mute. I try, but I cannot make a sound. I must, I must, I will die if I remain silent. I will myself to act.

And then a long loud scream breaks from me. The terrible constriction in my throat and chest is released. I wake myself and sit up, my heart pounding. It takes a moment to realize I am safe in my own bed. I hold a pillow in my arms and rock back and forth to calm myself. I am all right, I am safe, it's just a dream, it's all right, I'm safe, it's just a dream.

I have dreamt about Hilda for forty years, I have woken in terror regularly, but this seems different. The Mongolian soldier stays imprinted on my eyelids. I flick on the light to obliterate him.

A few family photographs are lined up on my nightstand: my sister in her wedding dress, little Boris at four on a rocking horse, Joe and I holding Boris's hands and sand pails on a beach, Boris again on the day he graduated from high school. Next to that is a picture of Joe, taken in a studio five years ago for a business promotion. The circle of light illumines the last photo most fully. Joe looks at me challengingly.

I pick up the picture and study it. He hasn't aged very much, I think, while I myself often feel faded and old. His dark springy hair is speckled with gray, there are wrinkles around his eyes, his chin and neck are fleshier. But in spite of how much he drinks or how late he stays out, his face still has a willful vitality. His black eyes are alive above his high cheekbones, his dark skin is glossy, his narrow lips are decisive, self-assured, a little contemptuous.

I catch my breath and hold the picture to the light to see it better, shut my eyes and shake my head to clear my vision, look at him again. Why have I never identified the familiarity I sensed when I first met him? How can I have failed to place him? Why have I not named the impassive cruelty of his slanted eyes? Why have I never used the word Slavic in describing Joe's high cheekbones? Looking out of the frame is Joe, but also the Russian soldiers of my childhood as well as the Mongolian soldier of my dream. The similarity is so undeniable that anyone else would see it immediately. I must have been asleep or bewitched not to recognize it.

"Even the black leather boots, like the Nazi Cowboy's, that Joe used to wear," I whisper and stop, half terrified.

It is as if something has happened to time, or at least to what I have always thought is time, as if widely different years have inexplicably come together, mirroring and reflecting each other. Has the soldier in the dream illuminated Joe, has he come to remind me of the Mongolian soldiers, did the soldiers foreshadow Joe? Or did the soldiers bring Joe into being? Is that why I recognized him when I first saw him? Did I need to live with him for twenty-two years in order to exorcise the soldiers?

It is frightening but very exciting. I know I have been given a miraculous vision that I must use. I have caught a glimpse of another reality with which I lost touch in Lobethal, when the soldiers shot Pastor Braun and I learned that reciting prayers was pointless. But now a meaningful benign world, the source of my dreams, glimmers briefly.

I pick up the photo of Joe and me on the beach with Boris. And then I see the last resemblance I am meant to see. My own patient eyes are like the mare's and Hilda's, I see that right away, but in their determined, implacable gaze they also remind me of Joe, the Mongolian soldier beating the mare, Nazi soldiers guarding the camp gates, drunk Russian soldiers dragging Hilda behind the partition. I reach for my hand mirror for confirmation.

The similarity is slight, but unmistakable. It shakes me. I am not only the victim. I am also the one who has silenced myself, who has mercilessly forced myself to wait here in silent misery, in Joe's house, for much longer than I had to. I am the one who has cruelly reined myself in. I have imprisoned myself, I myself have constricted my life. I have sealed myself into amber.

And then I know what I must do. I wrap the two *vāceles* filled with soil in my apricot-colored satin underwear, then toss them with other clothes and photographs and books into a suitcase. I write a note for Joe and prop it against the scotch bottles on the bar. I reach under my pillow and take out my mother's amber pendant. It is one of the very few things I have that was hers, but it is crucial.

I lock the front door and start to slide the key automatically into my purse. I pause, kiss it and like Uncle Jaša in Latvia, lay it carefully on the windowsill for whoever will come after me. Someone else will have the house and most of my possessions. I hope they will tend my flowers. I believe some of the flowers will flourish after I am gone.

Part V

♦♦♦

· 20 ·

After the Funeral

The day after her husband's funeral, my sister and I must go to Bloomington to close up the apartment, to pack Beate's things for storage, to deal with the apartment manager, the bank, the car, the phone, the utilities. My sister has been living in Louisiana for a few months, where she has a new job as a library administrator, while Uldis had stayed in Indiana to pack and to get ready to move south as well. Beate adds to the list between us on the front seat as we drive. Ragged leaves circle desultorily, mud is frozen in raw gashes by the road. The sky is gray but not soft enough for snow.

Walking up the stairs to the third floor, we hold hands. We have talked too many times about what we will find to delay now, or for only one of us to go in and then to report to the other what she sees. The hair around our temples is gray, we are a little short of breath, our legs tremble.

Beate fumbles with the key. "Do you smell anything?" she says, not expecting an answer. I nod.

When the door finally yields, the smell is overpowering, even though the balcony door has been left partially open to the chill December afternoon. We breathe in the sweetish odor of human decay, like a mixture of unwashed hair, coagulating blood, stale perfume, but really like nothing else in the world. We have smelled it before, in Lobethal, though we are not thinking of that now.

We climb over stacks of newspapers and empty boxes to pull aside the sagging drapes shutting out the light, to push the glass doors open wide for more fresh air. A dozen or so houseplants, left out during a hard frost, blackened and dry, huddle against the railing of the porch. A few have been overturned, their delicate roots exposed.

We move close again and hold on to each other. We survey the piles of scattered clothing, unopened mail, old newspapers, filled ashtrays and broken eggshells that cover every surface in the living room. More dead plants are on the chipped formica coffee table and on a white metal washstand close to the glass doors. Several of these plants have been overturned as well, the soil ground into the green shag carpet.

Beate picks up a pot of dead Cape primroses. "You gave me these. So pretty. The shamrocks too. They really flourished and multiplied."

She rights several pots. "But Uldis kept stumbling into them and breaking them when he was drunk and I lost interest. Still, I thought he would have watered them."

Flicking light switches, we move through the dining alcove, the bedroom, the bathroom, but the rooms remain dark. The refrigerator kicks on noisily, car doors slam somewhere. We stand silent in the doorway of the dark kitchen, a small enclosed space in the heart of the apartment.

"We need light," we say simultaneously. I drag the only chair beneath the place where I can just make out the dim outline of a fixture. I balance cautiously, groping for the screws, patiently loosening them one by one, using the sleeve of my oversize sweater to help me grasp. Beate hands me a light bulb, and the kitchen springs into life around us.

The speckled brown linoleum floor is grimy around the edges, but an area in the center, about six feet long and three feet wide, has been recently sponged. Unwilling to stand in this space, we step together into the doorway again. The coroner's description stays vivid. We imagine Uldis's body, dressed only in underwear, lying face down for five days and nights, with the light bulbs blazing, then going out, one by one. We imagine the pool of blood around his head and shoulders, the bare arms raised pathetically, as if to ward off a blow. His legs and feet are bare, vulnerable, strangely familiar.

We would stand here forever, but the desire to know saves us. We move through the apartment, replacing burned-out bulbs, searching for clues, guessing at the events of his last day, last week, last month. The kitchen wastepaper basket is filled with empty wine bottles and cigarette butts.

"Wine?" I ask. "I thought it was vodka."

"It was."

"Where do you think these came from then? Did he have a friend? Did he bring someone home to drink with him?"

"No. Never. He always drank alone. He never went out to drink either."

On top of the green ninety-nine-cent wine bottles are plastic gloves, syringes and bloodied pads of cotton, probably left by the coroner and his assistants in their search for the answers they need: disease, accident, murder, suicide? Uldis's death certificate read, "Cause of death: liver disease. Secondary cause: chronic alcoholism. Probable time of death: four days prior to the discovery of the body." Two empty cans of light beer are at the very bottom of the wastebasket.

Beate stares at them, then gets down on her hands and knees and reaches into the back of the corner cabinet next to the sink. She brings out two tiny bottles of kirsch liqueur, both still full.

"Ah," she sighs, relieved. "He *didn't* drink these. He didn't. He gave me these for Christmas two years ago. I was saving them for something special. When things got better, maybe we would invite somebody in. He knew how important having friends was to me."

"Yes, I can see that. Where do you think the beer came from?"

"He was trying to taper off. He didn't drink these, and he was trying to switch from vodka to beer and wine. He must have been trying to quit. He was still trying. Poor Uldis."

"Maybe. Maybe he was just too sick to hold down vodka." I remember my ex-husband Joe in the hospital once, drinking wine from a shaving mug, or standing in the kitchen in his bathrobe, too sick to go to work, too nauseous to hold down scotch, pouring himself a sherry. The eggshells, the egg-stained frying pan, the saucepan caked with Cream-of-Wheat all suggest nausea. In the refrigerator are moldy loaves of bread and chunks of cheese, torn open, bitten into, not rewrapped, as if a sick animal had gnawed them.

The receipts on the kitchen counter show that he bought a little food now and then. But not a single receipt from a liquor store ever turns up in the kitchen, or the car, or in his coat pocket. In order to deny his drinking to the very end, he has carefully destroyed them all. No one will ever know exactly how much liquor it has taken to enable a tall, broad-shouldered, handsome, once-powerful fifty-eight-year-old man to drink himself to death.

The bare mattress on the floor in the bedroom is bloodstained, but the brown stains look old. The lamps, set on packing cases used as night tables, have been knocked over, the bulbs broken off at the base. Only the bare bulb in the ceiling has escaped the large liquor-laden body, heaving and stumbling. Everything has been pulled out of the bureau drawers, dumped on the floor, trampled. The incomplete tasks and deluded efficiency of drunkenness are everywhere.

"You must write about this," Beate says to me. "It's terrible how he lived at the end, no one could imagine such chaos and devastation without seeing. But it seems so familiar," she adds wonderingly.

"Like the basement in Lobethal, after the Russian soldiers," I say.

In a half-packed open suitcase, a box of rifle shells is partially concealed under a pair of black cotton slacks worn so thin the light shines through the seat. The pockets are empty, one of them pinned with a safety pin, the cuffs frayed. Uldis's other clothes, taking up no more than two feet of space in the open closet, are worn close to nakedness except for some stiff, indestructible polyester pants with flaring bottoms left over from the sixties, and a black suit for Sundays and funerals.

A knee-high pile of stained underwear spills from the bathroom closet. Beate draws in her breath sharply. "Uldis, how *could* you?" she asks the empty room. "How could you let yourself *go* like that?"

She gets down on her knees and starts cleaning the toilet bowl and the area around it. She scours the sink vigorously. The long dead branches of an ivy plant trail across the moisture-beaded, badly insulated window. They rustle sadly and get in her way.

"He was so meticulous. He *was*. He used to take a shower every night, no matter how drunk he was. He always put on clean clothes. He said it didn't matter how poor we were, we could at least be clean. How are we ever going to get this place cleaned up?"

"We don't have to. All we have to do is to pack the rest of your things and get out of here." I feel my sister freeze, so I add, "Then if we have time, we'll clean what we can. The manager said we were looking at four days' work here, if we're lucky."

We start picking through loose papers and keys, hoping to find some money, but except for some change on an ironing board in the living room, which is covered by debris like every other surface, there is none. Uldis's black wallet is there, the leather split and torn where the credit cards would be, but of course there aren't any. The plastic over the window for the driver's license is no longer transparent, it has thickened and whitened with age. Only the outline of his face is visible, its features obscure. The wallet is empty; even the sacred twenty-dollar bill he kept for crises is gone.

We find a stack of automatic teller withdrawal slips, which come to almost $800, but probably not all are there. Before leaving for her new job as a library administrator at a Louisiana university, Beate had given him her number for use in emergencies. The $800 was all the money she had in the world. Now that is gone too, and she has a new debt for the burial plot in the Latvian section of the Indianapolis cemetery and for the funeral itself, almost $5,000.

Uldis had been unemployed for nine years. There is no insurance, but when the death certificate comes, she will get a $250 death benefit from Social Security. She may get another $100 for selling the car and $50 for the guns.

Mixed in with the Tyme machine slips are two pawnshop tickets.

"Oh," Beate says, "he must have pawned my bracelet and his watch."

"Pawned your bracelet? How dare he?"

"It's my fault, really. I taught him how to do that. After we moved back from Texas, right after Mama got sick and I didn't have a job, I used to do that to pay for gas to go see her. So really, I showed him how to do it."

"Why didn't he pawn his guns? He shouldn't have touched your things."

"It's all right, really it is. He would never have pawned his guns. He said that if he couldn't . . . stand it . . . well, he could always shoot himself. So you see he couldn't pawn those. They were like life insurance."

"Death insurance."

A loaded gun had in fact been found under the pillow on the bare mattress, so that the policeman who had called Beate at an academic conference had told her he thought it was suicide. The real cause of death was not determined until the autopsy. In the past, whenever I had heard some new detail about my sister's hard life, only half joking, I had threatened to shoot Uldis myself. But now I realize I have known only a tiny fraction of what my sister has endured.

"Well, at least he didn't shoot himself," Beate says. "That's something to be thankful about."

"I'm glad that he didn't kill you, like Ivars did Anna. That's what really counts. I am so happy that you're alive. There isn't much else to be thankful for."

"Oh," Beate says, "it isn't so bad, really. Others have had it worse. Poor Uldis, if only things had been a little easier for him. I've had a charmed life."

"A charmed life?" I ask. "You will have to explain to me why you think you've had a charmed life."

Beate's gray hair is pulled back severely from her face, her coat is too short, the worn cuffs don't even cover her wrists against the cold, her eyes are red with crying and exhaustion, her shoulders slumped forward.

"Well, I have you. And Boris. And so far we've gotten through everything, the funeral and the meal afterwards."

"Yes, that's true. And I have you."

"Come, *māsiņ*, my little sister." Beate smiles the mischievous smile of the lovely, lively little girl she once was. She takes my hand. "We better get to the pawnshop before it closes."

Holding hands, solicitous of each other, we guide one another down the stairs and over patches of ice towards my car.

"That Uldis was a bastard," I whisper to myself. I am holding two small jewelry boxes, which we have just redeemed for $175. Beate's gold bracelet is in one and so is her wedding ring. In the other is a silver and amber ring left to Beate by our mother. "That bastard, how could he?"

"It's all right. The rings were too small for me anyway. My hands started swelling in the last two years, so I hardly ever wore them."

"Bastard, even your wedding ring. And the only thing you have left that was Mama's. Bastard."

"Well, he knew I could always get them back."

"Your wedding ring. It shows how important that damn liquor was to him. Come, *māsiņ*."

I take Beate by the elbow and gently guide her past the smudged glass cases filled with jewelry and silverware, past rows and rows of guns against the dingy yellow walls.

"What happened to Uldis?" asks the owner, an overweight young man with greasy black hair.

"He drank himself to death," I snap. "What did you expect?"

"I'm sorry." His eyes seem to tear, he fumbles for a handkerchief in the pockets of his stained leather vest and blows his nose. "He was a really nice man, I liked talking to him. He knew a lot about history, didn't he? He lived through a lot of history himself. It's too bad he died now; things are starting to change over there."

Beate's tired and resigned face breaks into a smile. "Yes, Uldis certainly did understand history. Thank you for noticing." She straightens her shoulders.

"Those little defenseless occupied countries—Latvia, Estonia, Lithuania—I learned about them in school," the young man recites with satisfaction.

I am ashamed of myself. The misery that has flowed in and out of this shop washes over me; the misery my sister has endured threatens to overwhelm me.

But Beate seems cheered by the encounter with the pawnshop owner. "You know, Agatiņa," she says, "actually Uldis *did* care what happened to me. He always encouraged me to go to school, he always encouraged me to try to enjoy myself. In Louisiana, the last time I saw him, he stood by his car and said, 'I'll come to see you soon. You take care. Remember that I love you.' He bought a chain for my door, he measured everything so carefully, then he stood there and watched while the maintenance man put it on. He knew he wouldn't live long. He did care what happened to me. He did."

He didn't even put the chain on himself, incompetent useless bastard, I think. But his motive touches me. I have to help my sister salvage something.

"Yes," I agree, "he wanted to make sure you were safe."

"And as desperate as he was, he didn't touch my two little bottles of kirsch."

"That's right."

"I knew you would understand, *māsiņ*."

Back at the apartment we continue salvaging. We dust and pack books, gather pennies and occasional quarters into an empty margarine container, sort and fold Beate's clothes. There are so few of them; most of them I recognize as presents I gave her years ago. We dump the dead plants into bags and add them to the mountain of debris ready to be taken downstairs.

I scour the kitchen counter and begin washing the accumulated dirty dishes. They are mostly emptied margarine containers used as bowls, plastic utensils from carry-out places that have been washed and saved to be used again, a few glasses with Bugs Bunny on them given away by Burger King years ago. The only picture in the apartment is a poster of a melancholy rabbit playing a cello.

The dinner service consists of three plain white china dinner plates, two of them chipped, four unmatched mugs, odd stainless-steel knives and forks. Half-used packets of soup, rice and noodles have been carefully resealed. One drawer holds ironed and folded wrapping paper from birthday and Christmas presents, ready to be reused. Bits of ribbon and a few pretty napkins with tiny roses that my mother splurged on at L.S. Ayres are in another drawer. So is a half-used, resealed package of Easter-egg dye.

I cry as I uncover each new bit of evidence of Beate's poverty. My own house, which I have just bought, is warm and spacious, my closets are bulging, my cupboards are full. And yet this is how my sister has lived—Beate, who loves pretty things, who in the 1950s saved for and wore Shalimar perfume, a swirling taffeta skirt and a tiny gold watch with a delicate black velvet strap.

Beate would have to climb the stairs of this apartment after her sixteen-hour day: the clerical job that fed her and Uldis, but also kept them below the poverty level, and then studying late at the library so that she could get an advanced degree in library science and an administrative position in a university. She would be tired, and maybe she would allow herself to feel just a little sad that she did not have money to complete her Ph.D. work in political theory. But she would climb the stairs, telling herself firmly that all it took was hard work and willpower. What courage it must have taken to come back to this every night, I think.

Beate would open the door to this poverty and desolation. Uldis would be passed out on the couch, the bare bulb over the dining-room table giving the only light. Or he might still be awake, surly, incoherent. "Who wouldn't be drunk living with you?" he might say. "You're crazy, I'm not drunk. You are obsessed with drinking, just like your sister. You have a lot of problems."

But that is what Joe would say, not Uldis, who was always kind.

The green shag carpet that Beate had vacuumed early that morning would be scattered with newspapers and cigarette ashes. The suitcase she had packed for him the last time she had asked him to leave would still be standing by the door.

"He came back," Beate would say to me on the phone.

"Well, tell him to leave again."

"I can't. What will happen to him?"

"He'll have to start taking care of himself."

"It's too late for him," Beate would sigh.

I scour another caked saucepan and wipe my tears. I will not, *will not* cry for Uldis, I will cry only for my sister.

"Oh, *māsiņ*, I wish I had known how hard all this was for you, I wish I had known how poor you were. I should have known. I know what it's like to come home to someone drunk, but I didn't know how hard the rest was too. You didn't have any pleasure. You probably didn't even have enough to eat."

"That's not true. We ate a lot of rice, but we only went to bed hungry once. It wasn't so bad."

"Oh, I wish I had sent you money. Oh, I wish you had told me more."

"I didn't want you to know everything. I wanted to protect you, just a tiny bit. I wish I could have protected you more. Remember, you're the littlest," Beate laughs.

"Besides, it wasn't that bad," she continues. "This was really a pleasant apartment. I kept it nice. The sun would shine through that balcony door, the plants would glisten."

Beate points to the only chair in the living room. "I would sit here and talk to you. I always talked to you on Sundays; I looked forward to that call. And Uldis wasn't always drunk. Sometimes he was sober for a week. And on Sundays the liquor stores were closed, so he didn't go down to Big Red's. We would sleep till nine, then we would sit in bed and talk. If we had money, we might walk to get the paper and read that. If not, we might go out in the field behind the apartment houses and look for dandelions. Uldis was always hoping to see a rabbit, and sometimes we did. Or if I had gotten a few hours' overtime, we might go to a matinee or to Hooks Drugstore and sit in a booth and have a cup of coffee. Sometimes when you sent me money for my birthday or Valentine's Day, we would walk over to the mall and I would buy nail polish, Estēe Lauder's Champagne Pearl. It was my only luxury; Uldis always encouraged me to buy it. Then I would go home and do my nails. I never went back to the library until late in the afternoon. Sundays were always so nice."

I pick up a photograph of Uldis taken a few years ago at Christmas at his mother's house. He is wearing his good black suit, a white shirt and black tie, his shoes are shining, his dark hair curls softly around his temples. He looks clean, sober, carefully dressed. All this has Beate temporarily achieved. She has made him presentable, spruced him up, polished him. His smile, so like Beate's, is delighted, as if something wonderful has just happened.

"We should take this down to Big Red's," I say, trying to hold onto my anger. "We should show it to them. I'm sure they'd remember him, they must have made a lot of money from his Dark Eyes vodka, he was probably their best customer. They should give you a contribution for the funeral expenses, as a professional courtesy."

"It's too late for that. Poor Uldis."

I am looking through a Dark Eyes vodka box filled with Uldis's papers, which Beate has asked me to sort.

On top are dozens of letters from his mother. Feeling intrusive, I nevertheless read two of the most recent. His mother has sent him money, $20 at a time, even though she herself lives on meager Social Security payments, bulk cheese and flour from a food pantry program, low-income heat subsidies. She has also renewed her prescription for Valium and sent it to him "for his nerves." Valium is particularly intoxicating when mixed with vodka.

Uldis's mother never believed that he was an alcoholic. "Don't listen to Beate," she has written to him. "A man takes a drink now and then, that's natural. Everybody does. If Beate hadn't been so selfish and taken that teaching job at Texas A&M, you would be working in a good job right now. She should get a different job and support you better now instead of trying to get her own library degree."

Under the letters are various old postcards and birthday cards. Figures have been cut out from several of these. Two rabbits and a rose are pasted on a four-by-six note card. "To my beloved wife on her birthday" is carefully printed in the center. He hasn't had the money to buy Beate a real birthday card. No, he hasn't chosen to spend his money like that, I tell myself sternly. But I know the ice in my heart is beginning to melt; I don't want to feel what I know I will.

The rest of the box is filled with rejection letters, from universities and colleges all over the country, hundreds of them. "After carefully reviewing your qualifications, we find they are not what we can utilize at this time . . ." The oldest letters are from good schools, the most recent from obscure colleges in North Dakota, Mississippi, Georgia. There are also rejections from sales jobs, writing jobs, clerking jobs, all kinds of jobs in the last two years. "After reviewing your application we find that we will be unable to offer you a position at this time." Useless.

I see Uldis climbing the stairs, anxious to open each letter, knowing that if there were a job offer, he would have received a telephone call, but hoping. He would wait until he read the letter, put it carefully back into the envelope, then in the box, before he would turn and make his way down the stairs again, this time to Big Red's. Or would he? That is probably too simple. He would have the bottle with him already, he would only have postponed opening it to read the letters. The rejection would give him reason for the first drink and all those after that, and he would have opened the bottle in celebration as well.

I hold the box, crying about the waste, crying about his pain. What started it all? What changed him from the handsome, promising, hardworking young man he once was? I remember Uldis on the bus, tipping his hat to Beate, delighted to be asked to sit next to her. Uldis dutifully asking me to dance whenever I was a wallflower at one of the Latvian parties. Uldis smiling about the A+ he had received on a paper. Uldis talking with my mother about *Moby Dick*. After reading it in a night class at Indiana University Extension, they both agreed it was the greatest American novel. My mother had expected a fine future for Uldis; she had been delighted when Beate married him.

Why could Beate never leave him, as I had finally left Joe? Beate had loved him, of course, and even in his last agonizing years Uldis was never belittling, as Joe was. But perhaps she shielded and supported him because she understood his past so fully. They had a common history; Uldis only expressed his pain differently. His self-destructiveness was the dark shadowy mirror image of the compulsively hard work, unvarying cheerfulness and high achievement of so many other Latvians.

Uldis spoke a heavily accented English that included both black and

Southern patterns. His parents had first settled in Mississippi, where he and his father, a symphony musician in Latvia, worked long hours in cotton fields. After escaping to Indiana—they had been threatened with years in prison if they ever left the plantation—Uldis worked at the Kingan meat-packing plant with black men, who laughed at him a bit, then accepted him and taught him about life in the United States.

When a professor wrote an encouraging note on a history paper, asking Uldis to speak up in class, he said, "Goddamn, I ain't fooled by de damn professor. If he hear me say somethin' he not gonna give me no A."

He had been sixteen when he arrived in Mississippi. One day, he was wearing his one good white shirt, because it was Sunday. The sons of the plantation owner convinced him to catch a skunk, saying it would make a wonderful pet. Not knowing anything about skunks, he did. He had to throw away all his clothes, even his shoes. He laughed when he told it, it seemed a funny story. And he could smile when he said, "So I be de only worker at Kingan wid' Phi Beta Kappa key."

I had known Uldis for more than thirty years, I had seen him sipping drinks and smiling pleasantly at countless tables, but I know absolutely nothing of what happened to him during the war. Is that where his self-destructiveness began? It is too late to find out.

At the bottom of the box are several old copies of his registration forms for aliens. Only two years after coming to the United States, Uldis received his draft notice for Korea. His parents pleaded with their only son not to go—they had seen what happened to too many other young men. After great conflict, he gave in reluctantly and refused military service. As a result, he could never become a citizen; he would always be a foreign national, an alien, trooping with other more recent immigrants to the post office after Christmas each year to sign the necessary forms. Not being a citizen excluded him from even being considered for most of the jobs he applied for.

Other young men from the Park Avenue apartments went to Korea; two died there. Then the next generation went to Vietnam and brought new pain back with them.

I close the box and open another. It contains his unfinished dissertation on nineteenth-century movements for independence in the Baltic countries. The box is mildewed, rough jottings and beautifully finished lyrical passages jumbled together, thousands of note cards clipped and arranged according to a system no one else will understand. He has never been able to finish it. Nor has he lived long enough to see the renewed struggle for independence in Latvia, after almost fifty years of brutal Soviet repression.

"Poor Uldis," I say, "such a wasted life."

"Yes, poor Uldis," Beate echoes. "Things were too hard for him."

"He had such a sweet quality, didn't he? He could be so dear. It's just that he made your life so terrible."

"Oh, it wasn't so bad."

"Poor Uldis," I say. But he has already had enough love and pity. Now I must help my sister to salvage what she can.

Beate and I stand in the nearly empty apartment. We have carried out piles of trash, garbage bags full of things carefully accumulated once, useless now. All three dumpsters in front of the apartment building are full; neat rows of black plastic bags stand next to them as well. The nicer pots from the dead plants are lined up on top of the dumpster lids. We hope someone will come along who can use them, but so far no one has.

The movers have come and gone. Beate's suitcase and a few small boxes are in my car. The usual wealth of things to be given to friends or donated to charity when someone dies is not there. Uldis's pocket watch, once his father's and his grandfather's before him, is in Beate's purse. It is neither silver nor gold, but it is old and from Latvia. It will be a keepsake for Boris. I am carrying the box of rejection letters, which I will keep until Beate wants them. We have to return a few books on Baltic history to the library. "He told me he had done that," Beate says about these with the same disappointment as about dozens of other tasks. "I am sure he wished he had," I reply.

We walk through the clean apartment once again. The odor of decay is still there, faint but perceptible after three days of soap and water, fresh air and light. But it doesn't frighten us anymore. It is part of Uldis, his agony, his addiction, which like an evil master contemptuous of everything else, had seized him, possessed him, destroyed him and hurt and scarred Beate as well. I worry that the smell will cling to us after we leave, but we will have to do something about that later.

Beate closes the plastic margarine container into which we have gathered the odd pieces of change we found. There aren't many. She puts them in her purse.

The couch in the living room, which once belonged to our mother, is the only thing we have not been able to carry downstairs. It spoils our temporary sense of completion, but not much. We feel again the satisfaction we felt at the end of the funeral.

Only three of the Latvian men attending were vigorous enough to serve as pallbearers, so they did not bury the coffin themselves, as men used to when everyone was younger. Then American grave-diggers would sit in their truck, smoking cigarettes and joking, watching someone else doing their work.

Uldis's grave lay behind the memorial statue in the section of the cemetery dedicated "To all the exiles, who lost their beloved free Latvia during World War II."

Beate and I held hands while the coffin was lowered. The sandy Latvian soil that Jim had brought from Riga was sprinkled on the coffin. "Soil from home, for you dying in a strange land." People stepped up and threw in a handful of earth or a flower.

The truck backed up and dumped a load of gravel onto the coffin. Beate's old folk-dancing partner smoothed the soil and made the shape of the cross with the spade handle over Uldis's face and chest. The flowers, expensive arrangements in red and white symbolizing the Latvian flag, were arranged over the grave.

This small exertion cheered everyone. We were suddenly ravenously hungry. We paused by our mother's and grandmother's graves.

"He's with them now," Beate said.

"Too bad Papa will be leaving early. I wish he could stay with you, to comfort you."

"Well, it's all right, really. I can manage. He said his 'little wife' was expecting him. She was angry with him for coming to the funeral at all. She said it was too close to Christmas, and that her children had bought a lot of presents. It was good of him to come."

"Still, I wish you had someone to help you."

"Oh well. Let's go now and drink the toast to wish Uldis 'light sand'," Beate said, reminding me of the ancient custom of wishing the dead person comfortable rest under the earth. "Poor Uldis."

"All right, but we better hurry. 'Come, come, *māsiņ*, I'm your little wife and I'm expecting you,'" I mimicked. We both laughed until there were tears in our eyes, then grew serious.

"What a brave girl you are," I said as I took my sister's hand.

"Well," Beate says, "I do feel bad about that couch. Papa let me take it when he got married again. His new wife didn't like it, wrong color. I wish we could find someone who could use it. I hate for them just to throw it out."

"Maybe the manager will do that," I say, "but still let's move it now. There might be some money under it."

But there isn't. Two empty bottles of Dark Eyes vodka and a liquor-store bag, carefully folded with no receipt in it, emerge. But as we move the couch away from the wall, we see something light caught under it. Beate gets down on her knees and patiently gropes underneath it. She brings out one of my mother's cups, with apple blossoms around the rim. I remember my mother buying one pretty cup a month; I remember this particular one well. The inside is darkly stained with tea. Uldis must have been using it when he got sick, then he must have dropped it and forgotten it.

We carry the cup to the sink. A good supply of cleaning materials is still underneath, where we have lined them up in hope that the next tenants can use them. We pour a little detergent into the cup and swish it around. It doesn't seem to make much difference.

"We'll have to try soaking it in bleach." I think that even if the stain cannot be removed completely, it will probably fade. We pour some bleach in the cup, let it sit for a minute and pour it out. The stain seems just a little lighter. The bleach makes our eyes burn. It is a good, clean smell.

Images move before my eyes as I swirl the bleach. Russian soldiers tilt empty vodka bottles to drain them to the last drop. They stagger drunkenly, their boots crush the snowdrops, their voices threaten. They stomp across flowerbeds, they trample narcissus, lilies and ferns. They turn towards two starving girls to urinate.

A bomb has fallen on the house next door. One corner is still smoldering, but the rain has put out most of the flames during the night. My sister and I climb over rubble, we sift through debris, searching for something intact. Everything is smashed, it seems like total destruction, but we keep working. "Look," I say, "look." I see a delicate china cup, miraculously whole. The tiny violets against the golden rim are the only color in the grayness. But when I pick it up, only half of it is there. It is useless. "Never mind," Beate says, "we'll find something else, we just have to keep working."

The soldiers seize our mother and push her ahead of them with their guns. "It will be all right," Beate says and squeezes my hand. "I'll take care of you. Remember, you're the littlest." She pulls the old heavy wool coat over me. I feel momentarily safe in this little nest.

It is almost as if both of us have known that the cup would be there. Like so much about this death, finding it has not surprised us at all. We are used to salvaging.

"And now," I say, "let's go back to the hotel. Let's each take a long, luxurious shower. And then I'll take you out for a really good meal, something warm and rich, like oxtail soup and brown crisp chicken and roast potatoes, and wine, and coffee with lots of cream afterwards."

"That sounds wonderful."

"And we'll talk about you for a change. What a time you have had. You've lived through another devastation, like the war, and now you have to go back alone to Louisiana, such a distant strange place, you might as well be going to yet another foreign country."

"It's all right, *māsiņ*. Really, it is. You've helped me so much. I can manage."

"It would be a little easier for you if you weren't in a new job and a new town, so far away from everybody."

"I'll be fine. It isn't so bad. I just wish I had been able to do more for Uldis."

"But you did. You loved him and you kept him alive for much longer than he would have lived by himself."

"But he died anyway."

"Too many things had happened to him—exile, war, unemployment, humiliation. You couldn't change that, no matter what you did."

"Do you really think the war may have started it?" Beate asks. During the last week, which is the longest time my sister and I have spent together since we married, we have speculated about this question.

"I believe that was part of it for Uldis. And for both of us too, as if the drunken Russian soldiers were imprinted on everything. We put up with so much in our marriages, as if we didn't believe we had the right to be happy."

"That's what Mother used to say about you, Agatiņa. She said you were suffering too long. She kept waiting for you to divorce Joe."

I am so surprised I cannot speak.

"As soon as you got your Ph.D.," Beate continues, "she started saying you should take your little boy and leave. She wished you would move to Indiana, closer to her."

"Closer to her? Oh, if I had only known! It would have made such a difference! Why didn't you tell me?" Although my mother has been dead for seven years, I am not finished grieving for her and for our strained relationship.

"She forbade me to say anything. You were married to him, after all, and we had no right to interfere."

"What an institution marriage is," I snap. "You can flail around all by yourself while you're at it, and no one will say a blessed word. Then when you finally get divorced and are exhausted to death with the struggle to build a new life, people start telling you, 'Oh, good, we were hoping you'd do exactly that.'"

"Oh, is that Feminism 101?" Beate laughs. "Mother had a lot of pride, that's all, just like you."

"And you too," I say. I change the subject. "Do you have to call Uldis's mother?"

"I'll call her tomorrow. Papa too."

"Well, you certainly have your work cut out for you. They'll both expect you to comfort them, not the other way around."

"It's all right," Beate says, "I'm used to them. It isn't so bad. Others have had it worse."

If I could have one wish, what would I wish for my sister? To be as happy as I am. But that seems far in the future for Beate.

After I divorced Joe, even with Ingeborg's encouragement, it took me a long time to stop saying "It isn't so bad," and to try to change those parts of my life that I could, to act rather than wait. Days after meeting John, I finally called him.

"I don't think you'll remember me, but we were talking about—" I started.

"Of course I do. The importance of dreams . . . and lilies . . . Black Dragon and Green Magic, weren't they?"

"Yes. What a memory you have. I'm glad now that I called."

"Actually," John laughed, "I was going to call you. I've got your number right here."

"Really?" I asked, disbelieving.

"Really. Here it is, taped to my stapler." He read it off to me. That was a fortuitous start.

Later, coming in from a long walk in the Wisconsin autumn woods, John lightly touched my hand.

"How hard it must be for you to pretend to be an American all the time. Surely the Latvian part matters too? I'd like to be around when you're ready to talk about it."

He stayed with me as we took the hundreds of small but courageous steps necessary to establish a relationship between two people with complicated pasts. We had been walking through the autumn woods again when John gave me a piece of amber set in gold, to mark our commitment to each other. The almond-shaped amber feels alive, it warms my hand. Smooth as a stone, it is nevertheless much lighter. Amber is resin preserved from ancient pines, hardened and polished by sea and wind and sand, like a crystallized tear. By happy coincidence the piece John gave me is similar to that in my mother's pendant. After her funeral my father gave it to me. My parents found theirs on the shore of the Baltic Sea, the first year they were married, when they were happy together, with peaceful lives seeming to stretch in front of them. Both pieces are the rich color of dark honey, and each has a subtle dark streak at the base. I have not noticed before how similar these streaks are in texture and form. I touch John's piece of amber again and feel energy flowing into me.

Ancient Latvians believed that amber was magic. It could protect against illness, heal wounds, guide one to another world after death. It mirrors the sun and love and life in the present, but it also preserves the past as it encloses grasses, insects, seeds, needles of long-extinct trees. It floats in saltwater, so perhaps it can cure sadness and dry tears. I wish such a piece of amber for my sister too.

At the bottom of the stairs, Beate stops. "I'm really tired," she says. "Sometimes I think I can't . . ." She begins to cry silently.

Something about Beate's gesture is totally familiar. Suddenly I am six, back in the train station with my mother. I am on the platform where my mother sets down her heavy suitcase and says, "I can't go any further." Her face is flushed with the effort of carrying the huge bag and trying to hold my hand, so that I will not be swept away and trampled by the crowd. She starts crying. "I can't go any further," she repeats, "I cannot . . ." Hundreds of people swarm around us, shoving to get into the train, angry that we are in the way. My mother's tears fall on my neck, but I am too frightened to comfort her, all I can do is to hold on. Finally she wipes her eyes, takes me by the hand, lifts the heavy suitcase and continues, step by determined step.

When I return from my reverie, Beate has already wiped her eyes. She picks up her suitcase at the bottom of the steps and straightens her shoulders. She is exhausted, but she is doing what she has to. She is putting one foot in front of the other. She is moving forward.

· 21 ·

Trains

I dream a lot about trains. Almost nightly I move through the bleak countryside, hearing the guns in the distance, hiding from soldiers. There is a train that I must catch; if I do I will be safe. Gradually, John enters my dreams. Sometimes he helps me carry a bundle of warm winter clothing, at other times he holds the baby I must keep safe or leads the starving boy by the hand. But most of the time he is simply there with me, walking along the sandy path, leaving the old oak tree and the orphanage behind, pointing to a way to get through the barbed wire to the train that will take us to safety.

At other times I am with my sister or mother, and getting to the train is much harder. I dream that I am packing winter clothing and food and cooking utensils in a huge hamper. If I forget something, others in my family will starve or freeze. I hunt frantically for matches, for a book of fairy tales and a flute for Boris, who is just a little boy and will need something to give him pleasure in the camps. I can hear the black boots of the soldiers strike the stones in the courtyard, I can see tanks crushing lilies and ferns. I hurry as fast as I can and run, breathless because of the heavy hamper, to the train station. Crowds push and surge against me. I must get to the others, we must all get on the train.

It is the same train station where my mother cried, the same surging crowds, the same terrible urgency, the same fear of separation. I see my mother moving towards the train purposefully. Ōmīte is there too, leaning on Beate, who is holding Boris by the hand. My father is further back in the crowd. I feel hopeful, light is just beginning to flow through the huge windows overhead, we will all be saved. The train doors open right in front of me, I swing up on the high step and reach back to help my mother.

But at that instant the train moves forward violently, our hands are pulled apart, the doors close tightly between us. I try to pry them open, I strain and beat until my fingers bleed, but the doors stay shut. Through the heavy glass, I see my mother and son and sister and grandmother left behind on the gray platform, and my father even farther away somewhere in the crowd. My mother reaches towards me and says something I cannot hear. I try to open a window to give her my keys, my money, my watch and my maps, but the window is painted shut. The train moves forward, I know my mother cannot hear me. Across the street from the station tanks are lined up, waiting to move on those left behind. The train carries me, alone and guilty, towards safety.

Sometimes the train station in the dream looks more like the Greyhound bus station in Chicago, where I waited with the same terrible urgency ten years ago. I was on my way to see my mother, who lay dying in a hospital, far away from Russia and Latvia and Germany, all places more real to her than America. I had missed the final plane that night and so was taking this slow and frustrating way to her.

It has been a gray day, the floor of the lower level is strewn with useless straws and empty paper cups flattened by hundreds of feet. The walls are a dirty yellow, slashes in the worn plastic seats have been clumsily mended with tape, the air-conditioning isn't working. The plastic sticks to my damp soiled clothes, my body and face are covered with grime. The bus is late, and I know that once it arrives it will move much too slowly through the Indiana countryside.

I have been estranged from my mother for twenty-two years, ever since I married. I now share my mother's opinion of Joe, but that has not brought us any closer. Although I often wish that I were not, I am still married to him. But I know the break with my mother is sharper than that; it reaches back further into the past, back to the sandy path leading to the old oak tree where I struggled with her, back to my mother's eyes resting on the distant apple trees in the twilight. It goes back also to Žanis riding into the courtyard, reining his horse so hard that it rears backwards, raising a cloud of dust behind him, disturbing her peaceful afternoon and announcing the first of her many losses and displacements to come.

I am wishing for the bus to arrive, to move faster, to take me to my mother's bedside in time for her to say something to me. I passionately long for some kind of deathbed resolution between us, which I have learned to expect from books, and which I am terrified to miss.

The cool white foyer of the hospital; the pale light pouring through the windows hold out possibilities. Early morning routines are being carried out already: food trays are being pushed down the corridors, black women weighed down by cleaning supplies walk tiredly ahead of me, impeding me.

When I get to my mother's room, the door is ajar, and my mother is lying very still, breathing shallowly. Her skin is yellow and transparent, the palms turned up at her sides even thinner than they were two weeks ago when I had last seen her. She is unconscious, well beyond speaking or hearing.

I have been prepared for my mother's silent polite disapproval or for her reproaching me for being so late. I have imagined her lifting her book to read or pretending to read while I waited for her to look at me. But in all my worst fantasies of what it would be like when I saw her, I have not expected her to be unconscious. Her courage, her intelligence, her words would always be here.

A nurse asks me to go into the waiting room so that my mother can be bathed and the bed changed. She offers a cup of coffee, then hurries along the corridor to other patients in this wing reserved for the dying. I wash my hands and face, sip the surprisingly delicious coffee from a paper cup and sit on yet another plastic seat, this time cool and clean and restful. But the anxiety to hear my mother speak, to have something significant happen does not leave me; it is more intense than in the bus station, the urgency even greater.

The nurse has told me to wait at least fifteen minutes, but I walk down the corridor to my mother's room anyway and stand silent by the partially open door. Two middle-aged black women, with heavy, soft, calm bodies, are bending over her. One is sitting on the bed. My mother's shoulders lie in her lap, her head rests against the woman's breast, her cheek nestles against her. She is wiping my mother's face with a soft white cloth. "There, honey, there," she is half speaking, half crooning. The other woman bends over my mother's thin white legs, rubbing them with a firm circling motion.

The women are not aware of anyone watching, so that their movements are unhurried and formal, and as it seems to me, full of tenderness. The woman washing my mother's feet pauses for an instant by the scar filled with sand from Russia on the bottom of her instep, then carefully washes that. A brief flash of anger rises in me. This woman has no idea who my mother is, she knows nothing of the hardship and complexity of her life, of her being scarred by two wars, of losing Russia and Latvia both, of her struggle to get her Ph.D. in America, of her great store of languages and words, which will disappear with her death. These women do not understand the first thing about her. No one does.

"There, honey, there," the woman croons, stroking my mother's feet and calves with competent hands. The other woman is humming, either echoing those words or saying others so indistinct that I can only hear something steady and gentle, like the buzzing of bees. Rocking rhythmically back and forth, the woman strokes my mother's hair. Their movements are accepting and gentle, so that the anger I feel towards them for not understanding my mother ebbs away. They seem to know exactly the right thing to do, something that she needs, something that others—something that I myself—have failed to do. The washing takes only a few minutes, but it seems much longer, laden with meaning that I cannot put into words.

Someone touches my elbow and I turn to see Beate, who has come up quietly behind me. I have not been expecting my sister, who has moved back to Indiana from Texas. She and my father have been spending most nights at the hospital and need some sleep. Beate's gesture startles the two black women and their movements grow hurried. One rises hastily from the bed and lays my mother's head on the pillow, the other draws the blanket tightly over her body. They look at us questioningly, as if we have caught them in a misdemeanor rather than surprised them in a ritual that we do not understand. Suddenly they look only like two tired, underpaid hospital workers worried about being reported to a nurse for sitting on a patient's bed, instead of two women helping my mother die. They smooth her pillow, then with lowered eyes they push the cleaning trolley past us. I take Beate's hand, wondering how I am going to explain to her what I have just seen, or imagined.

"I know," Beate says before I can speak, "I was here. I saw what they did for her too."

For the next two days and nights I waited for my mother to speak, but she did not. Once I thought she whispered accusingly, "You are too late," but now I believe I may have imagined that. My mother was totally past movement and words in every other way. I did not know then that the comatose and dying may be able to hear, and so I did not try to speak to her. Even if my mother could hear me, I didn't know that I could say to her what I needed to say. I did not know then what that was.

During the time I had my recurrent dreams about trains I told John dozens of stories. At first they seem to be in no order at all— scattered, safe, unrevealing. But they move closer to the basement, closer to the old oak, closer and closer to the sandy path where I struggled with my mother and forever lost my sense of safety and worth. He asks me another question, listens to me, believes me, accepts what I say. When I cry, he doesn't tell me not to, but gives me his handkerchief and holds my hand. He does not say, "It wasn't so bad."

He tells me stories of his own. Some are about trains too, in America rather than Europe. When he was seven he had to leave his family and live with strangers in the city during the week; he rode the train back and forth. Once he set the clock back to miss the train. Our stories do not compete, nor do they cancel each other out. They make patterns around us, enter our dreams, gently bind us together. Sometimes I see us as two blond seven-year-olds, separated by a vast meadow, speaking different languages, but smiling at each other in recognition. Sometimes I dream we are the twins in *Twelfth Night*, pale in their dark green velvet, but reunited after all. We have come safely past storms, we can hold hands, tell each other our stories and dreams.

Gradually the silent oppressive images inside me have become words. The past takes on meaning and shape, loses its power to paralyze, silence and shame. I am startled by parallels between my mother and me, I wish to shield the girl she was, I understand why she could not give me more than she did. Our fathers powerless to protect us, we survived displacement and war. I imagine her as a twelve-year-old when she lost her beloved Russia because I was twelve when I secretly mourned leaving the fragile safety of the camps in Germany. We were both outsiders, both scarred. We both inflicted our sadness on our children.

Because I can tell my stories to Ingeborg and to John, my love for my mother becomes less jagged, and reconciliation and forgiveness grow. John's gestures can touch me to my core. He tells me stories as I fall asleep. He really sees me when he looks at me. He smiles without pretense. He is separate, complete in himself, yet he can do for me what I longed for my mother to do.

Finally one night I tell him about struggling with my mother on the sandy path, about Heidi and her mother not touching, not even in death. He knows everything about me now. He knows my mother wanted me to die, he knows now that all my life I have felt worthless and afraid. He knows my shame about my past.

I wait for him to leave, but he does not. Instead, he gently draws the blue quilt around us both. I feel his warmth around me as I fall asleep, he is there while I sleep, he will be there when I wake. It is comforting to have him there, next to me, safe in bed.

That night I have another dream about trains.

I am running across an open field towards a train that is already moving. I see the house with the door ripped off the hinges, I hear the black boots of the soldiers on the pavement, but I have escaped. I run as hard as I can, reach the railing and swing myself up. I am elated, I am on the train taking me to safety. I have survived. I sit down on a polished wooden seat and look around me.

It is a beautiful old train with gleaming brass fixtures, beveled-glass windows and ornate carved mirrors, and it is taking me to safety. I sit luxuriating in my escape. But something haunts me, there is something I have forgotten to do. Sitting across the aisle is a twelve-year-old girl, dressed in black, thin, foreign looking, someone from long ago. Seeing the girl jars something in my memory, and I know what it is. I have caught this train to find the corpse of my mother.

I go from compartment to compartment, looking for my mother's body. It is terribly important I find it, yet I see that the compartments are too small to hold a coffin, and the luggage car is far away. I move up and down the train, searching. I step into a compartment filled with people; only one seat is empty. My mother cannot be here, there is not enough room for a coffin anyway.

Sitting by the window, her face turned towards the late afternoon sun, is a blind nun. She is wearing a black habit and black sunglasses. Her face behind this disguise is serene. With a shock I realize this is my mother. Her hands, her skin, her hair, the curve of her cheek are all the way I remember her. Only the nun's habit and the glasses have confused me.

I sit down next to her and whisper, "Is that you?"

"Yes." My mother is pleased I am here.

"But, *mammiņ*," I say, using the diminutive, full of affection and intimacy, a name I can remember calling her only in Latvia, "*mammiņ*, I thought you were dead."

"No, precious," she says, "I am not dead, I am only blind. That is why I always looked at others, away from you, while you tried so hard to find another mother—Mrs. Saulītis, Mrs. Čigāns and others too— but they all left you as well. But you can understand that now."

She takes off her glasses and hands them to me.

"I've been blind for a long time. It happened in the war." She caresses my cheek.

"Forgive me, precious," she says.

"Forgive me, *mammiņ*," I say. "Forgive me for only remembering that you pulled me forward to be shot. But you saved me so many other times. Without your courage I would have died. We all would have."

Tears spill out of her dark eyes, which do not look like a blind woman's at all, but as intense and deep as when she really looked at me when I was small. We can see each other now.

I am overcome with such love and tenderness as I have not allowed myself to feel for my mother for years. I stroke my mother's face, her hair, her temples, her hands. Our tears mingle. Our eyes rest on each other.

"It's all right, precious," I say. "Precious, it is all right."

The miraculous feeling of love is so strong in the dream that it wakes me. John is already awake; two cups of fragrant coffee and two oranges are next to the bed on a tray. A letter from my son, who is bravely struggling with some hard issues in his life, is there too. My body feels wonderful, rested and supple and strong. I open the blinds above the shelves filled with my favorite books, and light pours into the room.

It is very early, but I can see it is going to be a clear sun-filled day. Under my window are spikes of sky blue delphinium, white daisies and deep purple Siberian irises against a white fence. At the other end of my garden is a solitary birch. Daffodils bloom beneath the white birch in the spring; the purple asters and pale yellow chrysanthemums that my mother loved will bloom there later. One of the madonna lilies has opened during the night. More lilies will follow.

A shadow crosses the garden, I am afraid it will cloud over. I remember I was not a happy mother to Boris. I wish again I had not inflicted my pain on him. Latvia is far away, its clear rivers polluted, its birches cut down. I will never live there again, nor will I really belong there if I return. I will tell my stories in English, not in Latvian, my mother tongue. I have been granted the gift of happiness in myself and with John, but others still suffer. In their own country and in exile, so many Latvians, my sister and father among them, live brave gray lives. And I, too, still bear scars, I will have to continue to struggle against depression for the rest of my life. I understand my mother, love and forgive her, but the pain is real too. As for so many others, family relationships and historical events intersected to inflict wounds. Nor can I ever change the long aftermath of war, when I waited, rather than lived, the forty years spent in a motherless universe.

Even more, nothing can change my mother's suffering. She died doubly displaced, embittered, worn out. She lost too much.

◆ ◆ ◆

But the whole world is full of pain. Anne Frank, Heidi and Hilda are dead, but Kurds still freeze on the hillsides, Bosnian women have to live on after rape, Rwandan children stand waiting, too emaciated to beg. My mother's and my story is only a tiny stinging particle of ice, not even the size of a snowflake, in a driving, cruel blizzard.

But then the sun touches the blossoms again. We have to believe that dreams are meaningful, we have to believe that even the briefest human connections can heal. Otherwise life is unbearable. The two black women did ease my mother's dying, Ingeborg did give me great gifts, John did gently draw his blue quilt around us both, my mother and I did touch each other, if only in a dream. We have to believe that matters.

Now John is turning towards me again, I am turning towards him, we are looking at each other.

"Did you have a dream?" he asks as he hands me a full blue cup. The orange he has peeled reveals itself; the sections open like the petals of a flower.

"Yes, precious," I say, and I begin telling him.

I am lucky to have had this dream, to have it again in telling him, to hear his dream afterwards. I *have* had a charmed life.

We continue talking in bed.

*In honor of my grandmother,
Līna Kness-Knezinskis
my mother, Valda Nesaule
my sister, Beate Nesaule K.
and all the other women and girls
who have experienced exile and war*